CW01637224

Building (

Building Contract Law

First Edition

John Murdoch LLB ACIArb

and

Will Hughes BSc (hons) Ph D MCIOB

LONGMAN

ISBN 0 85121 7273

First Edition 1992

Published by
Longman Law, Tax and Finance
Longman Group UK Ltd
21-27 Lamb's Conduit Street
London WC1N 3NJ

Associated Offices
Australia, Hong Kong, Malaysia, Singapore, USA

A CIP catalogue record for this book is available from the British Library

Printed in the United Kingdom by
Hobbs the Printers Ltd, Southampton, SO9 2UZ

Contents

Preface

The purpose of this book is to introduce the subject of building contracts to solicitors in general practice, many of whom become involved from time to time with such contracts or sub-contracts. This may come about as an aspect of commercial property work, where building contracts form part of the general package of development documentation. Alternatively, it may be a litigator who finds that he or she has become embroiled in a construction dispute. Whatever the reason, there is no doubt that increasing numbers of lawyers require at least some understanding of what makes building contracts special, and it is that need which this book aims to fulfil.

The aim of the book dictates its structure. This is not a commentary on a particular form of contract, but rather an analysis of the context of building contracts and their typical content. The early chapters describe the construction industry, with particular emphasis on its fragmentation and the different interest groups within it (a factor which, though frequently overlooked, accounts for many disputes). Attention is also paid to the various 'procurement methods' which can be adopted and the range of standard-form contracts applicable to each, and guidance is given as to which method and contract may be appropriate for different types of project.

The remainder of the book is concerned with the substantive law of building contracts. Where this in fact consists of general principles of contract law (for example offer and acceptance or remedies for breach) we have concentrated on those aspects which are of the greatest relevance, such as letters of intent, tenders or determination clauses. In other areas no such selection falls to be made — in such fields as sub-contracts, variations, contractors' loss/expense claims or the problems of liquidated damages and extensions of time, the law is almost exclusively construction-based. We have on occasion strayed beyond the strict territory of contract altogether, most notably when considering the thorny problems of liability for defective buildings, given the current restrictive judicial attitudes to tort claims for negligence.

It should be emphasised that this book is introductory rather than encyclopedic, seeking to complement rather than to compete with such major works as *Emden* or *Keating*. Those specialist construction lawyers who visit the Official Referees' courts on a regular basis may find it useful for their trainees, and for colleagues who are only occasionally involved with construction matters. While avoiding the detail of weightier tomes, we have tried nonetheless to concentrate on those topics which are currently the subject of debate amongst construction lawyers (retention moneys and the defence of set off being two notable examples), and hope that an up-to-date treatment of such issues will prove to be of assistance to the profession in general.

Table of Cases

Table of Statutes

Table of Statutory Instruments

Chapter 1

The UK Construction Industry

The construction industry of the United Kingdom is unique and complex. There are several definitions of its constitution, but they differ in many respects. This is because construction encompasses such a wide range of activity that the industry's boundaries are inevitably blurred. The term 'construction' can include the erecting, repairing and demolishing of things as diverse as houses, offices, shops, dams, bridges, motorways, home extensions, chimneys, factories and airports; it certainly encompasses building, civil engineering and much offshore work in the oil industry.

Many people approach the construction industry with mixed feelings. Building sites can seem primitive and arbitrary, yet even a cursory survey reveals a complex and mysterious technology. However, although many disputes hinge on technical matters, an understanding of the human factors is crucial. Whilst there are a plethora of experts who can advise on technical issues, these issues need to be considered against the backdrop of the industry's organisational culture.

The industry is best seen as a combination of five distinct groups of participators; builders, designers, regulators, purchasers and users of buildings. These groups, and the links between them, are becoming increasingly complex as technology develops and people's expectations change. More particularly, each of these facets is increasingly subdivided into specialist interests, such that any building project will bring together a variety of specialists from different sources. The way in which they combine is unique to each project. This uniqueness arises from the individual demands of the project coupled with the continuing evolution of specific roles.

The construction industry can only be understood if its inherent flux is confronted and accepted. For example, even the notion of a 'builder' has been constantly evolving, as industrial society has developed and placed differing demands on builders at every stage of that development. The five groups of participants are introduced below, with a brief account of their history to help put their current roles into perspective.

1 Builders

Construction is not a new activity; mankind has been fabricating shelters for thousands of years. However, for the purposes of understanding the modern construction industry, most of the significant developments have taken place in the last 200 years. The work done by craftsmen before the Industrial Revolution involved only a handful of technologies. The building trades consisted of little more than bricklaying, carpentry, thatching and stone-masonry. Some buildings were of sufficient artistic or cultural significance to warrant the appointment of a specialist in the art of architecture, but few building or civil engineering projects employed other than craft skills.

Many buildings at that time were *evolved* rather than consciously *designed*, involving incremental modifications as each new project utilised the lessons learned from experience. Pre-industrial projects were totally organised by an architect or by a master mason. The few crafts involved interacted in predictable ways. Each craftsman had an intimate knowledge of a particular technology and knew precisely what to expect of the other trades. As a result, integration and co-ordination were achieved by these people making mutual adjustments to their own work. This resulted in minimal demands for organisation and control because all of the participants knew what was expected of them and of the others.

The Industrial Revolution brought new technologies and new ways of working. New materials, and novel uses of old materials, enabled more adventurous and innovative buildings which would better reflect the spirit of the time. For example, 1770 saw the first use of cast iron as a building material when it was used as columns in churches. As materials and transportation developed, so new skills emerged and rapidly spread. As a result, building sites became more complex, involving increasing numbers of trade and sub-trades. The modern technological building process involves many complicated technologies and very few people can know and understand all of them. Particularly, the craftsmen can no longer be left to sort out the interfaces between work packages; these are the responsibility of the designer or of the building contractor.

As skills and materials emerged, and the pace of development accelerated during the Industrial Revolution, the demands for integration also grew. This demand led to the emergence of the *general contractor*, a role first undertaken by Thomas Cubitts of London in 1870. Prior to this, architects or master masons co-ordinated the work on behalf of the employer, who recruited the necessary tradesmen directly. The general contractor offered to employ all the necessary skills, provide all the materials and own the plant and equipment needed for the whole project. Hence the employer took the responsibility for design and the contractor took the responsibility for fabrication.

The extra demand for management and co-ordination is evident from Figure 1 (*below*). This shows that two people can have two communication links. The addition of a third person increases the number of links to six; a fourth to 12 and a fifth to 20. Clearly, each additional person adds a proportionally larger burden to the communication and co-ordination demands of the project's management structure. It is a fact of organisations that as technological complexity increases, so more skills are needed. The traditional skills of the building industry are long-established; each a lifetime's specialism in its own right. These have to be integrated with each other, and with newer skills, and it is the task of the builder to ensure that this takes place.

2 Designers

As materials and skills developed, and clients demanded more modern facilities, designers too had to embrace new techniques. The demand was for specialists who understood the emerging technologies. While this called for designers with a *deeper*, more detailed knowledge, their role was also *narrowed* by the emergence of general contracting, which relieved them of their management co-ordination role during fabrication of the building. The increasing need for specialisation led to the emergence of design disciplines such as structural engineering and services engineering. In domestic buildings the input of these specialists is negligible, but it is very significant in the case of commercial buildings.

An associated development which also narrowed the role of the designer was the emergence of *quantity surveying*. As commercial clients sought increasingly firm prices and tighter budgetary control, so demand increased for frequent site visits, comparing progress with the plan and valuing work done each month for the

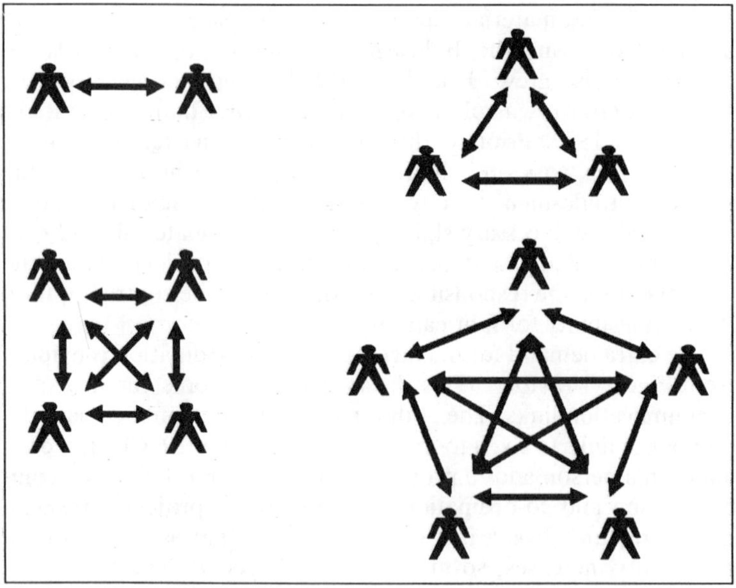

Figure 1: Communication links in different sizes of groups

purposes of making stage payments to contractors. From these beginnings the profession of quantity surveying emerged which concerned itself primarily with *accountancy* functions in the building process. Increasingly, quantity surveyors are more involved with *economics* rather than accountancy. The profession has grown to dominate the UK construction industry, not least because the client's employment of a quantity surveyor for cost planning and control encourages contractors to employ quantity surveyors in order to be able to respond.

The designer's role has thus become a complex management task. The use of an ever-larger number of specialists in the design stages makes the generation of information a co-ordination problem. The magnitude of the communication problem cannot be over-emphasised, with literally hundreds of designers involved before any work takes place on site. Because of this, the design cannot be truly said to emerge from one designer, even if one designer is notionally responsible for the process.

Strong management of a project by an architect will be evident when the architect elicits a clear brief and establishes an acceptable design policy for the project. Such a policy becomes the bench-mark against which all decisions are taken. Unfortunately, such clear and strong leadership rarely emerges. As a result clients often appoint project managers to manage the project. In this situation design is reduced to an advisory role, equal in status to the other professional roles.

This analysis reveals a fundamental crisis of identity for the architectural profession: is architecture art, or science? If architecture is art, then it is based upon the subjective feelings of the artists who should not need to articulate reasons for doing things, but should simply have their instructions carried out. Such an appointment demands complete trust by the client in the artist. On the other hand, if architecture is science, then it is a systematic application of objective techniques which can be managed by a third party in the same way as cost planning and control, for example. Observers frequently see the emergence of an artistic building as fortuitous rather than planned. The fact is that there is a real ambiguity within architecture which the profession (RIBA) has not fully confronted and resolved, and which currently generates lively debate.

3 Regulators

Increasing demands from clients for quicker, cheaper and more reliable buildings have always been accompanied by demands from the public to curb the voraciousness of the property developer. Public concern about the safety of buildings—and about the changing built environment 'spoiling' the scenery of the countryside—led to the establishment of building regulation and planning control respectively. These functions are administered by local authorities acting under powers conferred by statute. Recent changes to building control legislation have opened the way for privatisation of building control, albeit still overseen by the local authority.

Building control is a process whereby minimum standards are laid down by central government and enforced by local government. A new approach to building control, which surfaced in the Building Act 1985, concentrates upon functional requirements rather than dimensional and material specifications. One of the disadvantages of the earlier legislation was that it laid down minimum sizes and specifications; these minima came to be treated as the standard, leading to much criticism of the basis of building control. The result of the discontent was the adoption of a new approach which has two advantages:

(*a*) The regulations refer to *approved documents* which give advice on how to satisfy the functional requirement in the regulations. These approved documents are not in themselves statutory instruments, so revisions do not need the approval of parliament.

(*b*) A contractor can choose to achieve the functional requirements by methods other than those in the approved documents, but this may necessitate him having to prove that he has satisfied the requirements. This option provides opportunities for innovation in a way which was not possible under earlier legislation.

Planning control is a much more subjective and emotive endeavour than building control. Because of ever-increasing pressure to develop a finite amount of land, there is a need to control the erection of buildings, especially in urban areas which would otherwise become hopelessly congested. This is accomplished under legislation starting with the Town and Country Planning Act 1947, which established a process of development plans outlining the intentions for the future, and a requirement that all potential developers apply for permission to build.

There are appeal procedures built into the planning legislation which enable disgruntled developers to appeal ultimately to the Secretary of State. This appeal structure is frequently said to make a mockery of the system because the Secretary of State may take decisions based upon political criteria rather than planning criteria, which robs the system of much of its consistency.

The result of these two types of legislation and control is that all building projects automatically involve local government and often involve central government in key decisions affecting the development. Other legislation, such as the Health and Safety at Work Act 1974 and the Occupier's Liability Act 1957 also have an impact upon the organisation and management of building. These latter statutes, however, rarely have the political overtones associated with building control and planning legislation.

4 Purchasers

The purchasers of buildings do not form a homogeneous group. They range from the householder who wishes to provide shelter and/or prestige, to the corporate client who needs to provide some sort of facility for generating income, in addition to public sector clients with their own special circumstances.

The variety in client types explains why there are so many different motivating factors behind people's wish to buy buildings, and goes some way towards explaining why there is such a wide range of client satisfaction with the outcome. Whilst the aim from the point of view of the industry is to satisfy the client, this glib statement belies the complexity of many of the clients of construction. Consider, for example, the erection of a simple branch library in a suburb of a city. The county council's libraries department may be paying half of the building costs, whilst the district council pays the other half; sometimes money is endowed from some philanthropic third party; the library committees at county and district levels will have a voice about what goes into the building, as will the staff who are going to work there (if they are already on the payroll); the public are the users, and therefore they may feel that the library is theirs.

The problems of identifying the client are not restricted to public sector agencies. For example, where a property developer wishes to erect an office block speculatively, one might regard the 'client' as any or all of the developer's finance department, its design department, the future tenants or the local community.

5 Users

The fifth category of people involved in a project are the users. These have already been mentioned in connection with the difficulty of identifying the client, but it is necessary to describe users in a different context. Every building affects more people than those who choose to become involved. People pass buildings as they travel from place to place, and they move in, through and out of built facilities as an indispensable part of modern life. Roads, bridges, hotels, factories, houses and dams affect all of us as users at some point or other. There is an issue in deciding when, if at all, to involve the potential users of a facility in the process which produces it.

Users of buildings are frequently excluded from the construction process; many would say they are disenfranchised from it. Much of the legislation mentioned earlier is an attempt to give voice to such people via their elected representatives. The fact remains that the bulk of people who are affected by the output of the construction industry have no say in the production of these facilities. This is another of the unique characteristics of the construction industry.

6 Partial involvement of participants

The description thus far illustrates the variety of different pressures on a project. Each participator joins the process for a different reason, and many of them are unexpected, even uninvited! The demand for integration means that the process requires organisation, which leads to the creation of what is described by some writers as a Temporary Multi-Organisation. This phrase highlights the notion that each of the people involved in the project organisation is also involved with another organisation of some kind. Therefore, to be part of a construction project organisation is to be a member of at least two organisations, usually more if the role of professional institutions is also considered. It is a fact of organisations that people do not partake in them wholly and exclusively, but retain outside interests, even if those interests only include home-life, sports and hobbies. Most people are ordinarily engaged in a variety of formal and informal organisations and cannot therefore be expected to be *totally* committed to any one. This partial involvement is a feature which is exaggerated in construction due to the phenomenon of temporary multi-organisations.

7 Stages of a project

All projects go through a similar series of stages, and people are involved in different ways at each stage.

(a) Inception

The first stage, that of *inception*, includes the processes through which a potential client arrives at the decision that some form of built facility might be needed. This frequently informal process may only result in an exploration of possibilities and may thus not involve a professional consultant from the construction industry. It is of interest only in so far as it is the trigger for the process of building procurement.

(b) Feasibility

The second stage is *feasibility*, during which the client appoints an engineer, surveyor or architect to organise and manage the project. This stage includes developing the client's requirements, investigating alternative solutions and enabling the client to decide about the nature and magnitude of any development.

The client should aim to produce a 'brief' which describes what is wanted clearly and unambiguously. It will usually be rewritten many times in the early stages of a project as more information becomes available and the client's objectives are refined. One aim will be to develop the ideas sufficiently to enable the selection and appointment of consultants (such as architects and other designers). Their selection may be by competition or by negotiation. The prime objective of this stage is to see whether the scheme can indeed go ahead and whether finance is available. Secondly, clear problem definition is fundamentally important. The project will seek to overcome some perceived problem for the client, whether it is shortage of space, dilapidated buildings, infrastructure needs, or simply development for the purposes of making money. Having defined the problem in these terms, further constraints will be put upon the problem by the nature of the site itself. This leads to the other type of feasibility study, namely the technical feasibility of developing a particular site.

(c) Scheme design

If the outcome of these studies is positive, *scheme design* can proceed. This is also variously known as *sketch scheme*, or *outline design*. In this stage the idea for the design is developed, along with the cost plan, programme for completion and further development of the brief. The client's initial ideas are translated into one, two or three outline schemes to select the aesthetic approach and define the design philosophy most acceptable to the client.

The outputs of this stage are drawings of elevations and site layouts, specifications of quality, cost plans, suggestions (often implied) for the major areas of risk allocation and definite ideas about the function of the building and how the aims within the brief will be achieved. The suggestions about risk allocation should apportion the risks between the client, the consultants and the contractor, but this is rarely done adequately. By the end of this stage the brief should have been finalised and all further refinements or revisions prevented unless unavoidable. The primary objectives of this stage are to be sure about the client's future commitments for the project, the nature of the professional services required of the consultants (and therefore their fees), and the generation of sufficient information to enable the client to secure the site, possibly purchasing it, secure the finance either by budgeting or borrowing, and make the decision to take the project through to its conclusion. It is important that such full commitment is acknowledged early in the process, otherwise the client may waste resources in working up a scheme that ultimately does not go ahead.

(d) Detail design

At the next stage the concept is more comprehensively developed, and the individual sub-systems of the building (such as lifts, lights, floors, walls, foundations, cladding and roof) are developed into a series of documented packages. The main purpose of this phase is to ensure that all the individual parts of the building will interact adequately, and that any functional or spatial clashes are avoided. Much of this detail will be undertaken by specialists who will eventually fabricate the parts of the building for which they are responsible. Because of this, detail design is fundamentally different from scheme design. This stage becomes an enormous information co-ordination exercise. Modern, highly serviced buildings involve tremendous logistical management during this stage, but a simple traditional building will not. Indeed, on simple building projects this stage may not exist at all, because simple projects use the established skills of craftsmen. The key factor in using skilled craftsmen is that they not only know their own job well, but also appreciate and understand the skills of the other craftsmen. Hence, the most detailed information is not required because the tradesmen will be able to integrate their own work on site. This point highlights a key factor about the nature of the designer's task.

Design consists of three essentially distinct types of activity: innovation, choice and co-ordination. It is quite usual to think of designers in the same way as inventors: brilliantly innovative people who are able to create new visions and ideas. In reality, however, the bulk of a designer's innovation is not in creating original inventions, but simply choosing from a range of alternatives. When a designer takes a decision, it involves a choice. This is what civil engineers, architects, structural engineers and services engineers have in common. The interesting thing is that craftsmen, if given enough autonomy, also exercise choice; where to put a nail, or what kind of joint to fabricate. The increasing reliance on modern technology means that the craftsmen on site do not have the experience to be able to make choices concerned with new materials and components, and so these choices have to be made for them by the designers during detail design. This shows how reducing autonomy of the site operatives increases the demands for information during the detail design stage. An appreciation of this interaction helps to shed light on many construction disputes.

(e) Contract preparation

The purpose of the detail design stage, then, is to ensure that the building and all of its sub-systems will work in an integrated way. The next step is to produce sufficient documentation for the construction of the building to be commenced, which takes place during *contract preparation*. This stage is often called *production information*. The output of this stage is information which is sufficiently detailed to enable the contract to be let. This means all of the contract documents: conditions of contract, which form the agreement between the employer and the contractor; drawings, which show what the building will look like; specifications, which describe the quality of the various elements and pieces; and some sort of pricing document such as 'bills of quantities', which are a detailed set of descriptions of every piece of material in a building. Bills of quantities are prepared in accordance with a standardised code of measurement, called a Standard Method of Measurement (SMM), which shows the client's quantity surveyor how to describe all the material content of the building. Building contracts are usually based upon SMM7 (meaning the seventh edition) and civil engineering contracts are usually based on CESMM2 (Civil Engineering SMM, 2nd edition). The documentation from this stage is intended to enable contractors to price the work competitively, in order that one of them can be selected for the work. By enabling all contractors to tender on the same basis, and thus regulating the way in which the tendering process is undertaken, fairness is assured.

(f) Construction

Once the contractors are selected, the *construction* stage can commence. The fabrication of the whole building and all of its parts has to be co-ordinated to ensure that each part is built right first time and in the right sequence, so that people are not delayed and waiting on site to get on with their own part. This takes much planning and co-ordination, frequently demanding the skills of an experienced construction manger. This manager may or may not have been involved in the project before work has started on site. On traditional projects where little detailed information has been produced because of the high reliance on traditional skills, it makes sense not to appoint the manager of the process until the site work starts. In this circumstance a 'general contractor' would be used. As mentioned above, a general contractor is a builder who employs the full range of craftsmen and labourers to deal with all of the requisite tasks on a building site, and who will own most of the required plant. The general contractor, on receiving the contract documentation, will set up the site, use his own direct labour force for most of the work, and sub-contract parts of the work to specialists for some of the more technical or unique specialist sub-systems.

By contrast, more complex projects may have involved many specialists in detailed design. In this case, the co-ordination of the various parts of the design packages will have entailed a lot of negotiation and revision of ideas. This process of development forges a team who may well resent a new person being appointed to co-ordinate them (and possibly to insist on further changes) at fabrication stage. For these, and other reasons, it makes sense to appoint the manager at an earlier stage in the process. This is one reason for the development of management contractors and construction managers. In this way, early consideration of the fabrication stage reveals important aspects of how to manage the design stages.

(g) Commissioning

The final stage is *commissioning*, which is when the building is made ready for occupation. In traditional buildings this entails cleaning the building; switching on and testing (and repairing if necessary) the services (electricity, water and gas supplies); and making sure that everything works properly (for example that the windows and doors can be opened and shut, locked and unlocked). In more complex buildings the services may be extremely complex, and testing and repairing may also include balancing and tuning. This process may take many weeks in some buildings and can therefore represent a considerable expense which has to be allowed for if buildings are to be satisfactorily completed.

A final activity which ought to take place, but rarely does, is making sure the client gets what he wants. Ultimately, the client should be consulted about the extent to which the building satisfies the original objectives. It is not good enough simply to dismiss a project from one's mind as soon as one's involvement has come to an end. All those who take part should endeavour to discover what is good and bad about the completed building. They should identify those parts of their own contribution which affect the success or failure of the project, and constantly try to improve the service they offer to their clients.

The way in which the various parties participate in construction projects is called the *procurement method*. It depends largely on historical precedent, but is increasingly influenced by informed decisions about risk apportionment and effective control and management. The next chapter examines in more detail the roles of the professions in construction, and this is followed by an examination of some of the more common procurement methods.

Chapter 2

The Role of Construction Professionals

The intention of this chapter is to examine some of the underlying reasons for the current structure of the industry, before describing the roles of the various actors in the process of building. It is intended to dig deeper than a description of what can be observed, and to examine some of the forces which produce the distinctive elements of the construction industry.

1 The unique nature of professionalism in construction

The construction professions are characterised by their high level of fragmentation, their degree of institutionalisation, the specific difficulties in managing projects and the political influence of UK professionalism in construction. Each of these is discussed in detail below.

(a) Fragmentation

It is a fact of organisation that as a technology becomes more complex, so an organisation dealing with it needs to become more complex. Research has shown that there should be a fit between organisational complexity and the complexity of the environment in which the organisation operates. The same research has shown that, whilst complex building projects need diverse skills, the increasing diversity of skills demands higher levels of integration and co-ordination. This is essentially why a single standard form of procurement, and/or a single standard form of contract, is out of the question in the construction industry—the variety in the circumstances surrounding construction projects is simply too great for there to be a single standard solution.

There is a clear and well-established need to employ a number of specialist organisations, each with its own set of needs and objectives, within the temporary project organisation. Specialisation frequently results in fragmentation, a situation where the various interest groups in a project each have their own reasons for taking part and thus pull in a different direction. In such circumstances successful project completion can soon cease to be the top priority for many contributors. For example, the people responsible for designing and fabricating one part of a building may only be interested in the performance of their part. It is frequently the case that the individual parts of a project have to work less than optimally in order for the whole building to achieve optimal performance (a concept known as 'satisficing' in the literature on organisation theory). Fragmentation can prevent the holistic view necessary for effective optimisation. The task of construction project management is to co-ordinate and integrate the various parts of a dynamic and changing team so that the client's requirements are satisfied.

(b) Institutionalisation

A further consequence of an increasing diversity of skills is professionalisation, ie the identification of a discrete discipline by those who practise it joining together in an institution, which then becomes the controlling and qualifying body for that discipline. This happens for a variety of reasons, not least of which are the need for peer-group recognition and wider acknowledgment of the special nature of one's skills.

Professional institutions also have a role in regulating the conduct of practitioners, distancing their members from sharp practice. The chances of a secure workload are greater for members of a professional institution, and there are important benefits to clients and the public in terms of reliability, ethics and accountability.

There are, however, disadvantages in professionalisation; institutions are inherently conservative, membership does not guarantee excellence and the institutional definition of roles creates particular problems for construction projects. Because roles are fixed in terms of the practitioner's relationship with the institution, people come to construction projects with preconceived notions of their own roles, and the roles of others, in the team. This creates a further demand for integrating the various professional contributions, because such roles are defined for the purposes of the institution, whereas each project has unique objectives and involves unique combinations of skills. The inherent inflexibility of professionalism can prevent appropriate control procedures from being developed and appropriate tasks from being identified. When the need is for flexibility and dynamism in the organisation of construction projects, uncertainty, and hence insecurity, conspire to send people running for the cover of their familiar terms of engagement and fee scales. Thus, just when the need for adaptability is greatest, the likelihood of its emerging is least.

(c) The problem of management

Most businesses seek to limit their exposure to unnecessary risk. There is a commonly held view that this leads to all firms being 'risk-averse', but a moment's reflection soon reveals the fallacy of this conclusion. Entrepreneurs are in the business of taking risks in order to make money, and insurance companies take risks on behalf of people by spreading those risks across a sufficient number of events. Risk-aversion is, therefore, merely a disinclination to accept any more than a specific, and limited, responsibility. To clarify responses to risk, it is necessary to distinguish between *commercial* risk, which is the hazard of things not turning out as expected, and *contractual* risk, which is the deliberate allocation of duties and rights to specific parties. All firms take commercial risks, such as the risk of non-payment for work done, and would seek to minimise this, but contractual risk demands an inherently different analysis and response, since rather than mere uncertainty it involves the acceptance of particular responsibilities. Such analysis rarely happens in practice, leaving most construction projects with a vacuum in their management structure—caused by inappropriate responses to risks, coupled with the lack of people willing to accept responsibility for the whole of the project.

Projects frequently suffer from the lack of a clear or 'natural' owner for the problem of management, ie the problem of co-ordinating the various contributions so that the client receives the best overall performance. The best the construction industry can usually offer is the ascendancy of one professional interest over all of the others. Clearly, architecture (for building projects) and engineering (in civil engineering projects) are inherently design/management orientated, with the view that the project is managed through the nature of the processes of design and hence co-ordination. In this sense, the traditional view is that design is the overarching co-ordinating activity, and that leadership has arisen from the integration which results. Clients have become increasingly dissatisfied with traditional ways of working, especially where for example, what they want is not *architecture*, but rather a weatherproof box which will enable them to make a useful return on some investment of capital. This is a recurrence of the perennial debate about whether architecture is an art or a science.

The problem of management is also a matter of dealing with interfaces. As mentioned earlier, the construction industry is very good at specialising and developing new techniques and technologies. The fragmentation and institutionalism which follow this result in a series of narrow beliefs, each of which seeks to dominate the process. Whilst this can be handled with good management and political awareness, there is still the problem of interface management. This is what is needed to ensure that all of the pieces of the building fit together properly. For example, there are specialist steel frame erectors, and cladding specialists who are extremely advanced, but it is at the junctions between them that the greatest problems lie. Most of the junctions, interfaces and boundaries between technologies are poorly understood and the industry invests little effort in understanding these things. This is a symptom of over-specialisation and a problem which may not be solved simply by appointing a member of the established professions as a project manager.

(d) The state of professionalism in the UK construction industry

There is no doubt that professional institutions dominate and largely benefit the industry. However, there are problems arising from the ever-increasing political struggles between them for ascendancy. Most of them, at some time, have claimed to be best qualified to provide project managers. Most have drafted their conditions of engagement with little reference to others involved in construction, least of all their clients.

There have been many moves to bring the construction professions closer together. These moves are accelerating as the UK moves closer to the rest of Europe because the threat of competition from our trading partners is so great. As a result, the UK professions will probably never again be able to enjoy the protected position which they have occupied until now, although the legacy of that protectionism will be around for some time. Attitudes may not keep pace with commercial reality. This brief critique highlights the way in which the subsequent description of professional roles may be subject to dramatic change in a short space of time, indeed from project to project.

2 The established roles of the professionals

Chapter 1 described the various categories of contributors to the process of construction. The aim here is to expand upon that description into the basic roles of each of those who take part in construction projects.

(a) Architect

The architect has traditionally been the client's key agent on building projects. The role is often poorly understood, because architecture is understood by many to be an art form as well as a science. Whilst most people can identify the presence or absence of art in an old building, few are able to cope with the creation of art in a new building. If this issue is not explicitly addressed at the outset of a project, problems may arise because there is a potential conflict between the articulation of aesthetic developments and the economic constraints of creating a working or living space which has specific performance criteria.

An architect, then, is trained in the art of design, and much of his or her training is taken up with developing an ability to see whole problems and develop whole solutions. This is by stark contrast with the training of some of the other construction professionals (see *below*) who learn about construction by disaggregating the whole into parts. Whilst this distinction is somewhat over-simplified, it does highlight how far removed architectural training is from that of the other disciplines. It is frequently based on an understanding of light, form and space. Such concepts mean little to those who have to make a building work as a functional, wealth-generating unit. Understanding the gulf between the professions helps in dealing with the disputes which result.

Architects focus upon eliciting a brief from the client; developing the brief so that priorities can be identified; proposing schemes to the client; developing the client's chosen scheme into a detailed design in conjunction with other specialist designers; making recommendations to the client about whom to appoint to the team; co-ordinating the production of information; supervising the fabrication work on site to ensure that the contractor is producing what was specified; and ensuring that the building is completed, tested and handed over properly.

The architect's role within a project is complex and frequently somewhat ambiguous. Whilst being the originator of the design, and the main source of co-ordination and interpretation for all the other project participants, the architect's authority to act on behalf of the client is nonetheless a limited one. In particular, unless specifically authorised the architect cannot commit the client to a contract, for example by promising that a sub-contractor will be paid directly (*Vigers Sons & Co Ltd* v *Swindell* [1939] 3 All ER 590). Nor does the architect have any inherent power to order variations; whatever power exists must be found in the contract conditions (*Sharpe* v *San Paolo Railway* (1873) LR 8 Ch App 597).

Matters which an architect clearly *is* authorised to carry out fall into two clearly defined categories. First, there are those functions (such as the provision of design information to the contractor) which the architect performs as an agent of the employer. Any failure of reasonable care and skill by the architect in such matters is likely to have an adverse effect upon the contractor; however, it seems unlikely that this would give the contractor any direct claim against the architect under the tort of negligence. Instead, the architect's failings will put the employer in breach of contract to the contractor. Such failure is also likely, if delays result, to lead to the contractor being entitled to claim an extension of time and financial compensation for loss/expense.

The second important aspect of the architect's role relates to the responsibility for making certain decisions which will be binding on both employer and contractor. These decisions concern such matters as the certification of work as being properly executed, the achievement of practical completion, the granting of an extension of time and so on. In carrying out these functions the architect is required to act as an independent and impartial adjudicator, rather than as the employer's agent. In consequence, as shown in Chapter 10, the employer's responsibility for the way in which the architect acts is of a much more limited kind in this context.

The idea that an architect, despite being paid by the employer, is nonetheless expected to act independently can be a rather difficult concept to grasp for inexperienced clients. Indeed, the general lopsidedness of the picture is increased by certain judicial decisions defining the extent of the architect's liability for professional negligence. These decisions have established that, while the architect owes a duty of care to the employer when carrying out this 'independent' role (*Sutcliffe* v *Thackrah* [1974] AC 727), no equivalent duty of care is owed to the contractor (*Pacific Associates Inc* v *Baxter* [1989] 2 All ER 159).

The ambiguity of the architect's role is difficult to rationalise on projects where what is to be built has been fully specified and objectively measured. It is somewhat easier to understand where the aim is to create an original aesthetic manifestation of the values of the client, the architect or society. Such an aim cannot be reduced to a set of measured specifications, any more than can the creation of a painting or other work of art. If the aim is to give body to some ephemeral aesthetic principle, then it seems clear that the architect needs to act for the building *project* itself, rather than for the client.

The use of an agreement for architectural services is mandatory for all members of RIBA, although the actual conditions are not specified, even though RIBA publishes a standard memorandum of agreement and Schedule of Services and Fees. At one time a minimum scale of charges was laid down, but the Monopolies and Mergers Commission declared that such minima were no longer in the public interest and should be abolished. In consequence, the mandatory conditions of engagement were abolished in 1982 and the document 'Architect's Appointment' came into force on 1 July of that year. The 'Architect's Appointment', which was substantially revised in 1992, gives guidance about how to appoint an architect, decide upon what services are to be undertaken and how to calculate the fees that ought to be charged on projects. The document departs from earlier ideas about appointing professional consultants in that it acknowledges that different types of project call for different levels of services.

(b) Civil Engineer

Building is generally distinguished from civil engineering as a different kind of activity. Historically this is because building was essentially a *domestic* activity, whereas engineering encompassed all forms of infrastructure and thus had to be more or less centrally organised, frequently by government. At some point, military engineering was distinguished from civil engineering, and thus civil engineering encompassed infrastructure development undertaken for non-military purposes. Since all such work is now undertaken outside the military, the term has only historic significance.

There are many different ways of distinguishing civil engineering from building—perhaps one of the simplest is to ask whether the structure has a roof! Examples of structures which fall into the category of building are houses, offices, factories, shops, railway stations, airport terminals and so on. Examples of structures which fall into the category of civil engineering are roads, bridges, tunnels, large earthworks, railways, airport runways, dams and so on. Clearly, many projects will encompass aspects of both industries and the dividing line is fuzzy and flexible. Thus, while building and civil engineering are two fundamentally separated parts of the UK construction industry, notwithstanding the reasons for this division, it often seems totally arbitrary.

The civil engineer undertakes a role not dissimilar to that of an architect, the major differences being the nature of what is going to be fabricated, and the extent of the engineer's authority over the contractor. In civil engineering works, it is quite normal for the engineer to have the power to issue instructions about anything, whether or not it is mentioned in any of the contract documentation. This is by stark contrast with the architect's role under building contracts, where the authority to issue instructions is limited. Civil engineers are professionally represented by the Institution of Civil Engineers (ICE).

(c) Structural Engineer

As structures have increased in complexity, their analysis has become a discipline in its own right, and it is considered beyond the power of one person to be well versed in the principles (and application) of architectural design as well as structural design. The specialism that has consequently emerged is that of structural engineering—governed by the Institute of Structural Engineers (IStructE)—whose members are frequently consulted at the design stage of projects. The function of the structural engineer is to analyse a design in terms of the way in which the structure will function, and to determine the size of each of the structural components (beams and columns in a building for example).

Most construction professionals have been taught some structural analysis, and this enables two things. First, architects and civil engineers may be able to undertake structural analysis of simple structures to an extent sufficient to judge their safety. Secondly, they will have learned enough to know when advice from a structural engineer will be needed. In most projects, the interdependence between the structure of a building and its form means that designs pass back and forth between architect and structural engineer until a solution is derived which is satisfactory to both parties.

While a structural engineer will normally be employed under a direct contract with the client, this is not always the case. It is quite possible for the 'lead designer' on a particular project to employ an independent structural engineer for this part of the work, while retaining legal responsibility for the overall design. In such circumstances the structural engineer is effectively engaged as a subcontractor to the architect, or to the contractor under a design and build contract.

(d) Services Engineer

A services engineer specialises in the 'sub-systems' of a building, that is those parts which control or affect the internal environment, including the mechanical and electrical installations. This is a wide-ranging discipline, the relevant professional institution for which is the Chartered Institute of Building Services Engineers (CIBSE). The services within a building are subdivided into mechanical and electrical and it is therefore usual for there to be at least two services engineers on a project.

The role of services engineers has a significant impact on the design process. They each have a separate role during the design stages, and their proposals are, necessarily, highly interdependent. In turn, these proposals also have implications for the structure of the building, which has to carry the weight of the installations, and for its form, the shape and size of which must accommodate the space taken up by these installations. In addition, a forward-thinking services engineer will be able to accomplish much without the need for expensive machinery if alterations can be made to the shape and form of the building. The interplay between these design disciplines creates a huge demand for co-ordination and integration, which is usually accomplished by taking the design through a series of complex iterations. The idea of construction as a series of sequential stages (briefing, design, fabrication) rapidly loses credibility in such circumstances.

Like structural engineers, services engineers may be employed on a project either directly by the client or as consultants to other participants such as the architect or the main contractor. In addition, there is the strong possibility that the design and installation of certain services will form a single package let to a nominated subcontractor. In this case the services engineer will be either an employee of or a consultant to that specialist sub-contractor.

(e) Quantity Surveyor

The role of the quantity surveyor—usually a member of the QS division of the Royal Institution of Chartered Surveyors (RICS)—has been alluded to in Chapter 1, where it was pointed out that this discipline emerged from the increasing need to monitor the works and to control progress and expenditure. The discipline has developed a long way since then, becoming one of the most dominant forces in the industry. Many quantity surveyors regard the term 'building economist' as more accurate in describing the role that they undertake.

There is a wide variety in the types of services offered by those who call themselves quantity surveyors, but a traditional QS practice sees its purpose as taking a set of architect's drawings and developing from them a list of descriptions and quantities of every item in the building. This list, known as a 'bill of quantities', serves a range of purposes. It is first used for the selection of the contractor through a process of competitive tendering. Each of a number of contractors prices this bill of quantities and this forms the basis of its bid. In order to do this, each contractor also employs its own quantity surveyor (although these are often called estimators). Once appointed, a contractor will use the bill of quantities for a variety of other purposes, such as cost control, progress control, buying materials, discovering the precise location of parts of the building about which the drawings are vague and so on. The employer's agents also put the bill to further use in the valuation of work which the contractor has been instructed to do differently from what was originally envisaged (variations).

Since a bill of quantities has developed into such a comprehensive multi-purpose document, and since it is the vehicle of the profession of quantity surveying, these professionals have become involved in an ever-wider field of activity. For example, the aim of cost control on behalf of the client can be served by selecting materials and specifying methods which are economical. On the other hand, the client's overall expenditure in using the completed facility after it has been built will dwarf the initial capital cost. Therefore, the client may be better served if provided with a building which is more expensive initially, but has lower running costs. Such considerations require an understanding of accountancy, economics, construction technology and negotiation. Thus, what emerged as a relatively simple role has become a significant and comprehensive influence on the way in which construction projects are perceived and managed.

(f) Building Surveyor

Building surveyors are another of the disciplines which fall under the aegis of the RICS (Royal Institution of Chartered Surveyors). This is a specialism which evolved from general practice surveying in terms of the way in which people manage their assets, particularly land and whatever stands upon it. Building surveyors originally were the people who examined buildings to ascertain their condition. This is a distinctly different discipline from that of general practice surveyors who examine buildings in order to determine their value. In the UK these two activities have become so specialised that it is rare to find them practised by the same individual.

Because building surveyors have developed their specialism in terms of analysing the condition of properties, they have also tended to expand their role into specifying the remedial works necessary to repair or maintain buildings. In this sense they frequently take on the role which would otherwise be filled by an architect in designing, specifying and supervising the works on behalf of their client. However, this project management role, whilst still expanding, is generally restricted to smaller projects, and certainly to commercial and domestic property. A third role undertaken by building surveyors, as a further extension to this, is the management of a client's built assets with the aim of ensuring that the client gets the best use out of a building.

(g) Facilities Manager

Like some building surveyors, a facilities manager (or premises manager) also takes on the responsibility for managing the client's building. The difference is only one of emphasis. Facilities managers consider the building as one of the many facilities which a client uses in order to achieve the purpose of its own business. Therefore, much of what facilities managers do is not part of the construction industry. They would, for example, concern themselves with the maintenance of security systems, computer installations and every aspect of the facilities which a business uses. However, buildings are part of a firm's facilities, and the role of a facilities manager becomes particularly significant when they recommend that a new building is required, or that some other construction work is needed. In this way, it is increasingly the case that the facilities manager is the interface between the client and the construction industry. Whilst there is an Association of Facilities Managers, it is currently more a learned society than a professional institution and is not a qualifying body.

(h) Project Manager

Another discipline which has emerged recently is that of project management. Clearly, if a construction project requires special skills because of its impermanence and the transient involvement of the contributors, this is not the only industry in which this is the case. Those who hold themselves out as project managers frequently claim to have accumulated those skills which would enable them to manage any project, be it computing, aerospace, research or construction. Indeed, there are people who can move with ease between these industries. But, generally, a project manager is industry-specific because of the need to control technology rather than people.

Project management has also been fuelled by professionals who envisage a greater role for their profession in the future than has been the case in the past. For example, many quantity surveyors, aware of the growing importance of their discipline, maintain that their profession ought to provide project managers. Clearly, none of the professions can claim to be the 'correct' profession to lead all projects, and the real issue is how to decide what skills are needed to lead a particular project.

This discipline, then, counts amongst its members many who are already practising professionals from other disciplines. The aim is to represent the client's interests, and to act as the interface between the client and the industry. As such, there is no specific professional institution, although the Association of Project Managers is a body which is beginning to be a representative organisation.

(i) Construction Manager

The discussion in Chapter 5 develops the ideas behind construction management as a procurement method. This has led to the emergence of construction managers who hold themselves out as being experts in managing and co-ordinating the construction (design and fabrication) process. Frequently, their primary concern is time. In construction management projects, design takes place under the control of the construction manager, who should normally be appointed at an early stage. Their aim will be to ensure that the client's wishes are effectively converted into a building as quickly and economically as possible. The simple act of identifying this role highlights the idea that there are many in the industry who feel that the construction process tends to be dominated by the exigencies of design, rather then by the exigencies of 'just getting the job done'. Construction managers will, therefore, only be found on certain types of project, and will tend to be the 'leading consultant'.

(j) Clerk of Works

The clerk of works is a person whose role is frequently ambiguous on site. In contracts, the role is usually quite clear; the clerk of works may be permitted on to the site by express terms of the contract, but has no authority at all. A common description of this role is as 'the architect's eyes on site'. However, this reference to the architect may be misleading, for it is clear that the clerk of works is the employer's responsibility, not the architect's. It has for example been held that, where a clerk of works failed to notice defects in certain fixings, the employer's damages for negligence against the architect were reduced on the ground of contributory negligence (*Kensington & Chelsea & Westminster AHA* v *Wettern Composites Ltd* [1985] 1 All ER 346).

The purpose of appointing a clerk of works is to monitor progress of the works, conformance to standards and proper carrying out of the contractor's obligations. On some sites a clerk of works may be permanently employed, but frequently this is a roving commission, with the clerk of works taking the responsibility for visiting several sites. Where provision is made for the clerk of works to issue instructions to contractors, such instructions normally have to be confirmed by the architect in writing within a specified time period.

Overall, the clerk of works is in a good position to be able to advise the contractor and indicate the nature of what might be reported back to the architect, as well as being able to negotiate to a certain extent about acceptability of work (subject, of course, to the architect's approval). Thus, whilst the clerk of works has no legal authority, it is easy to imagine how such a person may wield a certain 'power' on site.

This discussion demonstrates why there are problems of coordination in the industry. Many people are needed to ensure that each aspect of the project contributes effectively to the whole. Because so many interactions need to take place, there is a huge demand for management, which is increasingly being filled by 'newly identified' roles. Many construction disputes, whilst not necessarily being caused by these factors, are clarified by knowing how the industry has come to be like it is.

Chapter 3

Traditional General Contracting

Traditional general contracting is the *usual* method of procuring buildings in the construction industry. This has been the case since 1870, when Cubitts in London first began to offer the services of a general contractor, before which time building work tended to be procured as a series of direct contracts between client and trade contractors.

The emergence of general contracting was a response to the increasing sophistication of construction technology during the Industrial Revolution. An ever-increasing number of new techniques and new materials caused increasing problems of co-ordination on building sites. Coupled with this, there was a general move towards clearly identified and protected crafts whose members, to become fully trained and qualified, needed continuity of employment. Economies of scale in the use of plant and the disposition of labour, and the development of a transportation system which enabled contractors to increase the base of their operations geographically, all combined to create a demand for a contractor who would take on the entire responsibility for a building project. This relieved architects of much of the demands for close site supervision, and enabled them to devote more time to coping with designs which would harness the new materials and techniques. At the same time, the burden of measuring work in progress and preparing documentation for tendering purposes fuelled the demand for what became quantity surveying.

1 Features of traditional general contracting

The essence of general contracting is that the contractor undertakes to build what is described in the contract documentation. In other words, the designer designs and the builder builds. The historical antecedents are clear, but in order to achieve this disposition of responsibility, the architect must co-ordinate all of the design input from the various technological design specialists, so that a single comprehensive set of documents can be put out to tender. The documents used for this purpose become very important in distinguishing design faults from fabrication faults and it is for this reason that the standard forms of contract tend to oblige the builder to produce what is in the documents. This effectively removes design liability from the contractor.

As mentioned in the previous chapter, the main pricing document, and the main cost control mechanism, is the bill of quantities. The central role which this plays in the process has made the quantity surveyor a dominant contributor. The system has evolved around the relationships between clients, architects, quantity surveyors and builders; these contractual relationships are summarised in Figure 2 (*below*).

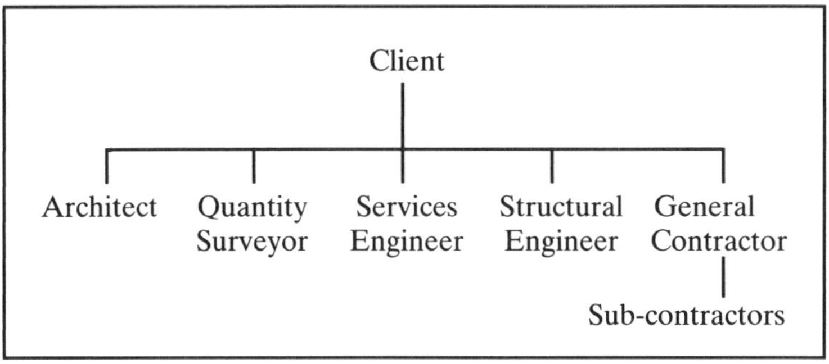

Figure 2: Contractual relationships in general contracting

The role of engineers is to contribute advice to the design team, led by the architect. They will also take on some supervisory duties on behalf of the client to ensure that their intentions are carried out adequately. The problem of what to do when the product fails to match the designers' intentions can only be resolved by looking at the means by which those intentions were conveyed to the builder.

The problems with the general contracting method of procurement revolve around the issues outlined above, ie complexity of technology, reliance upon contract documents, role of the quantity surveyor and co-ordination of specialists. For example, when the technology becomes very complex, general contracting cannot cope with the demands for management information. Any procurement system should only be used on projects for which it is suited, therefore it is important to understand the circumstances which are appropriate for general contracting. This theme is developed in the next section.

The bill of quantities is a key contractual document which relies upon the design being substantially complete before the contractor is selected. Because of time constraints and other uncertainties, there are projects where this is not possible. Such projects are likely to run into enormous problems under the general contracting approach. Another key idea under traditional general contracting is the assumption that the contractor's organisation contains all the necessary resources, including skills, for undertaking the work. Where the nature of the project is such that it is unrealistic to expect a single organisation to contain such a range of skills, some other form of procurement should be adopted.

2 Use of general contracting

The commonly used form of contract for general contracting is produced by the Joint Contracts Tribunal, the JCT Standard Form of Building Contract, 1980 edition (JCT 80). The Institution of Civil Engineers (ICE) produce a standard form for works of civil engineering, the ICE conditions of contract, 6th edition (ICE 6). However, there are many other standard forms of contract which are appropriate for general contracting and, whilst these differ in detail, many of the principles are transferable because they all deal with similar issues.

Such general contracts can be recognised by the following characteristics:

— the design is assumed to be substantially complete at time of tender,
— the bill of quantities has a contractual role,
— the employer's agent (whether architect or engineer) has a dual role of agent and impartial certifier,
— the contractor has no design responsibility,
— the majority of the construction resources are owned or directly employed by the contractor,
— payments to the contractor are calculated on the basis of the contractor's tender, *not* on the basis of the contractor's costs.

Clearly, there cannot be one universally 'right' method of construction contracting, because there is so much variety amongst construction projects. This leads to a consideration of the circumstances which are best suited to traditional general contracting (TGC).

It seems that general contracting should be used where:

(*a*) the employer has commissioned, and taken responsibility for, the design of the works;

(*b*) the design is complete at the time of selecting the contractor;

(*c*) the client wishes to reserve the right, via nomination, to select the sub-contractors for certain parts of the work;

(*d*) prime cost sums (those items which will be provided by nominated sub-contractors and suppliers, and for which the contractor will be reimbursed on the basis of actual cost) do not form the major proportion of the contract sum (subject to the previous point);

(*e*) the client wishes to use a quantity surveyor to plan and control the finance of the project, in conjunction with the architect;

(*f*) the client wishes the contractor selection process to be based upon the contractor's estimate of price and for the contractor to bear the risk of costs exceeding prices;

(*g*) the architect appointed by client is adequately experienced to cope with the co-ordination of the design team, to lead the design effort, and to co-ordinate the interface between design and fabrication;

(*h*) the client does not know what else to do, and the consultants do not raise the choice of procurement method as an issue.

Strictly, these are not selection criteria, but a combination of one or more of them occurs on projects following the general contracting path. It may happen that a general contract is let under circumstances which do not accord with those given, but it is suggested that such projects would be better served by consideration of alternative procurement methods. These ideas are discussed below:

(a) Employer must commission design

Under TGC the employer commissions the design and, therefore, has a responsibility for that design when appointing a contractor to produce it. This employer-sponsored design is the most distinctive feature of general contracting. It means that the contractor is only responsible for fabricating what is documented, which may be significantly different from what the client actually wants.

(b) Design must be near completion at time of tender

The selection of a contractor is usually based upon price, so it is essential that the employer can describe, with some degree of accuracy, what it is that the contractor is being invited to carry out. This means that the design must be fully worked out, detailed and documented and it must be measured, precisely or approximately, in order for a bill of quantities to be prepared. The documentation of the design consists of drawings, specifications, schedules and bills. The relationships between these documents are complex, and are dealt with in Chapter 9.

A further point about the completion of the design at tender stage is that it is sometimes desirable for the contractor to be involved in the design process itself. If novel construction techniques are being considered, it is sensible for the contractor to liaise with the design team so that the influence of the fabrication process can be taken into account. If this is indeed required, then general contracting will not be appropriate.

(c) Nomination important to employer

There are many aspects of construction work which the employer will not wish to leave to the contractor alone, but for which the employer will select specialists. For example, a new supermarket will need the very latest refrigerated display equipment in order to compete adequately with its competitors; the cheapest capital cost is simply not good enough. Again, where a building is to house equipment which may take longer to design and fabricate than the whole building project, such equipment must be specified and ordered before the contractor is even selected. Yet again, the employer may simply not trust the contractor to use competent sub-contractors.

The fact that the contractor will be reimbursed for nominated sub-contractors, whatever they cost, means that the risks are very different from those associated with domestic sub-contractors. The latter are entirely an arrangement between the contractor and the sub-contractor, and the contractor must find the money for them from within the bills.

Nomination must be used judiciously by the employer, as it is the single biggest cause of building contract disputes. Indeed, some commentators have suggested that nomination should never be used, because of these problems.

(d) Prime cost sums must not dominate

Because the bills allow prime cost sums for nominated subcontracts (those whom the employer selects and the contractor is instructed to use) the contractor will not be putting in a price for those parts of the work. The aim of competitive tendering is for the contractor to price the works competitively. Therefore, not only must the design be substantially complete, it must also be work for which the contractor is pricing. Large numbers of prime cost sums will mean that the general contractor is little more than a general manager/co-ordinator, in which case an alternative such as management contracting should be considered.

(e) Traditional architect/QS axis

It is not simply the choice of designer that leads to TGC, but also the cost planning, cost control and contractor selection mechanisms. General contracting should be used if the client wishes to let the contract by competitive bidding. It should also be used if the client wishes to appoint an independent professional quantity surveyor to plan the expenditure on the project, prepare detailed cost control documentation and to control the budget throughout the project. A bill of quantities is the traditional document for this purpose, but increasingly it is far from the only choice, competing as it does with more recent developments such as a contract sum analysis, or a priced schedule of activities. However, the division of responsibility, such that the architect designs, the quantity surveyor controls finance and the contractor controls fabrication is a key feature of general contracting. Increasingly, quantity surveyors are offering their services as the leading consultant in the team, influencing the choice of designer, as well as the choice of procurement method. This may be a prudent route to take where finance is the main or only criterion for success.

(f) Price

General contracts come in a wide variety of versions, and can be used whether the employer wants to commission the builder for a fixed lump sum, or if the employer wishes only a guide to the price, with the actual amount to be calculated after completion, or anything in between these extremes. Therefore, the extent to which the firmness of price dictates the type of contract is not an issue for TGC. What is an issue is that the contractor is selected on, and undertakes to work to, some sort of price offered to the employer based upon some indication of the work. The final price to be paid will be calculated on the basis of the contractor's offer. The risk of the work costing the contractor more than was allowed in the price is generally a risk taken by the contractor, subject to some important exceptions discussed later. It is because the contractor is selected according to price that the documents relating to the price—usually the bills—are so important.

(g) Architect sufficiently experienced

General contracting allows the architect flexibility in choosing the design team. Since each consultant is in direct contact with the client, the architect merely needs to instruct the client whom to appoint. The architect then supervises and co-ordinates the team.

In order for this to work, the client must be assured that the architect has the relevant integrative skills. Although many architects have proved themselves sufficiently professional and adequately skilled to meet the demands of this situation, it is important for the client to understand how much power is being delegated to the architect. Because of the demands for integration and management, architects should not be selected solely on their design skills; management skills should also play a major part.

(h) In the absence of any other suggestion

It is probably true to say that, if a procurement method does not immediately suggest itself, and the project does not clearly demand some specific approach, then a general contract is best. What is undoubtedly true is that, if no consideration is given to the method of procurement, habit will almost inevitably result in the adoption of TGC! As to what *form* of contract should be chosen, this depends upon a further set of criteria, and these are examined in Chapter 7.

Chapter 4

Design and Build Contracts

Design and build is a long-established procurement method which is not unique to the construction industry. From ships to micro-electronic components, it is commonplace to buy things which have been designed and fabricated by a single organisation. Indeed, before the emergence of architecture as a profession distinct from fabrication, pre-industrial society used to procure building work through a process of design and build. It was the separation of responsibility for fabrication from responsibility for design that led to the emergence of so-called traditional general contracting in the nineteenth century. This separation of design from construction in the building industry has been the source of many problems for a long time, and remains so today.

A contractor's design responsibility can take a wide variety of forms. These range from merely finalising details of a design which has been substantially completed by the employer's agents, through to a complete package deal involving the contractor in complete responsibility for the whole of the design and fabrication processes. Because of this, there are a variety of standard form building contracts to choose from for design and build, and it is important to understand the purposes behind each of them.

1 Features of design and build contracts

The essential features of design and build contracts can best be dealt with in terms of how the requirements for the job are defined by employer and contractor; the pricing mechanism; and the roles and responsibilities within the process.

(a) Employer's requirements and contractor's proposals

The first essential feature, that of defining the work, begins with the *employer's requirements*. This document defines what it is that the employer wants built. The tendering contractors respond with proposals which will include fabrication as well as design work. The scale of design work depends on the extent to which the employer has already commissioned design work during the process of drawing up the employer's requirements. The contractor's design input varies from one contract to another, and will usually involve refining or completing whatever design work has already been undertaken by the employer's agents. Occasionally, the contractor will be invited to submit design proposals from scratch. Clearly, there is tremendous flexibility in this approach.

There will usually be some negotiation between the employer and one or more competing contractors, with the aim of settling on an agreed set of *contractor's proposals*. Competition between contractors may be part of this process, resulting in a final choice from a limited number of bidders, whose proposals will include a price as well as the manner of its calculation. Once the employer's requirements and the contractor's proposals match, the contract can be executed and the contractor can undertake the work. The contractor will be totally responsible for undertaking the design work outlined in the contractor's proposals, for fabricating the building, and for co-ordinating and integrating the entire process. This includes the appointment of consultants if the contractor does not have the necessary skills in-house. The employer may also choose to appoint consultants in order to monitor the various aspects of the work, but this is not always the case.

One way in which standard forms of design and build contracts differ is in the definition of the contractor's obligation. Some (like the JCT 1981 design build form) oblige the contractor to build what is defined in the contractor's proposals, whereas others oblige the contractor to build what is in the employer's requirements. However, if the two documents match, as they should, this is not a significant difference.

(b) Price

Whether the contract sum is derived by negotiation or by competition, it is a price for the whole of the contractor's responsibilities, including design, fabrication and the obtaining of any necessary statutory approvals such as planning permission, except where the employer's requirements exclude this. The financial risk associated with this work is purely the contractor's, in that the contractor must do whatever is necessary to achieve the employer's requirements, whether or not particular items of work or materials have been specified. This makes the client's financial commitment very clear, with the risk of the cost exceeding the price lying squarely with the contractor. Of course, any changes in the employer's requirements, or any hindrance by the employer, will result in the employer being liable for extra money. However, out of all of the procurement procedures, design and build offers the highest confidence in the contract sum.

A feature that is sometimes present in design and build deals is a 'guaranteed maximum price' (GMP). This helps clients to feel reassured that they are not signing 'a blank cheque'. As an incentive to the contractor, any savings made by completing the project for a price below the GMP may sometimes be shared between the client and the contractor.

The price may be governed by means of a 'contract sum analysis' (CSA). This obviates the need for a bill of quantities by replacing most of its functions. The nature of a CSA is very different from that of a bill of quantities, its form not being prescribed by any of the contracts. The major difference is that rather than following a prescribed method for allocating prices to rates for pre-measured quantities, the contractor chooses the most appropriate method for describing and pricing the work (which will, of course, include design). A CSA can be presented in any form appropriate to the circumstances of the project, but some of the purposes of a CSA have their parallels in bills of quantity. These are calculation of stage payments (in some circumstances), valuation of employer's change instructions, and exercising the fluctuations clauses (where applicable). The CSA should enable the design content of the work to be reflected in any estimation of the value of variations.

(c) Roles and responsibilities

One of the most significant features of design and build arrangements is the lack of an independent certification role in the contract. There is no architect or contract administrator to issue certificates or settle differences between the parties, and there is no independent quantity surveyor responsible for preparing the basis upon which contractors tender. The absence of such roles, which would be incompatible with the contractor's exclusive responsibility for the project, changes some of the basic assumptions about what roles are required on construction projects. Whilst there may be provision for appointing an adjudicator for the project, such a role is not intended to be anything other than an expedient measure for temporary settlement of disputes, pending completion. In any event, the power of an adjudicator has been severely restricted by the decision in *A Cameron Ltd* v *John Mowlem & Co plc* (1990) 52 BLR 42.

Figure 3 shows the contractual relationships encountered in design and build contracts, the key feature being the contractor's 'single point responsibility' to the employer. The role of the quantity surveyor is shown in parenthesis because there is not the need for traditional quantity surveying in this form of procurement. There is no standard method of measurement, no bill of quantities, and no *contractual* role for the quantity surveyor. However, since cost information and economic advice remain important, contractors frequently choose to employ the skills of the quantity surveyor. Alternatively, or in addition, the employer may choose to employ architects, quantity surveyors, engineers and so on.

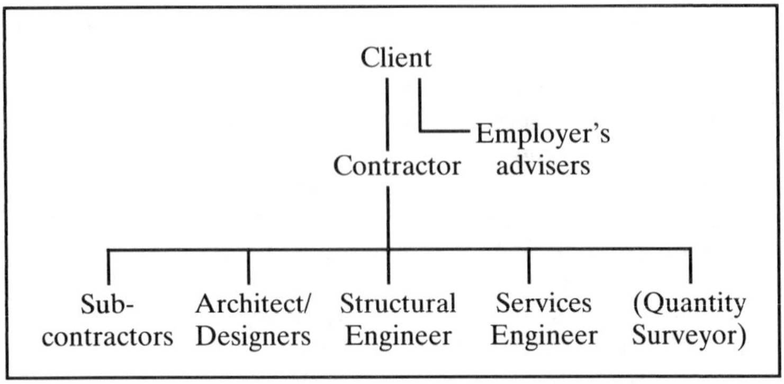

Figure 3: Contractual relationships in design and build

Many quantity surveyors have welcomed the departure from traditional bills of quantities and the British approach to cost control, which some claim to be counter-productive in serving the best interests of the client. Such quantity surveyors have seized the opportunity of becoming specialist client advisers in all aspects of the economics of building and the procurement process. There are a large number of consultants who are qualified to advise the client during the whole of the process. These consultants come into the category of employer's advisers and would be used by the employer when dealing with the contractor. It is often the case that employers who are more experienced in traditional general contracting will set up their own project team, with a counterpart for each of the professional advisers in the contractor's project team. The contractor's team may or may not be in-house.

The contractual relationships in design and build offer some advantages over other methods of construction procurement. The most important advantage is that the contractor is responsible for everything. This single point responsibility is very attractive to clients, particularly those who may not be interested in trying to distinguish between a design fault and a workmanship fault. It also means that the contractor is not relying on external firms for execution of design, or for the supply of information. By removing these blocks to effective communication, experience has shown that programmes and budgets are more likely to be adhered to, and the speed of building is likely to be quicker.

One of the benefits of the design and build process is the increased opportunity for harnessing the contractor's experience during the design stages of the project. Many of the developments in procurement processes, and much of the work in the field of study known as 'buildability' have been undertaken with this purpose in mind. The benefits of the integration of the designers and builders are more economic buildings as well as a more economic and effective fabrication process. However, this integration may also produce a disadvantage in that, where there is a conflict between aesthetic quality and ease of fabrication, the requirements for fabrication will dominate.

A further criticism of design and build has been that a contractor will put in the minimum design effort required to win the contract. This criticism, together with the previous point, is a strong indication that quality, particularly architectural quality, will suffer under this procurement process. However, the criticisms are not unequivocal, since they are aimed as much at the people practising the system as the system itself, and, as such, can be made about any process. Much of the criticism of design and build from within the construction industry is based upon institutionalised ideas about roles and responsibilities, and it therefore suffers from the same weakness as all stereotyping.

2 Use of design and build forms

Frequently the only advice given by those who draft design and build contracts about the circumstances under which they should be used is that they are *not* for use where the employer has appointed an architect or contract administrator to act as employer's agent for the duration of the project! Considering the range of uses to which these forms have been put, and their inherent flexibility, it would not be sensible to define circumstances for using it in terms of specific types of construction project. Rather, the overriding features should be the client's requirements regarding risk apportionment, the nature of the client's experience, and the availability of suitable contractors to undertake the work.

The characteristics of projects where design and build would be suitable can be considered to be as follows:

(1) the client need not be familiar with construction,
(2) the relative importance of client priorities (time, cost, function, quality, value for money, etc) can be considered, rather than selecting contractors on price alone,
(3) technical complexity of the project is such that specialist nomination is not required,
(4) there is no need to make variations to requirements as work proceeds,
(5) patterns of responsibility and communication are focused through a single organisation, which has responsibility for design and fabrication,
(6) there is a need for an early start on site.

Each of these are discussed below.

(a) The client's experience

Unlike some other forms of procurement, it is not necessary for the client to be an 'expert', although it should be remembered that the traditional approach has evolved as a response to the lack of trust endemic in the construction industry. Clients employing the traditional approach like the feeling of control that the high degree of documentation gives them. However, a high level of documentation does not guarantee greater certainty, and the price of this level of information may well be the difference between achieving pessimistic cost targets and over-running optimistic ones.

Novice clients who know nothing of the construction industry will often stumble into design and build without realising it. It is the usual approach when engaging a jobbing builder for repairs. Modifications are made to requirements and proposals until they match, and prices are discussed until the client feels that the most economical and effective job will be done. Therefore, whilst design and build clients may be very sophisticated, it is equally likely that they may not be so.

(b) Relative importance of client priorities

Whatever system of procurement is used, the client ought to make it clear to the tendering contractors what the objectives of the project are, and how they relate to each other. It is generally believed in the construction industry that quality is the first thing to suffer in design and build contracts, but there is little evidence to support this. No one has yet established any correlation between procurement method and perceived quality of the product.

Cost certainty for the employer is one of the advantages of design and build. It is a fixed price contract so the risk associated with pricing is entirely taken by the contractor, except to the extent that fluctuations clauses apply. Notwithstanding the cost certainty, design and build is not necessarily cheap. Single point responsibility and fixed price contracts mean that the contractor carries more risk than a general contractor, and it is to be expected that a design and build contractor would add a premium to allow for this. Similarly, design and build encourages economical solutions, and enables value to be considered as well as price. A truly economical approach to the employer's problem may not produce the cheapest building in terms of capital outlay. In this respect, design and build may cost the client more than traditional general contracting in capital outlay. Some of this extra capital cost arises because more economic use of the client's revenue will follow when the building is used; some of it arises because the design and build contractor has a higher level of risk to absorb. On a high risk project the premium paid for the contractor's risk element may be too high and it may then be inappropriate to pass so much risk over to the contractor. If the cost of transferring the risk is unacceptable, then other forms of procurement (with less risk to the contractor) should be considered.

As a procurement method, design and build offers different possibilities in combinations of priorities. A client whose highest priority is aesthetic quality can appoint a design and build contractor with a reputation for architectural merit, perhaps a specialist design and build firm which includes architects as directors. A client whose highest priority is speed or money should appoint a design and build contractor with a track record of hitting such targets. Clearly, there are numerous ways of configuring the priorities for a project, and the client should make explicit decisions about these before inviting contractors to respond with their proposals. It is essential that the client takes the opportunity to look at the contractor's previous work and clients. Different contractors have different skills, and the selection process should take some account of this.

An element of competition is usually seen as advantageous when appointing a contractor. Traditionally, contractors submit tenders based upon a description of the works. In this sense they are competing on price alone, since they are all pricing the same description of the works. One of the strengths of design and build is that the contractor's proposals will include design solutions to problems posed in the employer's requirements. In this way, contractors are competing not only on price, but also on any other criteria which the client thinks important. This presents opportunities for making the quality or level of accommodation the selection criteria, where a client can put forward a budget and ask the bidders to demonstrate how much building they can supply for the money (a technique frequently used by local authorities when procuring sports centres, for example). Clearly, the element of competition is far more flexible in design and build than in traditional arrangements.

One of the biggest disadvantages of design and build is that the brief (ie the employer's requirements) must be clear and unambiguous very early in the process. If the contractor is to undertake the whole of the design, the employer is committed to an outline statement of requirements at a very early stage. This is by contrast with general contracting where the architect and other design team members help to refine and develop the brief in conjunction with the refinement of the design. Obviously it is possible for the employer to commission early design development before letting a design and build contract, in which case this particular problem is very similar in both procurement methods. The key issue is for the client to make a deliberate choice about the extent of design work to be undertaken prior to the appointment of the design and build contractor. In any event, the brief should not be subjected to major or frequent change during the project. Although variations to requirements are not such a problem in general contracting (because the brief can be developed alongside feasibility studies and sketch schemes), it must be remembered that the quantity of variations brought about because of the client's change of heart is tiny compared to those brought about by the design team refining and revising their earlier decisions.

(c) Technical complexity of the project

When dealing with technically complex projects, the solution rightly adopted by the construction industry is to specialise. The range of specialist sub-contractors in construction is extensive and comprehensive. Design and build is one of the few procurement processes which reduces the employer's choice of those specialists. In general contracting the process of nomination has emerged so that the employer may reserve the right to select particular specialists which the contractor must employ. The employer under a design and build contract who wishes to specify particular sub-contractors to undertake particular parts of the work cannot nominate a sub-contractor in the traditional way, but can specify a sub-contractor in the employer's requirements. In such circumstances, the employer picks up the responsibility for this choice, but there are seldom provisions in the main contract to deal with the complex legal relationships which arise from the practice of nomination of sub-contractors. Therefore, without very carefully drafted additional provisions, the employer is taking on a considerable risk. This means that if the technical complexity is to be confronted by use of specified (nominated) specialists, then design and build may well be unsuitable.

Technical complexity of a project may lead to solutions and approaches which are more akin to process engineering than to building. A client with a high degree of technical knowledge about what is to be procured, who wishes technical demands to drive the project, would be well advised to consider other forms of procurement. Whilst this does not mean that design and build is necessarily unsuitable, it is likely that in such circumstances the use of other forms of procurement will be favoured. This is because of the more comprehensive precontractual documentation which may be required.

(d) Variations to requirements as work proceeds

Variations to requirements are a constant source of problems for any form of contract, being one of the most frequent causes of claims and often leading to disputes. A client who wishes to reserve the right to make extensive alterations to requirements during the fabrication process should *not* use design and build. It is a process which demands early agreement between employer's requirements and contractor's proposals. A change in either of these documents makes it awkward, although not impossible, to bring the project to a satisfactory conclusion. The valuation of variations can be difficult without a comprehensive contract sum analysis and the employer's insistence on time and cost targets becomes less convincing if the requirements are altered. Therefore, a client who needs to retain the right to make variations should either consider an alternative procurement method, or should consider allowing the design and build contract to be completed on its original basis, making variations the subject of additional contracts after the conclusion of the project.

(e) Patterns of responsibility and communication

Single point responsibility is the most obvious advantage offered by design and build. There is no division of responsibility between design and fabrication, so the finished building should reflect the trade-offs made between these occasionally conflicting demands. In terms of choosing the procurement method, it is essential to appreciate that design and build does *not* necessarily mean poor quality. It is a method to be used where the project is one for which it makes sense to combine responsibility for design with responsibility for fabrication. The types of project for which design and build contracts are suitable are those where the contractor's responsibility for design extends over the whole project, whether the design is partially completed by others or not. This is distinct from the situation where the contractor's responsibility for design only covers a particular portion of the works.

The communication patterns observed in design and build projects are amongst the most effective to be found in any form of procurement. Since institutionalised roles are reduced in their importance, there is less likelihood of there being institutional axes to grind. The scope for adversarial games with the client in the middle is greatly reduced, and consequently separate firms will not be vying for ascendancy. Single point responsibility, therefore, reduces much of the guarded and ambiguous communication which often takes place when parties have one eye on the possibility of litigation.

(f) Early start on site

Since the contractor is undertaking the design work, there are opportunities to overlap the design and construction processes. This will give the benefits that any form of fast-track construction will give, but carries the same penalties. The benefits of fast-tracking are that the overall construction process can be speeded up by not having the fabrication process delayed until the whole of the design is completed. However, too much overlapping will result in penalties arising from the need to revise early design decisions as the design is refined. If the project has already started on site by the time these revisions are made, it is often the case that some work has to be undone before further progress can be made. Extreme cases of this phenomenon can lead to the problem of a fast-track project taking longer to complete than a conventional one. However, under design and build such things are purely the contractor's responsibility.

There are clients who need to start spending their budget within a short time of the money being allocated. This happens particularly in the public sector. For such clients the appeal of an early start on site is that they can spend some of the budget before the money is withdrawn in favour of departments with more urgent needs.

Chapter 5

Management-based Contracts

The term 'management-based' might be taken to imply that other forms of contract do not encompass management. This would be unfair, since building projects have been 'managed' by those who organise them for many years. Nevertheless, it is true to say that certain procurement methods start from the assumption that 'management' is an activity which is distinct from design, and that in certain circumstances management is more effective if it is separately identified as a contractual responsibility. This idea has found favour with many commercial clients recently, resulting in two categories of procurement method; management contracting, which is a development of general contracting, and construction management, which has its origins in North America. There are other methods, such as 'design, manage and construct', which are refinements of the basic methods described here but these are beyond the scope of this book.

1 Characteristics of management-based procurement

One of the main purposes of a management contract is to limit the exposure of the 'main contractor' to risk. The types of project that are most suitable for management contracts involve a high degree of commercial risk. Under the traditional approach, a tendering contractor would have to make an allowance to accommodate such risk, resulting in inflated tenders. The contractor who fails to appreciate the level of risk will submit the lowest tender, and under these circumstances, the likelihood of insolvency and cash flow problems for the contractor is increased. Insolvency of contractors can be very expensive for the client. Therefore, it is in both the contractor's and client's interests for there to be low risk contracts. Many employers who use management contracts are developers. Not only are they used to building, they also build frequently. Constant exposure to hazards reduces the level of uncertainty and, therefore, risk. Clients who regularly engage in building are well placed to absorb some of the risks attached to the process.

The two management-based methods achieve similar results in terms of project organisation, but they have very different origins. These are reflected in a number of significant legal differences between the systems.

(a) Management contracting

Management contracting has been in existence for some time but it is only since 1987 that it has had its own standard form of contract. Before this, modified standard forms or contractors' own forms were used. In some cases, what was intended to be a management contract simply adopted the same conditions as those which operated between contractor and sub-contractor, even though these were entirely inappropriate to the main contract.

The characteristics of a management contract are that the client engages the management contractor to participate in the project at an early stage, contribute construction expertise to the design and manage the construction. Because of these requirements, it is normal for the management contractor to be an experienced builder or construction company, but this is not essential. To avoid the client having to make a premature commitment to build, the standard form of management contract distinguishes between pre-construction and construction phases, thereby creating the opportunity for the employer to terminate the management contractor's employment after the design stage, but before work actually commences. The management contractor is not employed to carry out any of the works, but solely to manage the process. Management contracting is thus a procurement method that consists of 100 per cent sub-contracting. Every item of building work is sub-contracted to 'works contractors'. The contractual relationships in management contracting are shown in Figure 4.

These relationships allow the contractor to become part of the consultants' team, on equal terms with the other professionals. This is one of the main reasons that the contracting side of the industry has been promoting its use. The modern form of management

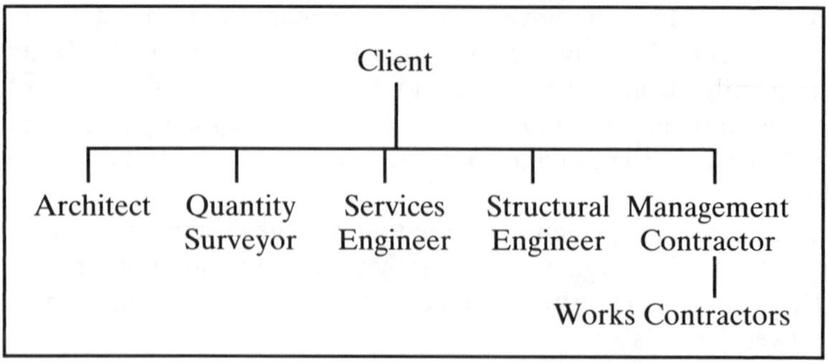

Figure 4: Contractual relationships in management contracting

contract also reduces the contractor's risk to a level equivalent to that of the design consultants, enabling contractors to dispense with a labour force, plant and equipment, and hence to reduce their operating costs significantly. These features have helped to push management contracting to a dominant position in the industry.

(b) Construction management

By contrast with management contracting, in the construction management form of procurement the client places direct contracts with the specialist and trades contractors. This is the single most important distinguishing feature of construction management. In order to do this, the client buys in the expertise of a construction manager who acts in the role of consultant. This technique overcomes many problems of management contracting which are associated with the direct contractual link between the management contractor and the works contractors.

Construction management has its origins in the United States, where there was a need for large buildings to be erected quickly and reliably. Coupled with increasing technical complexity, this led to the emergence of an ever-higher number of technical people being involved in the design, programming and construction of the building, which meant that the management of these people became a more important issue than that of design.

Figure 5 shows how the contractual links combine in construction management. However, it should be noted that the figure only shows the *contractual* links and cannot hope to convey the implications of construction management for a project's *organisational* structure.

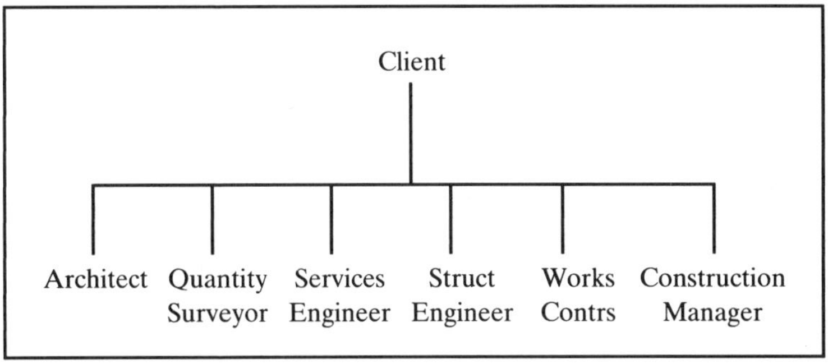

Figure 5: Contractual relationships in construction management

2 Background to management-based procurement

Evidence that the US construction industry could perform better than that of the United Kingdom, and increasing dissatisfaction with the output of the UK industry, prompted an examination of the management techniques used in the United States. Management contracting seems to be the result of an initial attempt at implementing construction management in the United Kingdom, but this development was severely curtailed by the inflexibility of an industry whose professional institutions were at the time restricted by compulsory conditions of engagement and mandatory fee scales (since outlawed under restrictive practices legislation).

As management contracting has grown in popularity and become more generally acceptable, the basic problems of the UK construction industry have re-emerged to show that management contracting is unsuitable for most British building projects. On the other hand, it is also clear that the 'traditional' forms of procurement are unsuitable for the increased technical complexity of modern construction projects. The construction industry has found it very difficult to accept management contracting wholeheartedly, and this has been evident from two trends. First, management contracting became more of a marketing tool for ambitious contractors, rather than a real alternative management strategy, and secondly, clients modified many clauses in the contract to displace contractual risk back to the contractor. The combination of these two factors resulted in the situation where many so-called management contracts were in truth no different from the traditional method of procurement. As expected under these circumstances, the same old problems emerged and management contracting rapidly fell into disrepute.

The basic problem with management contracting lies with the contractual links, information links and authority. The construction professions have their roots in systems of authority that date back to the middle of last century and, consequently, professional traditions are well established. This makes it difficult to form quickly a team of people who have not worked together in the past, and then to expect them to modify their traditional roles. Therefore, it seems that novel forms of procurement work best when the members of the team have worked together before.

To overcome the problems of management contracting, construction management emerged on major commercial development projects in London during the last few years. It is a system which involves a fundamental reappraisal of the familiar 'pecking order' in building projects. By subjecting the design team to the same management regime that the fabricators have long been familiar with, it is intended to ensure that the client's wishes predominate over all other interests in the project. As we shall see, this calls for clear project objectives from the client, as well as rapid and comprehensive responses to the project team's requests for information and instructions.

3 Use of management-based contracts

These procurement methods are most suited to various combinations of the following circumstances:

(*a*) the employer wishes the design to be carried out by an independent architect and design team;

(*b*) the client is familiar with construction and knows some or all of the professional team;

(*c*) the risks associated with the project are dominated by timeliness and cost;

(*d*) the project is technically complex, involving diverse technologies and sub-systems;

(*e*) the client needs to retain the right to make minor variations to requirements as the project proceeds;

(*f*) the nature of the project is such that it makes sense to separate professional responsibility for the design of the project from professional responsibility for the management of the project;

(*g*) the client requires an early start on site, and/or early completion of the project;
(*h*) the cost to the client needs to be competitive, but the control of cost in terms of securing 'value for money' is more important than simply securing the least possible cost.

They are commented upon below:

(a) Independence of architect and design team

This means that the employer wishes the architect and design team to be independent of the contractor. This is not a new idea, but the special point about management contracting is that it is offered as an alternative to, and perhaps in competition with, design and build packages where independence of the designer from the builder is not assured. The reason that this aspect is singled out is that in design and build contracts, there is no independent certification role, and this alters some very basic assumptions about contracting.

One of the main thrusts behind the development of the management-based methods is the idea that the traditional problems of construction procurement are fuelled to a large extent by the arbitrary ascendancy of members of the team over each other. The traditional 'pecking order' has given the architect authority over the builder. Design and build overcame this by turning the tables. Management-based methods are specifically designed to place the construction manager on an equal footing with the architect.

The separation of design from management requires that the manager be a specialist in management. This calls for skills quite different from those of a general contractor, and probably different from those of a management contractor. The prudent client should perhaps avoid firms who claim to be specialists in all of these things. In any event, the client should always be wary of contractors using the appellation as a marketing tool, rather than as an accurate description of the services which they are competent to offer.

(b) Client's familiarity with construction

These procurement methods demand an active role on the part of the client in the management of the process. There must be regular and effective feedback from the project team to the client. The appointment of a client's project manager may help this process, but that (of itself) does not transmute the procurement process into a 'project management' model. The idea of familiarity extends across not only the product of the construction industry, but also the idiosyncrasies of the process of construction. In particular, management-based procurement methods demand a responsive and authoritative contact in the client's organisation, otherwise a potentially quick process may be subjected to delay every time a decision is needed from the client. In order fully to appreciate this, it is essential that the client has some previous experience of working with the construction manager and with some of the other consultants.

(c) Relative importance of categories of project risk

Risk is very difficult to identify in construction projects. If this were not the case then construction would not be a difficult and interesting industry. In order to be able to configure an appropriate management strategy for the project, the client must make some explicit decisions about the nature of the risks associated with the project. For construction management to be most effective, it is essential that clients understand that they are commissioning a process that is intended to be speedy by comparison with other procurement processes. The need for speed may compromise decisions about least cost. This must be understood very clearly by the whole team, including the client.

(d) Technical complexity of the project

Large and complex projects involve enormous levels of risk, and it is precisely these circumstances for which the management-based procurement methods were developed. For example, on a development project in the heart of London on a restricted site, with high levels of building services and a very high level of finishes, the risk for the contractor is so high as to lead to tenders which will be inflated to cover the risks. In such circumstances the client may be in a stronger position to bear the risk, particularly if the client is a property developer and builds frequently.

Interestingly, construction management seems to have been used mainly on 'shell and core' projects. This reduces the level of technical complexity and eliminates many site co-ordination problems. It may, therefore, seem inappropriate to quote technical complexity as a strength of construction management. The main point is that complex building projects need to be managed more organically, rather than hierarchically. Therefore, a high level of technical complexity demands a procurement system that allows for dynamic and flexible working relationships. By this it is implied that the management structure will be adaptable throughout the life of the project, and that the significance of each contributor's input will vary from one stage to another.

(e) Client's right to make minor variations to requirements

There are provisions in most standard forms of contract for the employer to change the requirements of the project. This can involve the client in enormous cost and delay and it is essential that variations are kept to a minimum if claims, prolongation and disruption are to be avoided. Since variations to requirements cause so many problems with contractual claims, it is odd to find that the guidance notes to the standard form of management contract almost encourage them. The structure of management contracting does allow the freezing of design decisions to be left to a later stage than with traditional contracts. This is because the work is let in packages. As a result, the earthworks and substructures packages can actually be let and started on site before much of the detail of the superstructure has been finalised.

The need to be able to make variations should not be paramount, but minor changes must be accommodated. If frequent changes are envisaged, their administration can snarl up the communicative and supervisory processes, and make the project more like a traditional general contract. Such a project should be designed and specified with flexibility in mind, so that late decisions can be accommodated. If no changes are envisaged then approaches such as design and build may be relevant, and should be considered.

(f) Separation of responsibility for management and design

Not all projects are suited to management-based methods. Sometimes, design is such an intrinsic part of the project that it cannot be separated from management. In this situation, design *is* management. However, there are many commercial buildings where design is not the overriding feature of the job. In such situations, the designer's role is reduced to that of a manipulator of relations between spaces in the early stages. Once these are fixed, the only design activity is the manipulation of the façade. If all other activities related to design have been delegated to consultants, then the problem of co-ordination ceases to be a design problem and becomes a pure management problem. This is the situation most suited to construction management.

(g) Early start on site and/or early completion

Many clients are driven by the need to optimise their use of finance. When finance dominates the project, early letting is essential. In order to get started on site at the earliest opportunity, questions relating to the fundamental design issues must be settled and resolved at an early stage. The comments in the preceding paragraph are also pertinent here. If the project must generate income at the earliest opportunity, then the client cannot afford the luxury of having a comprehensive design statement translated into a sophisticated architectural concept. The need is simply to house economic operations in a shell that is marketable. In order to make the whole process work in a competitive business environment, an early start on site can become critical to the success of the project.

There are many fast-track approaches available to the client seeking early completion. With 'fast-tracking' the contract tends to be let as soon as sufficient work is documented and ready to start on site. Although this encourages faster overall times, due to the overlapping of design with construction, it causes severe problems of communication. Information needs to be very carefully co-ordinated if site problems are to be avoided. There are those who claim that the overlapping of design with construction actually slows down the process of construction because of variations, disagreements and the escalation of disputes. It is these added problems associated with 'fast-tracking' that management contracting is possibly designed to avoid; not just the lack of speed experienced with the traditional approach to contracting.

(h) Value for money is more important than least possible cost

Although economic competition is often advisable, it does not mean that least cost is the primary objective. In order to compete successfully in the market, business premises need to be attractive, integrated with their surroundings, and flexible. In addition, their provision must be timely. Therefore, value for money becomes more important than least cost. There must be some mechanism where alternatives to competitive tendering may be considered and incorporated. Construction management has the capacity to allow for contracts to be either put out to bid or negotiated.

Chapter 6

Standard Forms of Contract

It is common practice when procuring a building to use one of the standard forms of building contract. These forms have emanated from various parts of the construction industry, for various reasons, and each of them has a role to play in the choice of strategy. To many in the industry, it is important that an acceptable negotiated form is used in order to ensure a fair and familiar distribution of risk. In order for the construction process to work effectively, it is essential that the way in which the standard forms distribute risk is clearly understood. Unfortunately, this issue remains obscure to many in the construction industry, who may feel that the contract need not be looked at unless and until a dispute arises. Such attitudes are the source of many of the absurd difficulties experienced by those who engage in construction; parties frequently sign contracts which bind them to promises they either do not understand or do not intend. Unfortunately for them, building contracts are so comprehensive and specific that the courts tend to interpret them literally.

1 Standardisation of contracts

One reason for standardising the contracts used in building is because of the contractual complexities involved. Many in the industry feel that the use of a standard form will help to increase familiarity with all of the contractual provisions. In addition, those who appreciate the complexities of construction place a high value on particular standard forms which their own interest group has had a hand in drafting, and this has a major influence upon their choice.

Standard form contracts are frequently negotiated contracts, in which representatives of the various interest groups contribute to the drafting process. When this happens, the parties are treated in law as if they had individually negotiated the particular terms of their own bargain. Therefore, in the event of a dispute over interpretation of the conditions of contract, the courts will interpret any ambiguities fairly between the parties. If, on the other hand, a contract has been prepared by only one of the parties, any ambiguity will be interpreted against that party, in accordance with the principle of *contra proferentem.*

Unfortunately, the benefits of standardisation are seldom achieved, for at least two reasons. First, the standard forms are rarely used as printed; it is common for amendments to be made, by striking out unwanted clauses and adding in preferred clauses. Secondly, the way in which the industry is structured encourages people to concentrate on particular types of work, so that, for example, consultant civil engineers and architects rarely interact. Consultants can thus fall into the trap of only knowing about one standard form. If this happens, their understanding of the contractual issues involved may become myopic, with a failure to see these in their general legal context. This in turn leads to misunderstandings which are perpetuated simply because, once such consultants realise how complex the standard form is, they do not wish to add to that complexity by using a different one. For these reasons, inappropriate contracts are the norm, rather than the exception.

It is a fundamental principle of contracting that the transfer of a risk from one party to another should be accompanied by a financial premium. The passing of too many risks to the contractor ought therefore to result in inflated tenders. One of the perceived advantages of standard forms of contract is that they allocate risks fairly between the parties, and thus help to ensure that tender prices remain at a reasonable level. However, there are two reasons for suggesting that this picture is not an entirely accurate one. First, much of the risk apportionment in standard form contracts is implicit rather than explicit, so that it is difficult if not impossible to know what if any allowance has been made for any given risk in a particular tender. Secondly, there is much evidence to suggest that, in practice, contractors with very little time to prepare a tender on a batch of contract documents will price only for their costs and the market position, and will fail to add in any premium for the risks involved. Indeed, this appears also to be the case where tenders are invited on the basis of heavily amended standard forms or even on non-standard forms.

It might be thought that, if the risk element of a project is left unpriced, this must necessarily be for the client's benefit, in that it should produce a lower tender figure. However, any temptation to place an unduly onerous risk burden on a contractor who has *not* priced for this should be resisted, as it is not, in the long run, good business practice. What tends to happen is that the contractors and sub-contractors who least understand risk (and who tender in ignorance of it) are precisely those who are financially least able to absorb it. In consequence, inappropriate risk distribution (at least where it is not overt) tends to lead to insolvencies in mid-project, leaving the client with a half-built facility.

2 The importance of procurement method

Clearly, an appreciation of the range of standard form contracts is an advantage, and these are introduced in the next part of this chapter. First, however, the differences between the major types of procurement method are summarised, as demonstrated in the previous chapters.

Traditional general contracting has existed for a little over a century. It was ideally suited to the emerging construction industry between the Industrial Revolution and the post-war boom, but has suffered more recently from inflexibility and an attachment to outmoded ideas of construction organisation. It is served by the Joint Contracts Tribunal (JCT) who represent most of the interested parties in the building (though not the civil engineering) industry. There are many factors which come together to influence the form and content of JCT contracts, not all of which are in the best interests of the client. Unfortunately, the way that the risks are apportioned under a JCT general contract, whilst fair to all parties, is not well understood by many who use the forms. It seems as if the existence of a drafting committee, representing all of the major interested power groups in the industry, relieves many people of the responsibility for understanding the contracts they sign. Not everyone involved in the construction process understands the contracts they sign, even when they are using amended or unilaterally drafted contracts. The advantage of so doing is not to become litigious, but to understand better the positions from which adversarial conflicts develop. A good understanding of each other's positions would enable adversaries to resolve their disputes quickly and cheaply, without recourse to expensive litigation.

Design and build is a logical, clear and sensible method for procuring a wide range of buildings. Its increase in popularity has been steady, and there are very few reports of client dissatisfaction. As a procurement method it is a good alternative to general contracting or construction management, especially because of its high cost certainty. There is no real limit on the type or scale of project for which it can be used, but it is inadvisable to use it for high risk projects or for adventurous schemes. As with any procurement method, it is the selection of the personnel for the project team which is the most important thing but, if this is properly done, design and build is unlikely to compromise good practice. It has been used for centuries, and its use is likely to continue.

Management-based methods are more novel. Their most important feature is that they do not aim to be an automatic solution to the problems inherent in procuring buildings; they are rather a mechanism whereby the client can harness the experience and knowledge of a co-operative and highly motivated building contractor. They will not by themselves alter awkward people, nor re-orientate contractors who are habitual 'claimers'. The client has to be very careful about selecting priorities, and even more careful about selecting those to appoint to the project team, especially the management contractor or construction manager.

The two management-based approaches to procurement suffer from much confusion. The ideas behind the emergence of management contracting were of good intention, but were compromised by the institutionalised nature of the British construction industry. The development of a standard form of management contract, and the attitudes of many of the parties in such projects, has resulted in management contracting being little more than glorified general contracting. Construction management is a better approach to creating a project team which is conducive to teamwork and to the more effective fulfilment of client objectives. However, it needs an experienced and pro-active client, and the uncertainties over cost and duration are only justified on large and complex projects.

Whatever method of procurement is used, it must be appropriate and flexible. In choosing a standard form contract, the process is first to decide upon the method of procurement, then to identify the particular form of contract to be used. The next part of this chapter gives a brief introduction to the standard forms most frequently encountered, with some pointers as to their usage. Chapter 7 deals with the decision process.

3 JCT contracts

JCT contracts represent the vast majority of those used in construction. Despite its name, the Joint Contracts Tribunal does not sit in judgment on others. The use of the word 'tribunal' actually arises because it originally consisted of three groups; architects, builders and clients. It is an affiliation of interest groups within the construction industry which operates as a forum for discussing and determining the content of the clauses of standard forms of contract. It does not appear that this body was ever meant to be democratic, or even representative. Its origins lie in 1870, when the Builders' Society (now the CIOB) and RIBA together produced the first 'standard form' of contract. This was for use only in London and seems to have been an attempt to overcome some of the problems of the day which were caused by the use of *ad hoc* building contracts.

Over the years the meetings of the various interest groups continued and, after much argument, negotiation and debate, the first national standard form became available in 1909. This was drafted by RIBA and the NFBTE (now the BEC) with help in mediation by the Institute of Builders. It was largely based on the 1870 form, and much of the original 1870 style, if not the actual content, can still be detected in the latest JCT forms.

The current membership of the Joint Contracts Tribunal is as follows:

- Royal Institute of British Architects (RIBA)
- Building Employers Confederation (BEC)
- Royal Institution of Chartered Surveyors (RICS)
- Association of County Councils
- Association of Metropolitan Authorities
- Association of District Councils
- British Property Federation (BPF)
- Confederation of Associations of Specialist Engineering Contractors (CASEC)
- Federation of Associations of Specialists and Sub-contractors (FASS)
- Association of Consulting Engineers (ACE)
- Scottish Building Contract Committee

Examples of the forms produced by the JCT follow, along with a description of the circumstances for which they are intended.

(a) JCT 80: The Standard Form of Building Contract

This form of contract, called JCT 80 because it was issued in 1980, is regarded as the 'industry standard' against which all others are measured. It is a long and complex document which consolidated all the revisions to the earlier standard form (JCT 63), as well as making fundamental changes to such matters as the nomination of sub-contractors. It is published in six editions:

Local Authority edition With Quantities;
Private edition With Quantities;
Local Authority edition With Approximate Quantities;
Private edition With Approximate Quantities;
Local Authority edition Without Quantities;
Private edition Without Quantities.

JCT 80 is intended for use with building work which has been fully documented before tender, including a bill of quantities. In the 'with quantities' versions, the quantities are contractual, which means that the contractor is paid a lump sum for the whole of the work described in the bills, regardless of the actual quantity executed (unless specifically instructed to vary the quantity). This is by contrast with 'measure and value' contracts, eg ICE 6 (see *below* under section 4(*a*)), or JCT 80 with approximate quantities, where quantities in the bill are estimated, and all of them are remeasured on completion so that the contractor is paid for the actual amount of work done.

The detailed provisions of JCT 80 are intended for complex projects, larger than those for which IFC 84 (see *below*) would be used. It requires that the employer takes the responsibility for the execution and documentation of the design. An employer who chooses JCT 80 has also to decide which version to use. The choice between local authorities and private editions is easy enough. The decision about the status of the bill of quantities is more difficult. The first decision is whether the employer requires a lump sum agreement, or whether the price is merely indicative. In the latter instance, the choice is the 'approximate quantities' version. This is for use when the exact scale of the work is unclear at the time of tendering, and the employer does not wish to expose the contractor to the risks associated with this uncertainty. By taking this risk, the employer gains the advantage of straightforward, if not transparent, pricing by the contractor. An employer requiring a lump sum agreement has to choose between 'with quantities' and 'without quantities'. The former is used where the design has been fully documented in drawings and specifications, and the quantities of work have been extracted in the form of a bill. The latter is used where the employer's designers have prepared the design and documented it with drawings plus either a specification or a schedule of work. The contractor will submit a lump sum price for this work. Variations will be valued on either a contract sum analysis or a schedule of rates.

Among the major characteristics of JCT 80 are the requirement that an architect (or a 'contract administrator') and a quantity surveyor must be appointed. The architect has wide but strictly defined powers. These include the issuing of certain instructions on behalf of the employer, and also the independent certification of payments, quality of work, contractor's performance and so on. The quantity surveyor is responsible for the valuation of work done and the valuation of variations.

Another very important feature of the form is the provision which it makes for the nomination of specialist sub-contractors. This practice arose originally because complex electrical and mechanical services installations can take a long time to design and procure. By making provision for the employer to nominate such a specialist before the main contractor is known, it was possible to ensure that the specialist installations would be ready for inclusion in the building in good time. Without this provision, the contract could be subject to considerable delays whilst the main contractor procured these items. Unfortunately, the practice of nomination is now frequently adopted for different reasons, for example because the employer or the contract administrator wishes to ensure that specialist work is awarded to someone with whom they have worked in the past and on whom they feel able to rely. Whilst there is nothing wrong with this in principle, it tends to lead to the increasing incidence of nomination for the sake of nomination, rather than for the sake of expediting the works. Other reasons for nomination include its use as a device to enable dilatory design teams to delay their decisions until quite late in a project. By allotting parts of the project to nominated sub-contractors, the need to detail their work before the main contract is let can be avoided. Although this is bad practice, it frequently happens.

Further characteristics of JCT 80 are its elaborate provisions for dealing with delays to and disruptions of the work; lengthy and complex insurance provisions; and provisions for bringing the employment of the contractor to an end in the event of either party's insolvency.

(b) *IFC 84: Intermediate Form of Building Contract*

This form is growing in popularity, and is now being quite widely used. Its aim is to bridge the gap between the lengthy provision of JCT 80 and the simplicity of the Minor Works Form (see *below*), which was being used in place of JCT 80 for contracts for which it was totally inappropriate. IFC 84 is shorter than JCT 80 but is still fairly complex.

The main characteristic of IFC 84 is its flexibility. It can be used for either local authorities or private sector employers and either with or without bills of quantities as the cost control document. The employer is responsible for the design, which will be communicated by drawings plus other documents, which may be either bills of quantity, schedules of work, or a specification. The first two of these will be priced by the contractor, the last will involve the contractor in submitting either a contract sum analysis or a schedule of rates. In this way, the contract achieves the same range of possible applications as JCT 80, but through careful phrasing in the clauses manages this with only one version of the printed contract.

Although there are no provisions for nomination of sub-contractors as such, there is a different mechanism for achieving a similar result. This is the 'naming' of a sub-contractor or supplier, which involves either including their name in the contract documents or allocating a provisional sum. There are some important legal differences between named sub-contractors under IFC 84 and nominated sub-contractors under JCT 80, which will be examined in more detail in Chapters 17 and 18.

(c) *MW 80: Agreement for Minor Works*

This contract is designed for use only on very small and simple works. The conditions give a bare outline of the parties' duties and responsibilities, and allocate risks too crudely for more complex situations. It is very useful for such projects as domestic extensions, but generally should not be used on contracts exceeding £70,000. Its chief advantage is its simplicity, but this becomes a major disadvantage on larger projects, where its lack of detailed provisions will leave the employer dangerously exposed to many different kinds of risk. It is intended for use as a lump sum agreement, where the employer takes responsibility for the design work. The work will be documented with drawings and/or specifications and/ or schedules, but there is no detailed measurement. There are no provisions for fluctuations in market prices or nomination of sub-contractors.

(d) FF 76: Fixed fee form of prime cost contract

This form is a revision of one which was issued in 1967. Because it is substantially based upon JCT 63 (the predecessor of JCT 80), it is issued with a warning that some of its provisions may have become obsolete. The JCT is currently endeavouring to replace it with a more up-to-date version.

FF 76 is intended for use in situations where the exact nature and scope of the works is difficult to predict, particularly on alteration and repair work, and where it is therefore not possible to obtain a firm price for work in advance. The contractor is paid whatever the work costs, plus a previously agreed lump sum for overheads and profit. This lump sum fee is based upon an estimate of the probable cost of the works which the contractor is required to give, which indicates that, although the precise extent of the works is not known at the outset, a certain amount of design is assumed to have been done.

FF 76 envisages that the contractor will execute the majority of the work through directly employed labour and resources, rather than sub-contractors. As a cost-reimbursement contract, this is a precursor to the JCT Management Contract which was issued in 1987 (see *below*).

(e) CD 81: Standard Form with Contractor's Design

This form is used in situations where the client does not wish to take responsibility for the design of the work, and so requires the contractor to undertake the design of a building as well as its construction. It thus differs significantly from the majority of JCT forms. If the contractor is only to complete *part* of the design, rather than all of it, this contract is not suitable; there is instead a supplement, called the Contractor's Designed Portion Supplement, which should be used with JCT 80. The use of JCT 80 with this supplement is very different from the use of CD 81. For example, there is no provision in CD 81 for the appointment of either a contract administrator or a quantity surveyor, although there is an 'employer's agent' who has limited powers to act on behalf of the employer.

The CD 81 contract is let on the basis of a document called the 'employer's requirements', which specifies precisely what it is that the contractor is being asked to do. This will often take the form of a performance specification. 'Contractor's proposals' for meeting these requirements are submitted, and the winning contractor's proposal document is then used as the major control document on the project. Whilst there is no provision for the nomination of sub-contractors, this can be effectively achieved by careful wording of the requirements.

In other respects, apart from rewording to eliminate the contract administrator's responsibilities and to create a situation in which the contractor is responsible for self-certification of work, much of this form is very similar in style and content to JCT 80. It is a lump sum agreement, and has comprehensive provisions, enabling it to be used for a wide range of project sizes. Chapter 4 contains more detail about how and where to use design and build contracts. Particular issues of design liability, under this and other forms, are covered in more detail in Chapter 11.

(f) MC 87: Management Contract

The management contract was issued in 1987. There is nothing new about the idea, which in essence simply introduces a new level of management in between the employer and the 'builders'. It is similar in some ways to the traditional way of procuring buildings in this country, which is still sometimes used, known as 'separate trades contracting'. The only difference is that the management contractor decides how the work is to be broken down into packages for letting and undertakes supervisory and agent's roles.

Before the management contract was issued, a similar pattern of involvement could be achieved under JCT 80 by using sub-contractors. The problem with this was that the employer had to sue the main contractor for any defaults or faulty workmanship or materials, leaving the main contractor to sue the sub-contractor if this was possible. Under the MC 87 arrangements, the employer and the works contractors have a more detailed set of obligations, which means that the management contractor is relieved of much of this liability.

The arrangements within management contracting are designed to encourage the overlapping of design and construction. For this reason, the chances are that a building will be completed more quickly than under the traditional arrangements. There are some special provisions relating to time—in particular an acceleration clause, which is entirely new to standard form building contracts. However, this provision is somewhat strange in that, rather than entitling the employer to instruct the management contractor to speed up, it merely sets out an administrative procedure for renegotiating the basic terms of the contract (duration and price), an option which is in any event open to all contracting parties.

Under the standard form of management contract there are provisions for extensions of time for events similar to those listed in JCT 80, and there are extra provisions concerned with the works contractors. For example, an extension of time for a works contract does not automatically mean an extension of time for the main contract. A management contractor who is in delay is liable to the employer for liquidated damages, subject to an important provision in which the employer indemnifies the management contractor for *all* losses under the contract, other than those arising from the management contractor's own negligent performance.

MC 87 is intended for use on complex projects where management and co-ordination are paramount, and for which the management contracting procurement system has been chosen.

(g) JCT Measured Term Contract

This form of contract is designed for use where an employer needs regular maintenance and minor works to be carried out, and wishes to engage only one contractor for a specified period. The single contract will then cover a number of separate jobs, since the contractor carries out work from time to time on receipt of instructions from the employer.

4 Other standard form contracts

There are bodies other than the JCT which also produce building contract forms, but in most cases this is not through a process of 'debate until consensus'. Some individual interest groups simply produce a contract, although this is in many cases done after extensive consultations with other interested parties. Of these other forms, the most important follow.

(a) ICE conditions of contract

This is a negotiated form produced by the Institution of Civil Engineers, the Association of Consulting Engineers and the Federation of Civil Engineering Contractors. It was first published in 1945; the current 6th edition appeared in January 1991. There is only one version, for use with public or private clients, and it is intended for use on major civil engineering projects. These include a wide range of works, such as navigable canals, irrigation schemes, roads, railways, docks, harbours, dams, bridges and tunnels. Many civil engineering contracts include building works, and vice versa.

The essential feature of the ICE 6 conditions is that they provide a contract between a promoter and a contractor. The promoter becomes the employer under the conditions, and the engineer provides the technical aspects of design and specifications and effectively translates the contract. The engineer is not a party to the contract and thus has no legal rights or obligations under the contract. However, engineers have their own contract (conditions of engagement) with their employers.

The conditions create a 'remeasurement' contract, also known as 'admeasurement' or 'measure and value'. This means that the contractor is paid at the contract rates (which may be subject to variation) for the actual quantities of work carried out. This is recognised by the fact that the ICE 6 conditions, unlike JCT contracts, make no reference to a 'contract sum'; they refer instead to a 'tender total'.

Work under an ICE 6 contract is to be carried out to the satisfaction of the engineer, whose powers of control and direction are both extensive and apparently arbitrary. The conditions contain wide provisions for the adjustment of the contract sum, usually in favour of the contractor.

(b) ICE Minor Works Contract

This form is intended for use on contracts of less than £100,000, with a duration of less than six months. However, it is much more complex than the JCT minor works form MW 80, and there is no real reason why it should not be used (with care and possibly minor amendments) on larger contracts.

The Minor Works Contract is based on the ICE conditions, but is much more simple, much of the wording having been redrafted into straightforward English. There is no prescribed form of tender. The method of payment can be calculated by remeasurement, lump sum, day works, cost plus fee or any combination of these. There are no provisions for nomination of sub-contractors, and the provisions for extensions of time, liquidated damages, valuation of variations and the like are both simplified and more limited in their application.

An interesting new provision is the step-by-step procedure in case of disputes which is outlined in clause 11. The main aim is clearly to reach an agreed settlement; this is a refreshing change from many standard forms, which seem to assume that the target is a lawsuit!

(c) FIDIC conditions of contract

Produced by the International Federation of Consulting Engineers (FIDIC), in association with the European International Federation of Construction (FEIC), this contract is substantially based on the ICE form, modified to enable it to be used anywhere in the world. It contains special provisions to enable the parties to decide under which nation's legal system the contract will be executed. This has traditionally been the country of the engineer, but recently it has become more usual for it to be the country of the employer.

The basic characteristics of the contract are that an engineer is employed as the client's agent and representative, as well as having certification powers. Legally this role is similar to that of a contract administrator under JCT 80. There are provisions for nomination of sub-contractors, settlement of disputes, extensions of contract period, liquidated damages, and all the other complexities usually encountered in major standard forms of building contract. The provisions are not considered further in this book, and interested readers are referred to the guidance notes issued by FIDIC.

(d) ACA 2: The ACA Form of Building Agreement

This form, first published by the Association of Consulting Architects in 1982, is not a negotiated form but rather a response to widespread criticisms of the JCT 80 range of standard forms. A second edition, ACA 2, was published in October 1984. The conditions are remarkable in their use of standard alternative clauses, which can be used in a variety of combinations to provide a wide range of contract types. In this way, contractual arrangements can be provided which suit the parties to a particular project.

(e) BPF System

In 1983 the British Property Federation published its controversial *Manual of the BPF System*, which proposed major changes to the way in which building projects were organised from inception to completion. These moved much of the risk back on to the building team and suggested things which, to judge by the reaction of the construction industry at the time, were considered alarming. However, many aspects of the proposals, such as fee tendering by the professionals on the project team, now seem quite acceptable.

Part of the new package was a form of building contract conditions. However, it seems to have been discovered at the last minute the conditions in it would not be acceptable to any tendering contractors and so they were never published. Instead, the BPF adopted a particular version of ACA 2 with fewer alternative clauses. Although the BPF system produced a flurry of consternation at the time, its influence has mainly been in the way the building industry perceives its clients and differentiates between them. The system itself has had very little use.

(f) GC/Works/1: General Conditions of Government Contracts for Building and Civil Engineering Works

This contract, which is widely used for central government and PSA work, is issued by the government after consultation but without negotiation. It has been in use for many years and has recently been republished in a third edition. A significant characteristic is that many of the contract conditions give binding force to decisions of the employer, referred to as the 'Authority'.

The contract has some very unusual aspects, such as the employer's right to determine the contract without having to give any reason. Other provisions include the appointment of a project manager, unique payment provisions related to cash flow 'S-curves' instead of measured work done, acceleration provisions, extensions of time and liquidated damages. A notable feature is that many of the provisions are tailored to work for the central government and would be wholly inappropriate for other clients.

(g) GC/Works/2

This is a simplified version of GC/Works/1, intended for small and simple projects.

Chapter 7

Choosing the Right Contract

Clearly, the construction industry has a pressing need to develop techniques for tailoring contracts to suit particular jobs in a manner which is acceptable to the representative pressure groups. Until this is achieved, all that can be done is to offer guidance on how to select the most appropriate form from the range of standard forms currently available, and the best way to do this is to begin with choosing a procurement method. This chapter therefore develops a framework for choosing a procurement method, which leads in turn to the decision about contracts.

1 Selecting an appropriate form of procurement

Many building projects go wrong because the needs of the particular project are insufficiently considered. Much of the thinking behind the development of standard forms in this industry has been driven by the assumption that there is a 'best way' of doing business which will apply to all projects. This assumption has been found to be hopelessly misguided; there is much to be learned from studying the similarities between building projects, but the differences should never be overlooked. To take payment as an example, a project for a few hundred pounds which lasts for less than a week can be priced as a fixed lump sum which requires no adjustment. On the other hand, a project for hundreds of thousands of pounds lasting several years requires fluctuations clauses, variations clauses and interim payment provisions. In short, a single standard form of contract for the construction industry is a false ideal; each project is unique in at least some of its features.

The discussion in Chapters 3 to 5 has highlighted certain criteria for choosing procurement methods, the most important of which are:

(*a*) Client's involvement with the process of construction
(*b*) Complexity of the project
(*c*) Separation of design from management
(*d*) Reserving the client's right to alter the specification
(*e*) Speed from inception to completion
(*f*) Certainty of price
(*g*) Client's contractual remedies for defective work.

Each of these are developed below, in order to establish a framework for the decision. The six criteria are not represented in any particular order of priority, because a critical part of this decision process is deciding *which* of the criteria are important for a particular project. Clients are seldom aware that there are options for procurement, in which case the construction project personnel tend to revert to their own ideas of 'standard practice', whether or not this is in the best interests of the client. The best professional advisers take their clients through some kind of decision process at the outset of the project.

(a) Client's involvement with the process of construction

Experienced clients will have the knowledge and the procedures to deal with the integration of the various parts of a construction project team, and can therefore choose either to utilise their skill or to pay consultants to manage the project. This is by contrast with novice clients, who will have difficulties if they do not rely upon specialist project management advice. However, even an experienced client will need to delegate authority on a complex project. Since complexity influences other project organisation decisions, it is best dealt with as a separate criterion (see *below*).

It has already been made clear that the modern construction process demands a high degree of co-ordination and integration (although this has not always been the case—indeed, many in the industry still fail to appreciate it). The client should therefore understand that an active role requires responsiveness and authority if the project is to run smoothly. This means responding rapidly to requests for information or instructions, and delegating authority along with responsibility to those who must manage the project on a day-to-day basis. Each of the procurement methods is based upon assumptions about the role of the client, and the organisational demands associated with that role.

Traditional general contracting is based upon the assumption that the design leader will manage the entire process on behalf of the client, and that the contractor will take the responsibility for fabricating what has been documented and for supplying and co-ordinating all of the work on site. In this way, the bulk of the client's authority is delegated to agents.

Design and build is a form of procurement which demands slightly more from the client. The agreement with the contractor is for a specific product, for a particular price. This reduces much of the uncertainty surrounding construction projects but, according to the critics, it correspondingly reduces the opportunity for innovation and creativity. The absence of an independent certifier involves the client directly in many of the decisions that would be delegated to an architect or engineer in traditional general contracting.

Management contracting, being a development of traditional general contracting, reduces the main contractor's role to that of managing and co-ordinating, as well as contributing fabrication advice during the design stages of the project. The management contractor would normally be expected to have some responsibility for co-ordinating the designers, particularly during the later stages in the process. This has always been seen as advantageous by those commercial clients who feel comfortable when commercial exigencies override aesthetic exigencies. For exactly the same reason, it has proved unpopular with many construction professionals. However, the efficacy of this co-ordination is open to doubt because the management contractor has neither direct authority over the designers nor contractual responsibility for the design work. In addition, the management contractor does not have the authority to commit the client to additional expenditure. These factors combine to increase the client's involvement to a high level, in approving or sanctioning recommendations of the management contractor.

The construction manager's role is simply that of a consultant and client's agent, leaving the client as the chief co-ordinator and paymaster for every contract. Construction management is best suited to the client who wishes to take a pro-active role in the process. The fact that each of the specialists contracts directly with the client means that the client is exposed to higher levels of risk due to insolvency, trade interface clashes and mismanagement.

As an approximate guide, the relative levels of client involvement in each of the procurement systems are indicated in Table I, which shows the range of minimum to maximum client involvement as a continuum, along which the relative level for each procurement method is placed.

Table I: Relative level of client's involvement in each procurement system

MINIMUM			MAXIMUM
TGC	DB	MC	CM

(b) Complexity of the project

Any decision about management delegation must be influenced by the complexity of the project. However, defining the complexity of a project is not easy, since it is also a function of size and speed and, moreover, it really depends upon the background and experience of the person judging it. Assumptions about complexity are critical because they have important consequences for the level of specialist sub-contracting, and for the relative priorities for project success. The danger of choosing an inappropriate procurement technique is that the identification and appointment of particular combinations of established professionals brings with it stereotypical assumptions about roles and priorities, and these govern the criteria for project success. Such preconceived objectives have to be considered in the light of the client's objectives.

This becomes clearer if a large petro-chemical plant is considered: for the client it is critical that this complex installation works properly, so functional criteria are far more critical than budget or time constraints. However, although the correct functioning of the installation is the highest priority for the client, the particular clauses in most management contracts force cost to the top of the agenda at every step of the fabrication process. The client must be conscious of the way in which procurement methods for complex projects bring their own sets of objectives to the project: this may change the client's view of the whole venture.

Table II shows the relative suitability of each of the main procurement methods to differing levels of complexity. Both of the management-based methods have been specifically designed to suit the demands of large, complex and fast projects. Traditional general contracting lends itself to all but the most complex, whilst suffering from a poorer record for speed. Design and build typically lends itself well to the simplest projects, but there are different possibilities for management structures in design and build. For example, a management contractor who takes on the responsibility for a whole project, including the design, may well be suited to very complex projects. Therefore, design and build stands at both ends of the range of possibilities in Table II.

Table II: Complexity of project

MINIMUM			**MAXIMUM**	
DB	TGC	MC	CM	DB

(c) Separation of design from management

The extent to which design and management can be separated is a matter of debate. Some believe that these two skills are distinct and that one ought to prevail over the other in order to achieve financial and time targets for the project. To others, design, or more particularly architecture, is an art form which can only work as a whole and from which management is inseparable: to fragment the design effort, or to subjugate aesthetic exigencies to financial ones, is to reduce architecture to the status of mere ornamentation. It is important that the client should take a view on this issue, because each of the procurement methods presupposes one or other view. They each involve particular patterns of authority which influence the interaction between design and management.

Construction management introduces the client's management agent at a very early stage in the process, enabling fabrication and co-ordination exigencies to be accounted for from the beginning. This can have the effect of reducing the designer's role to one of an adviser, rather than a leader, but ultimately the extent of this change in dominance depends upon personalities of those involved.

Management contracting achieves the separation of management from design in two ways; with the specialist sub-contractors it is achieved contractually, but with the other consultants it merely introduces the management contractor into the design team so that fabrication exigencies are aired, without necessarily prevailing.

In design and build, the combination of all of the skills into one organisation does not usually result in a pure combination of management with design, because the basis of the contract as a lump sum agreement results in the economies of fabrication prevailing over aesthetic considerations. This happens because the client is effectively removed from these debates, which are internally resolved within the design and build firm.

Traditional general contracting does not admit a difference between design and management. In this form of procurement, design *is* management because the architect (or civil engineer) is in charge of the whole process as client's agent. This is a sensible choice in those circumstances which demand that design criteria should prevail over others.

Table III shows the relative separation of design from management for each of the procurement methods.

Table III: Separation of management from design in each procurement method

MINIMUM		**MAXIMUM**	
TGC	DB	MC	CM

(d) Reserving the client's right to alter the specification

Alterations to specification become necessary for two reasons. First, there may be a need to make changes to the client's brief as the project progresses, and secondly there is the need to revise the design, and therefore the contract documents, on those occasions where the design was incomplete or inaccurate at the time of the contractor's appointment. It must always be remembered that a client who takes on responsibility for the design by commissioning a designer also takes on an obligation to allow the contractor to build what has been specified, or at least to be compensated if the specification is altered.

Frequently, time pressures force clients to invite tenders on less than complete documentation. Under general contracting this is a dangerous practice because the underlying assumption is that the design is complete, and fully documented. Clearly, an incomplete design increases the reliance on provisional sums (building-contract jargon for contingency allowances). The duration of a project also influences this issue, because a long project is more likely to be subject to change than a short one. All of the procurement methods reserve the right for the client to alter the specification, but they are not equally accommodating because of the nature of the appointment of those who fabricate the building.

Table IV shows the relative capacities of each method for accommodating change. Design and build projects require early and definite commitment to the specification from both parties, and often lack the traditional contractual mechanisms for dealing with variations (ie detailed clauses covering the valuation of variations by reference to bills of quantity). Traditional general contracting tends to include comprehensive contractual provisions for instructing and valuing variations to the specification, but the scope for instructing variations is limited (despite any statements to the contrary) to those which do not go to the root of the contract. In management contracting, although the management contractor takes on responsibility for the whole of the project, the fact that the trade contracts are let progressively allows an employer more scope to alter specifications for later work whilst earlier work is already being fabricated. The same holds true for construction management, where the absence of a contractual intermediary probably increases the flexibility still further.

Table IV: Capacity for accommodating variations to specification

MINIMUM					**MAXIMUM**
	DB	TGC	MC	CM	

(e) Speed from inception to completion

Most developments in procurement methods have been spurred by the desire for speed. To public sector clients, the ability to spend money within the period for which it is allocated may be essential if the money is not to be lost to competing demands. In the private sector, everyone knows the adage ‘time is money’. For these reasons, increasing dissatisfaction with the performance of the UK construction industry, compared to others, has fuelled demand from clients for faster building. Because of the essentially linear processes of specification, design, manufacture and assembly, each following from the preceding one, the largest savings of time arise from overlaps introduced into the process. Invariably, this involves early selection of the contractor or sub-contractors.

Traditional general contracting is probably the slowest method of procurement because of the need to document the design before appointing the contractor. Large numbers of nominated sub-contractors, and the letting of separate earthworks and foundation contracts, are two common techniques for accelerating progress. However, these are merely symptoms of the underlying truth, that the system itself is too slow for certain types of project.

Design and build overcomes this lack of speed because the contractor is able to make some fairly safe assumptions about the design, since all responsibility lies in the same place. Such assumptions enable an early start on site.

The management-based methods are also likely to be quicker, because of the opportunities for large overlaps in the design, fabrication, assembly process. For example, the excavations can begin on site before the superstructure is fully designed. Indeed construction management has been known to produce the fastest rates of building ever seen in the United Kingdom. Under construction management, the obligations as to time are entirely related to the construction manager's programme. This means that the client who wishes to have the project completed quickly needs to appoint a construction manager who has proven experience of being able to complete projects quickly. Too ambitious a programme will result in inflated tenders from the trade contractors, and too conservative a programme will result in a slow project. The skill of the construction manager lies in judging the speed of construction.

The relative speeds of each of the procurement methods are indicated in Table V.

Table V: Speed from inception to completion

MINIMUM		**MAXIMUM**	
TGC	DB	MC	CM

(f) Certainty of price

Economy as such is not generally an issue which impinges upon the choice of procurement method, because it is usually simply a matter of making a choice from amongst priced alternatives. What may be important, however, is the question of price certainty, since some clients need to be assured of the level of their financial commitments.

Certainty of price relates to the way in which the payments to the contractor are calculated. There are only two bases for calculating payments; reimbursing the contractor's expenditure (which is essentially uncertain), or paying prices according to the contractor's estimate (which is relatively certain). In reality, all procurement methods consist of differing combinations of these two bases. What matters is which of these two payment regimes dominate, and this is shown in Table VI.

Design and build, as a fixed price, lump sum agreement, offers the greatest price certainty. However, whilst the client's financial commitment is clear and relatively certain, it may not be the lowest possible price for the work. This is because, since most of the risks are the responsibility of the contractor, there may be a premium in the contractor's price to cover these.

Under traditional general contracting, the amount to be paid is based on rates on the contractor's tender, *not* on the contractor's costs. This effectively holds the contractor to the original bargain throughout the contract, because the bill of quantities is used to calculate every sum of money paid. However, the apparent certainty which this offers may be undermined to a degree by the level of sub-contracting and the contractual status of the bills of quantity (the variability is indicated by the dots in Table VI).

Construction management, which involves direct contracts, can utilise any kind of contract for each of the bid packages but, no matter how certain each package may be, the client's total commitment is not clear until the project is well advanced. The aim of this procurement method is *not* to minimise the price, nor even to fix it clearly, but rather to ensure the maximum value for money to the client. Since each of the direct client-specialist contracts can be negotiated or bid, there is some variability in the certainty of prices. However, the fact that the trade contractors are in a direct relationship with the client often means large savings because the trade contractors do not have to budget for lengthy payment delays and spurious counter-claims from intermediaries.

Management contracting, as a pure cost reimbursement arrangement, has the least cost certainty. The original intention of management contracting was to create a 'no-risk' contract for the contractor. This was seen as the best way to encourage the contractor to act as a professional consultant, and to enable the client who builds frequently to take some of the risks and benefit from the savings in contractors' risk premiums. The frequent amendments made to management contracts, which move the burden of risk back to the contractor, eliminate the basic reason for choosing such a procurement system.

Any detailed consideration of price certainty must be based on particular contractual details and not simply on procurement methods. As projects become more complex and/or larger, so they move from the lump sum arrangements to greater proportions of the price relying upon a reimbursement basis. For example, any contract lasting more than a year will need to take account of potential rises in the prices of contractors' supplies. If no allowance is made for these market fluctuations, the contractor will have to guess the potential levels of prices, and this will result in inflated tenders. In order to enable economic pricing levels, fluctuation clauses move this item of risk to the client, by providing mechanisms for adjusting the contract sum each month in line with movements of prices in the contractors' supplies markets.

Complex projects frequently call for specialist sub-contract work. Nominated sub-contracts, whilst selected competitively on a lump sum basis, are fixed price arrangements between the main contractor and the sub-contractor. However, these items of work will be identified in the main contract as cost reimbursement items for the contractor. For this reason, projects which consist mainly of specialist work would be better organised on a management-based method, where the agreements reflect the reality of this situation.

The pricing policy is affected by the status of bills of quantities. Bills of approximate quantities might be used in building projects, and are the norm in civil engineering projects, resulting in remeasurement of work after execution. Whilst removing the risk of inaccurate or inadequate documentation from the contractor, these arrangements hold the contractor to the bargain struck over the *rates* of remuneration. Overall, they result in less price certainty for the client.

Table VI: Level of price certainty

MINIMUM			**MAXIMUM**
MC	CM	. . . TGC . . .	DB

(g) Client's contractual remedies for defective work

Since a procurement method is a network of contracts which reflect patterns of responsibility, each contains contractual remedies to enable the employer to ensure the acceptability of what is built. The degree to which the employer is enabled to pursue contractual remedies depends entirely on the particular contracts that have been executed. A useful part of the analysis of procurement methods is to identify the potential that each has for enabling the client to compel the project team to provide what was required, and the relative strengths of each procurement method are indicated in Table VII.

Table VII: Client's contractual remedies

MINIMUM			**MAXIMUM**
MC TGC	CM		DB

In traditional general contracting a client who is dissatisfied with the outcome of the project must first identify the extent to which the contractor has conformed with the contract documents. Since the client is responsible for commissioning the design, the contractor is only obligated to build what is documented. In some contracts, for example civil engineering projects, this is modified by a requirement to build to the satisfaction of the client's agent, regardless of what is specified in the documents. However, it is still not the case that the contractor has to build to the client's satisfaction. In any event, the argument usually revolves around whether the client's dissatisfaction is caused by design defect or by poor workmanship. In this way, the contractor's liability is restricted to workmanship and standards and quality of materials. Anything else is outside the terms of the building contract and is a matter for the client to pursue against the designers.

A further complication which may arise under traditional general contracting concerns the position of nominated sub-contractors. When, as frequently happens, these undertake work of design as well as installation, this is likely to go beyond the scope of the main contract (which may contain no design element). If this work proves to be defective, there may be considerable doubt as to whether the client should then pursue the main contractor (who can in turn proceed against the sub-contractor), or whether the client must take action directly against the sub-contractor under whatever collateral agreement exists.

Management contracts consist of a carefully linked network of interlinking agreements. In practice, they are rarely implemented without amendment, and the pursuit of contractual remedies can be fraught with difficulty. As a development of traditional general contracting, the difficulties are similar, but worse.

Construction management contracts form direct links between those paying for the work and those undertaking it. As a result, collateral design warranties between the specialist and the client are unnecessary, and recourse is assured provided that blame can be apportioned. This results in clearer contractual remedies for the client.

Under design and build contracts, it is not necessary for the employer to attempt to distinguish whether a particular problem is a design fault, a manufacturing fault or an assembly fault; the contractor is liable for the performance of the building. Depending on the contract terms, this liability may take the form of a strict warranty that the building will be fit for its purpose, or it may simply consist of an undertaking by the contractor to use reasonable care and skill. Either way, a single point of responsibility is tremendously appealing to clients of construction, and is often cited as the greatest strength of design and build.

(h) Balancing conflicting requirements

The key to choosing the most suitable procurement system, and hence the appropriate contractual clauses, lies in balancing conflicting requirements. The criteria offered above are summarised in Table VIII, from which it is clear that there is not a cohesive and decisive picture, but a complex interaction of objectives, each pulling in a different direction. A client should be taken through a series of decisions about what is important for this particular project. These requirements should then be ranked so that the suggestions from Table VIII can be rationalised with each other.

In addition to what is contained in this table, there are other factors to be taken into consideration, which do not fit into such a straightforward framework. For example, traditional general contracting is based upon a central role for the quantity surveyor in cost planning and cost control which is felt by many to increase the cost certainty of a project. The complexities of construction projects tend to justify much of the documentation and procedures which have been developed by quantity surveyors, whose skill is not to be done away with lightly. However, not every project requires this level of documentation and control, so it is valid to question the constitution of the project team. Certainly, there will usually be a

Table VIII: Choosing an appropriate procurement system

	MINIMUM														**MAXIMUM**
a		TGC			DB					MC					CM
b	DB								TGC			MC		CM	DB
c	TGC						DB							MC	CM
d			DB					TGC		MC		CM			
e	TGC										DB		MC		CM
f	MC			CM				... TGC ...							DB
g	MC	TGC				CM									DB

KEY:
- a Relative level of client's involvement in each procurement system
- b Complexity of project
- c Separation of management from design in each procurement method
- d Capacity for accommodating variations to specification
- e Speed from inception to completion
- f Level of price certainty
- g Client's contractual remedies

TGC—Traditional general contracting, DB—Design and build,
MC—Management contracting, CM—Construction management

need for cost advice, but the question is whether this should come from a quantity surveyor employed directly by the client, or whether such a consultant should be employed by one of the other consultants eg the architect. The authority given to the quantity surveyor should reflect the importance attached to this function by the client.

The client must further be aware of the influence that the choice of procurement method can have upon the contractors' pricing policy. In times of recession, contractors will probably work under any conditions of contract. However, in boom times many contractors will refuse to tender on some forms of contract, effectively taking the choice away from the client. In stable circumstances, professional contractors will add a premium to their prices to cover for risks, but this is not clear to clients, since there will also be a market premium. The danger of competitive tendering is that the lowest bidder may well be the contractor who has failed to appreciate fully the risks involved in the contract, and whose price therefore makes no allowance for them. Such a contractor will almost inevitably have difficulties, and these will usually adversely affect the client. Generally speaking, the greater the certainty for the contractor, the lower the price will be to the employer.

This discussion shows that the decision about which procurement system to choose must be based on an analysis of each of a large number of variables, not only in isolation but also in their interaction, choosing the priorities from amongst them and finding the procurement system which best fits the project.

2 Matching standard contracts to procurement decisions

Having considered procurement choice, it is a straightforward step to choose the contract. First, any project for central government will be let on their own contract, GC/Works/1 or 2, so the issue of choice is not relevant.

The widest choice comes under traditional general contracting, where any version of JCT 80 is applicable for building work, depending upon the nature of the client and the status of the quantities; small works are catered for by JCT MW 80, and larger projects not requiring the full machinery of JCT 80 are catered for by JCT IFC 84. If the work cannot be quantified at all, then either the JCT FF 67 contract, or the JCT Measured Term contract should be considered. The former is related to an indication of the scope of the work, whereas the latter is related to the duration (eg a maintenance agreement). Clients not wishing to follow the JCT route may alternatively choose the ACA form, with appropriate optional clauses selected. For works of civil engineering, the choice is between ICE 6 or ICE minor works, depending upon the scale of the project, unless the project crosses national boundaries, in which case FIDIC should be used.

Design and build can be achieved through the JCT CD 81 form for building work, or through the ACA form with appropriate optional clauses selected. The civil engineering contracts are also used for design and build, but this involves extensive amendments to many of the clauses.

Management contracting leads to only one standard form, the JCT MC 87 management contract, although the civil engineering contracts are again often amended to achieve a similar solution.

Under construction management, there are no standard forms, so bespoke contracts must be used.

The choice follows a clear pattern; the further one moves from traditional general contracting, the more one is forced to rely upon bespoke clauses, and ultimately on bespoke contracts. This phenomenon, associated with a general reluctance to pay attention to legal contractual issues, leads to a higher incidence of misunderstandings about the relationships between common law, contract rules and management practice.

Chapter 8

Contract Formation

The law which governs the formation of building contracts is in principle no different from that applicable to contracts in general. The usual elements of agreement, consideration, contractual intention and capacity must all be present, and the standard vitiating factors of misrepresentation and mistake may also have a part to play. It is not proposed to deal generally with such matters, but rather to concentrate on those aspects of contract formation which are of the greatest practical relevance in the context of construction. These naturally include the question of tenders, since most building contracts of any size result from some form of tendering procedure. Also of importance is the legal effect, if any, to be given to informal arrangements such as 'letters of intent', which seem to play a part in an increasing number of projects.

1 Tendering procedures

There are many tendering procedures, distinguished by the extent of competition which they involve. Tradition strongly favours competitive bidding, but there is increasing dissatisfaction amongst consultants and clients with such competition, because all this really guarantees is the lowest tender price, rather than the best product. What is more, it is precisely those contractors most desperate for work (because they are in financial difficulties) who are most likely to tender at suicidal levels. And, whilst a low tender may seem appealing to the client at the outset, the contractor's subsequent insolvency is likely to cost the client a great deal more than a higher initial bid would have done.

As tendering procedures have evolved to confront this kind of problem, they have been codified by the National Joint Consultative Committee (NJCC), which consists of the major professional institutions involved with construction. Their Codes of Procedure are briefly described below, before more novel forms of selecting a contractor are looked at.

(a) Open tendering

This long-established method begins with an advertisement in the technical press, carrying a brief description of the location, type, scale and scope of the proposed works and inviting interested contractors to apply for more detailed documentation. Open tendering, as an indiscriminate request for tenders, can be unprofitable, lacking as it does any reliable method of ensuring high quality building. Furthermore, since only about one out of twenty contractors' bids are successful, the preparation of such tenders places upon the industry a burden of time, effort, and expense which is ultimately passed back to the clients of the industry. Another drawback is that, because of the indiscriminate nature of open tendering, contractors can be awarded work for which they are not properly equipped in terms of either resources or experience. Although an employer is not legally bound to accept the lowest bid, a committee in charge of public expenditure is under a great deal of pressure to take this course. When the lowest bid is accepted, this can easily result in the employer awarding the contract to the builder who has the least appreciation of the complexities of the projects; or the greatest willingness to take risks; or the lowest current workload of all the bidders. It would be unusual, not to say fortuitous, if these factors resulted in the best value for money for the employer.

Because of the problems associated with open tendering, its use has been declining in recent years, and much progress has been made in developing the alternatives which are described below. However, it is still often used by local authorities to obtain tenders for building work. Indeed, the indications are that its use will increase for public sector work because of an EC directive (88/295/EEC). This covers any public procurement programmes in excess of certain (rather low) thresholds. The intention is that open tendering should become the main form of selection for such programmes, even though the directive will allow the use of restricted or negotiated procedures in certain circumstances. Since public procurement means procurement by any association governed by public law (central *or* local government) and includes health authorities, education authorities and the police, this directive will be extremely wide-ranging in its effect.

(b) Single-stage selective tendering

The first step away from the problems of open tendering is to restrict the number of tenderers invited to bid. This is the purpose of single-stage selective tendering, sometimes referred to simply as selective tendering. It consists of preselecting a limited number of contractors to tender for the work, as a process distinct from selection for a particular project. The preselection process establishes a list of contractors of established skill, integrity, responsibility and proven competence for work of the character and size contemplated. It is recommended that the number of tenderers should be limited to a maximum of six. The NJCC code of procedure gives the points which should be considered when considering a contractor for inclusion on the list.

Clearly, if the preselection process has been properly carried out, any of the contractors should be satisfactory to the employer. Thereafter, tenders may be considered on price alone, and the lowest one selected. Provided that tenders are checked carefully for mistakes by the bidders, and that the list of approved tenderers is regularly revised, some of the worst problems associated with inappropriate selection can be avoided.

However, other problems *may* still occur. Important difficulties arise because the design team do not have the benefit of the contractor's experience at a stage in the design when it would be most useful. Issues such as continuity of work, production cost savings, 'buildability' and subletting specialist items can have a significant impact on the final price of a project. The successful management of some types of construction project can be contingent on getting this kind of knowledge into the design team at an early stage in the process. A variety of techniques have emerged to deal with this, and their purpose is to separate selection of the contractor from the determination of the pricing mechanisms to be employed when paying the contractor.

(c) Two-stage selective tendering

One of the processes used to involve a contractor at an early stage is known as two-stage selective tendering, or sometimes as 'negotiated tendering'. It must be emphasised that the purpose is not to burden the contractor with *responsibility* for design, but rather to involve the contractor in an advisory capacity before the scheme has been fully designed.

In this system, the process is split into two stages. The first stage is a process for the selection of a contractor and for the establishment of a level of pricing for subsequent negotiation. This is the competitive part, based upon minimal information indicating simply the basis of the layout and design of the works. The detail need only be sufficient to provide a basis for competition and for the negotiation of the price during the second stage. In the second stage the precontract process is completed. The employer's professional team collaborates with the selected contractor in the design and development of production drawings for the whole project. Also bills of quantities for the works are prepared and priced upon the basis of the first-stage tender. The result of the second stage is an acceptable sum for inclusion in a form of contract, and complete contract documentation is prepared with the contractor.

This form of tendering is used where the building works are of a very complicated nature; where the magnitude of the work may be unknown at the time for selection of the contractor; or where an early completion date is paramount. In many ways it has emerged as a response to the same pressures which spawned management-based procurement methods, whilst retaining many of the traditional procurement habits.

(d) Selective tendering for design & build

Another NJCC codified process is intended for use with 'design and build' contracts. In this system of tendering, a price is submitted for which the contractor offers to carry out and complete the works, in accordance with the conditions of contract. The word 'tender' in this context is taken to cover the whole of the Contractor's Proposals including both price and design. It is expected that any tendering contractor will have been preselected to a certain extent, as in two-stage tendering.

(e) Negotiation

A more radical approach to the selection of the contractor is offered by negotiation, an approach well suited to novel procurement strategies. These newer forms of procurement demand a less adversarial approach at all levels and all stages in the building process. The inherent flexibility demanded by such approaches means that there is no standard method for negotiating a contract.

Experience has shown that one of the most effective ways of selecting a contractor under 'non-traditional' approaches is to negotiate the deal as the relationship develops. It seems that the single most important factor of such a relationship between the employer and the contractor is familiarity, and the preservation of continuing business relations. Because of this, it is essential that the client is familiar with the building process and with some or all of the professional team, the contractor and the specialists.

(f) Joint ventures

Certain construction projects are so complex that the distribution of liability between the consultants becomes a problem. One solution is to approach the design and implementation of the project as a joint venture between all the consultants and some or all of the specialist contractors. This is an even more radical departure from the so-called 'traditional' methods than are 'management-based' solutions. It involves all of the parties to the joint venture agreement taking on joint and several liability for the design and/or execution of the project. It is not necessary to set up a special joint venture company to do this, but it is possible. The agreements between the parties to the joint venture need careful preparation, and may be backed up by performance bonds and/or parent company guarantees.

2 The effects of a tender

Conventional legal analysis regards an employer's request for tenders as an invitation to treat and the tenders themselves as offers, which the employer is free to accept or reject. From this analysis a number of important consequences flow.

In the first place, the employer is normally under no legal obligation to accept the lowest tender submitted, or indeed to accept any tender at all. It follows from this that the costs of tendering, which may be considerable, are to be be borne by each contractor, unless the circumstances of the case are such that a promise by the employer to pay for this can be implied. This might be so where the work involved is greater than what would normally be expected (for example where it includes detailed design), and especially if the results can be put to profitable use by the employer (see *William Lacey (Hounslow) Ltd* v *Davis* [1957] 2 All ER 712; *Marston Construction Co Ltd* v *Kigass Ltd* (1989) 46 BLR 109).

The employer's basic unfettered discretion in respect of tenders (which is frequently, though unnecessarily, expressly reinforced in the invitation to tender) is however subject to the following qualifications:

(i) An express promise by the employer to accept the lowest tender will be binding upon him, once a tender which complies with any conditions set has been submitted (*Harvela Investments Ltd* v *Royal Trust Co of Canada* [1986] AC 207).

(ii) There may in any event be an implied undertaking by the employer that tenders submitted in accordance with published conditions will at least be properly considered (*Blackpool and Fylde Aero Club Ltd* v *Blackpool BC* [1990] 3 All ER 25), although the assessment of damages for breach of such an undertaking might give rise to difficult problems.

(iii) In relation to public procurement, European Community legislation seeks to ensure that contracts are let to the lowest or more economically advantageous tenderer following a freely competitive tendering process. This principle is also enshrined in the United Kingdom's Local Government Acts 1972 and 1988, although these are of more limited scope. In either case, however, the extent to which such legislation confers rights on an aggrieved tenderer is somewhat uncertain (see *Keating on Building Contracts*, 5th edn (Sweet & Maxwell 1991), Chap 14).

The second major consequence of treating a tender as a mere offer is that it can be withdrawn at any time before the employer's acceptance brings about a binding contract. This will be so even where the tender has been relied on by the other party, such as where a main contractor uses the prices of a tendering subcontractor in building up his own tender (*Cook Islands Shipping Co Ltd* v *Colson Builders Ltd* [1975] 1 NZLR 422). The only exception to this in English law would appear to be where a tenderer expressly and for consideration (or by deed) undertakes to keep his offer open for a specified time, although it may be noted that the Canadian courts have enforced such undertakings even where no consideration has been given (*Queen in Right of Ontario* v *Ron Engineering and Construction Eastern Ltd* (1981) 119 DLR (3d) 267).

The above discussion relates to the type of tender most commonly encountered—namely, an unconditional offer by the contractor to carry out certain specified work. Naturally, the acceptance of this offer by the employer creates a contract which is binding upon both parties, provided of course that the acceptance is unconditional. Where the employer's 'acceptance' expressly envisages that a formal contract will be drawn up at a later stage, it can sometimes be difficult to decide whether this makes everything conditional, or whether the intention is that the parties are to be contractually bound from the outset (*Lewis* v *Brass* (1877) 3 QBD 667).

A second type of tender which is sometimes encountered occurs where a contractor offers to carry out work of a defined character over a specified period. Depending on the precise terms used, the 'acceptance' of such a tender may create a contract under which the employer *must* employ the contractor for any such work which he wishes to have carried out, and the contractor *must* duly undertake it. However, the more usual result is that the contractor's tender constitutes a 'standing offer'. This does not bind the employer to use the contractor's services, and furthermore it can be revoked by the contractor at any time; until such time as it is revoked, however, the contractor must comply with any order placed by the employer within the terms of the offer (see *Percival Ltd* v *LCC Asylums & Mental Deficiency Committee* (1918) 87 LJKB 677).

3 Negotiated contracts

In the absence of a formalised tendering process, two questions arise: whether a contract has been formed and, if so, on what terms. Those questions fall to be answered in accordance with the general legal rules on offer and acceptance. These include the need to establish that the acceptance relates completely and unequivocally to the offer (see *Peter Lind & Co Ltd* v *Mersey Docks & Harbour Board* [1972] 2 Lloyd's Rep 234), and also that agreement has been reached on all the essential terms (*Courtney & Fairbairn Ltd* v *Tolaini Brothers (Hotels) Ltd* [1975] 1 All ER 716). This latter requirement is of considerable significance in construction cases, where it seems that the making of contracts, and more particularly sub-contracts, is often characterised by extreme informality—examples of contracts worth several million pounds being formed without any written evidence whatsoever are all too easy to find.

A purported 'acceptance' which does not match the offer in question will normally be treated as a counter-offer, and thus as a rejection of that offer. It then becomes a question of fact whether the original offeror has accepted the counter-offer or (as frequently happens) has in turn made another counter-offer. This problem is especially acute where the parties' 'communications' with each other are based entirely on their respective standard form documents, since these will almost inevitably be inconsistent with each other. The most common outcome of such a 'battle of forms' is that one of the parties will be held to have accepted by conduct whichever terms were last communicated. Thus a sub-contractor may, by delivering materials (*Sauter Automation Ltd* v *Goodman (Mechanical Services) Ltd* (1986) 34 BLR 81) or starting work (*A Davies & Co (Shopfitters) Ltd* v *William Old Ltd* (1969) 67 LGR 395), be held to have accepted the terms of a main contractor's 'order', notwithstanding that those terms were inconsistent with the sub-contractor's original tender. Conversely, where the last document to have been transmitted consists of a sub-contractor's standard terms, acceptance by the main contractor of materials delivered to the site may also constitute acceptance of those terms (*Chichester Joinery Ltd* v *John Mowlem & Co plc* (1987) 42 BLR 100).

4 Estimates and quotations

It should be apparent from what has been said above that contractual documentation in the construction industry is not always given a high priority, and that work is frequently commenced or even finished before anything resembling a formal contract is drawn up. For example, an employer may, on approving a contractor's 'estimate' or 'quotation', state that this is accepted and thereupon instruct the contractor to start work. Where this occurs, it may be necessary to decide whether the contractor's figure represents an offer (which the employer's acceptance has turned into a binding contractual obligation to do the work for the quoted price) or whether it is a mere indication of a likely figure. The answer to this question is one of construction in all the circumstances, and the term used is not conclusive; thus a contractor has been held bound by a document headed 'Estimate' (*Croshaw* v *Pritchard* (1899) 16 TLR 45).

An estimate or quotation which does not constitute an offer in the legal sense cannot of course give rise to any *contractual* obligation, even if the employer approves it and the contractor consequently begins work. The contractor's entitlement in such circumstances will be what the court regards as a 'reasonable sum', which may be higher or lower than the quoted figure. However, it has been held that a contractor who continues work in such circumstances, when he knows that the estimate which he originally gave was a misleadingly low one, may be liable in negligence to the employer for failing to correct it and thus enable the employer to cut his losses by abandoning the project (*J & JC Abrams Ltd* v *Ancliffe* [1978] 2 NZLR 420).

5 Letters of intent

There appears to be an increasing practice within the construction industry of commencing work before settling the contractual paperwork. This may be partly due to the growing use of 'fast-track' methods of building procurement; it also arises where the long lead times required by the suppliers of specialist components means that the manufacture of those components may have to start even before the main contractor has been chosen. Whatever the reason for the practice, however, it has undoubtedly led many contractors to seek some kind of assurance from the employer that, if they carry out work, a contract will indeed be forthcoming in due course. Such assurance frequently takes the form of a 'letter of intent' from the employer, indicating his firm intention to award the relevant contract to the particular contractor and requesting him to make an immediate start on the work. The question which can then arise is whether such a letter has any legal force.

As to this, the basic position must be that a letter of intent (like a 'comfort letter' issued by a parent company—*Kleinwort Benson Ltd* v *Malaysia Mining Corp Berhad* [1989] 1 All ER 785) is no more than a statement of present intention and is thus of no contractual significance. This will be even more strongly the case where the parties are still in negotiations as to important terms of the contract, such as the price (*British Steel Corporation* v *Cleveland Bridge & Engineering Co Ltd* [1984] 1 All ER 504). In such circumstances, it is not possible to spell out a binding contract from the letter of intent and the contractor's commencement of work; as a result, the contractor will be entitled to claim on a *quantum meruit* basis for the work which he does, while not incurring any counter-liability in respect of late delivery or other 'breaches'. What has not yet been decided (since the Court of Appeal in *Crown House Engineering Ltd* v *AMEC Projects Ltd* (1989) 48 BLR 32 refused to deal with it in Order 14 proceedings) is whether such defaults on the contractor's part would affect the amount of the *quantum meruit* claim.

Notwithstanding the basic position outlined above, there may be cases in which a letter of intent can be regarded as a definite offer by the employer to pay for the specified work. This is perhaps most likely to be so where the work in question can be seen as separate from the rest of the contract, for example where a design and build contractor is asked to carry out certain preliminary design work so that the employer can seek planning permission and obtain estimates (as in *Turriff Construction Ltd* v *Regalia Knitting Mills Ltd* (1971) 9 BLR 20).

6 The effect of a later formal contract

Although, as has been shown, a formal contract is not always regarded as essential for the commencement of building works, it is nonetheless common for parties who have begun work (whether or not on the basis of a letter of intent) to continue their negotiations and ultimately to conclude a contract. Where this is done, the question which it raises is whether the contract terms are to apply retrospectively to the work already done, or whether that work is to be governed exclusively by the letter of intent or by the rules of *quantum meruit*.

The answer to this question is, once again, dependent upon the intention of the parties as expressed in their agreement; however, the leading case of *Trollope & Colls Ltd* v *Atomic Power Constructions Ltd* [1962] 3 All ER 1035 suggests that a court will be fairly ready to imply a term giving the contract retrospective effect. In the case in question, this approach had the desirable result that detailed financial provisions in a civil engineering contract (dealing with both variations and fluctuations in the cost of labour and materials) were held applicable to the whole of the works, including that part which was carried out before the contract was executed.

7 Variation of an existing contract

If the original formation of building contracts is governed by general contract law, the same is true of any agreement by the parties during the course of a project to alter the terms of the contract under which it is being carried out. Provided that any agreed package of alterations can be seen as providing benefits for both parties, no problems should arise. Where, however, the benefits appear entirely one-sided (as for example where the employer unilaterally agrees to allow extra time for completion, or where he agrees to pay a bonus if the contractor merely keeps to time), the question which may be asked is what, if any, consideration the contractor is providing in return for the employer's promise, since the law does not normally regard the mere performance of an existing obligation as good consideration (*Stilk* v *Myrick* (1809) 2 Camp 317).

Of course, if what the employer undertakes is not a positive commitment (such as a bonus payment) but simply a waiver of his existing legal rights (as where he agrees to forgo a claim for liquidated damages), then it may in any event be enforceable under the doctrine of promissory estoppel (*Central London Property Trust Ltd* v *High Trees House Ltd* [1947] KB 130). However, received wisdom is that that doctrine is merely 'a shield, not a sword', and that any *positive* promise must, in order to be enforceable, be supported by consideration.

In a somewhat controversial decision (*Williams* v *Roffey Bros & Nicholls (Contractors) Ltd* [1991] QB 1), the Court of Appeal has recently held that there is no rule of law which prevents the performance of an existing duty from being regarded as valid consideration for another's promise; the crucial question is simply whether that performance *in fact* confers a benefit. Thus, where a domestic sub-contractor who had seriously underpriced his tender for carpentry work, and who was on the verge of liquidation, was induced to remain on site by the main contractor's promise of extra payment, it was held that the practical advantages of this arrangement to the main contractor were sufficient to constitute consideration. It is to be noted that the court placed great emphasis on the complete absence of evidence to suggest that the sub-contractor had been guilty of fraud, or that he had exerted any form of economic duress in order to secure this bonus from the main contractor.

Chapter 9

Contract Terms

1 Contract documents

Contract documents are the means by which a designer's intentions are conveyed to the client, the statutory authorities, the quantity surveyor, the contractor and the sub-contractors. All the design consultants add their own specialised information to the increasing body of documentation as the project progresses. From a management and administrative point of view, every item of documentation is important, because it describes and records decisions about the project. However, by no means every item comes within the more limited legal definition of 'contract documents', a special term used in construction contracts to describe those documents which define the contractor's obligations. Whichever form of contract is used, the contractor's basic undertaking is to carry out the works in accordance with these contract documents.

As to what the term 'contract documents' includes, nearly all the forms identify the articles of agreement, the conditions of contract, the appendix, the drawings and the bills as key contract documents. However, there are differences between the forms when it comes to such items as programmes, specifications and the like.

We will examine each element of documentation briefly, before considering how they relate to each other and how the conditions of contract integrate them.

(a) Articles of agreement

The articles of agreement record in general terms what it is that the parties have agreed to do. They identify the parties to the contract, what is to be built (the contractor's obligation) and what is to be paid (the employer's obligation). They tie these obligations to the conditions and to the other contract documents.

In defining the contractor's obligation, the articles do not descend to any great detail, but merely state, in a section starting with the word 'whereas', that 'the employer is desirous' of having the briefly described works carried out. Some standard forms also record that tenders have been accepted, that drawings have been prepared, and so on. This section is called the 'recitals' (although only JCT 80 specifically gives it this name). The purpose of the recitals is to describe the background to and the purpose of the contract. They help to provide a basis for interpretation of the detailed provisions contained in the contract clauses.

(b) Contract conditions

The conditions of contract are the very detailed clauses which follow from the articles of agreement. It has become common practice recently for standard forms to provide a table of contents to help in finding the various clauses, but until 1980 this was a rare occurrence. In addition to tables of contents, ICE 6 and GC/Works/1 also have indices which increase their accessibility.

The purpose of the conditions is to amplify and explain the basic obligations which the parties undertake by signing the articles of agreement. The conditions also provide administrative mechanisms for ensuring that the correct procedures are observed. Effective contract clauses of this kind deal efficiently with minor breaches of contract and thus help to ensure that the contract is kept alive.

(c) Appendix

Certain facts relating to the execution of a building contract will inevitably differ from one project to another. To enable standard form contracts to be used in spite of these differences, the particular facts can be summarised in an appendix to the contract. Thus, JCT 80 contains two pages, and ICE 6 three pages, which should be filled in when executing the contract. GC/Works/1 achieves the same effect with a document called an 'abstract of particulars' which is included with the tender documentation.

It is in the appendix (or abstract) that such matters as the base date, date for completion, defects liability period and amount of liquidated damages are entered. Some of the contractual conditions specify what is to happen if the relevant entry in the appendix is left blank. Some provisions are not applicable at all unless the appendix is completed, such as the employer's right under JCT 80 to delay possession of the site by up to six weeks.

The contents of the appendix are of fundamental importance in assessing the amount and duration of responsibility accepted by the parties. It is therefore essential that close attention is paid to the entries in the appendix.

(d) Drawings and plans

The production of drawings is generally, although not always, the responsibility of the design team. The technical complexity of most modern buildings results in a large mass of documentation, the production and control of which is frequently a management problem in itself.

Drawings have more than one function and, whilst these different functions are usually fulfilled by different drawings, it is as well to remind oneself of the exact nature and purpose of each particular drawing.

First, they form a model of the designers' ideas and help to rationalise and predict problems and conflicts with fabrication and with appearances. Isometrics, scheme design drawings and 'artistic impression' drawings help to fulfil this function. Although there is little information on them which would enable a builder to erect the proposed building accurately, they amplify and explain the basic nature of the required finished building.

Secondly, drawings are the vehicle by which the designers' intentions are conveyed to the contractor. The detail design drawings contain information which shows how the separate parts of the building interact with each other. The detailed information from specialist sub-contractors and from other designers is co-ordinated and presented through such drawings.

Thirdly, drawings form a record of what has been done. These 'as-built' drawings are essential to the building owner as a basis for future maintenance of the facility, and may not be the same drawings that were used for the purposes of fabrication.

The multiple uses which different drawings are called upon to perform, and the interaction between drawings and other types of documentation, have often been a source of problems for construction projects. A consequence of these problems was the setting up of the Co-ordinating Committee for Project Information (CCPI) which produced a set of guidelines for the production of drawings, specifications and bills of quantities. These currently represent best practice in the industry and should be essential reading for everyone concerned with the documentation of construction projects.

On completion of the work, the architect or building surveyor can insist that all drawings are returned because, according to their conditions of engagement, the copyright for this information is theirs. Neither the contractor nor the client is entitled to use the information again, by constructing an identical building, without first obtaining the permission of the designer.

Associated with the drawings and plans will be 'schedules'. These are tables of information which summarise the quantities and dimensions of certain generic items, for example windows or ironmongery. Although they will rarely be cited as contract documents, they will often be bound up and included with the sets of drawings, as they are invaluable in summarising detailed information. Clearly, a drawing will show all the windows in a building, but it is very useful to extract all the details of sizes and numbers on to one table. The aim of the schedule is merely to simplify the retrieval of information. It is not intended to supplant the bills of quantity, which will contain the full and final description of the work.

(e) Bills of quantity

The bill of quantities originated as a tendering document; indeed, engineering contracts still retain this emphasis. In the JCT contracts, the bills of quantity have an increasingly important role to play in the valuation of variations and interim certificates, and in the control of the works. In addition, various other categories of information are often gleaned from the bills, such as locational identification of work and formation of a basis for cost planning. Not surprisingly, bills of quantity are increasingly seen as incapable of fulfilling all of these conflicting needs. There are many ways of choosing a contractor, and many ways of fixing a price for the work to be undertaken. To use the bill as the sole vehicle for both these purposes is an over-simplification that can lead to many problems.

The bills consist of preliminaries, preambles and measured works. There is a wide variation in the application of these terms, and it is useful to clarify their meaning.

The *preliminaries* contain the definition of the scope of the works. They include, among other things, particulars of the project, lists of drawings, description of the site, scope of the work, details of documentation and management arrangements.

The *preambles* were originally a separate description of the materials and workmanship to be employed in assembling the building, and this was known as the 'specification' section of the bill. Nowadays, it is more common to include such information with the main bill of quantities and, as a result, it is likely that preambles will disappear from the vocabulary of building contracts.

The *measured works* are the detailed quantification of the works. This section should be presented according to the rules dictated in the contract.

Two further terms worthy of mention are PC and Provisional Sums. These terms are antiquated and their origins are now obscure, but their use is prevalent and seems likely to continue. Their use is as follows:

Prime Cost (PC) Sums are used for works under the building contract which are to be carried out under the direction of the main contractor by certain other persons, namely, nominated sub-contractors, nominated suppliers and statutory authorities. The nominated sub-contractors will usually have been selected prior to the selection of the main contractor. Since the contractor has no control over the pricing of this work, an amount of money is simply included in the bills, to which the contractor can add a price for attendance and profit.

Provisional Sums are used for work which has not been finalised, or for costs which are unknown, at the time the bills are prepared. They may simply be contingency sums, and their presence does not necessarily imply any obligation on the part of the employer to spend them. In effect, they are simply a method for the employer to express part of the budget for the project. The contract administrator must issue instructions to spend these sums.

Whilst drawings provide information about the shape, appearance and location of the various components which have to be assembled, they convey little about the methods to be used, the quality of finishes and the workmanship to be employed. Assuming that such things are to be specifically controlled by the contract, rather than relying on the terms which would be implied at common law, this is a matter for the 'specification', which is usually found as a discrete section of the bill of quantities.

Where bills of quantity are used for a project, information of this kind will be contained in the bills, and there will be no 'specification' in the sense of a separate document. However, not all projects need full quantification with bills of quantity; an increasing number of projects are being let by drawings and specification alone. Where this is done, the specification may be called upon to perform an even wider role.

(f) Other documents

Other categories of documents include certificates, instructions and programmes.

There are several types of certificate in building contracts, falling into two main categories: interim certificates, which certify the quantity of work done to date for the purposes of payment; and those which certify that an event has taken place.

Interim certificates are used in the great majority of building contracts, because it is not intended that the contractor should have to finance the whole of the building work. The contractor will be paid for the amount of work done at regular periods; usually one month. When each payment is made, a small percentage of the money due to the contractor (called the retention) is kept back, and this is released when the work is completed. It is also possible for other amounts of money to be withheld, under a right known as set off, for delay or defective work (see Chapter 13).

The second category of certificates consists of those which record an event (or non-event). They vary from one form of contract to another, but basically they are the certificate of practical completion, certificate of final completion and certificate of non-completion.

Additional contract information is contained in *instructions*, which contain information more detailed than that found in the tender documents. There are also other post-contractual documents (such as descriptive schedules, further drawings and setting-out information), which the contracts may describe as being 'necessary' or 'required' to execute the work. Such additional information should not impose extra work on the contractor but, if a contract administrator wishes to impose changes when issuing instructions, then a variation order must be issued to cover the changes.

Many contracts make it incumbent upon the contractor to provide a 'programme' of work. Although certain dates in the *contract* are legally binding, the programme is not. All the contracts make it clear that, even though the contractor must provide a programme soon after being awarded the contract, there can be no extra obligations imposed by it. The programme is essential as a management control mechanism because, for example, the contract administrator can use it as a basis for deciding upon dates for issuing instructions and information to the contractor, as well as for judging the effects of delay and disruption. In order for it to be effective in this role, it must be updated from time to time, and the contracts make this a requirement.

2 Priority of documents

The enormous quantity of documentation which characterises building contracts, at least those which relate to substantial projects, not infrequently leads to inconsistencies between documents. This possibility is no doubt enhanced by the fact that many of the contract documents will be drawn up by different people and for different purposes. Where this occurs, any conflict is to be resolved by application of the general principles governing the construction of contracts, which may themselves be amended by express provisions.

In particular, the principle of interpretation which makes printed contract terms give way to those specifically written or typed in is modified by many of the major standard form contracts. Most emphatically, JCT 80 clause 2.2.1 states that nothing in the contract bills shall override or modify what is contained in the articles, conditions or appendix. Thus the printed standard form conditions prevail over provisions in the bills of quantity, notwithstanding that the latter will naturally have been drafted with the specific circumstances of the particular contract in mind.

A similar clause in an earlier version of the JCT contract enabled a court to hold that an obligation to carry out design work could not be imposed on a contractor by the 'back door' method of inserting a performance specification in the contract bills (*John Mowlem & Co Ltd* v *British Insulated Callenders Pension Trust Ltd* (1977) 3 Con LR 64). However, that same provision has in other cases served to stultify what was fairly obviously the parties' intentions, for example where the contract contained a single completion date, but the bills showed clearly that staged completion was expected (*MJ Gleeson (Contractors) Ltd* v *Hillingdon London Borough* (1970) 215 EG 165); or as to the extent of insurance cover to be taken out by the contractor (*Gold* v *Patman & Fotheringham Ltd* [1958] 2 All ER 497).

The result thus achieved under the JCT forms of contract would presumably also apply to GC/Works/1, since clause 2(1) provides that the contract conditions shall prevail over all other contract documents. ICE 6 clause 5, on the other hand, provides somewhat enigmatically that the contract documents 'are to be taken as mutually explanatory of one another', which appears to replace the common law principle with the unfettered discretion of the engineer.

It is worth noting in the present context that most building contracts make specific provision for any discrepancies between documents, or between different parts of the same document, to be referred by the contractor to the contract administrator (see JCT 80 clause 2.3, ICE 6 clause 5, GC/Works/1 clause 2(3)). The latter is then required to resolve the discrepancy by issuing appropriate instructions; if these result in delay or disruption, the contractor will normally be entitled to an extension of time and to financial compensation.

3 Incorporation by reference

It is comparatively rare for the document which is actually signed by the contracting parties to contain all the terms of their agreement. In most instances, that document will incorporate by reference the contents of other documents, which will thereby also acquire the status of express terms. Even in the case of a formally executed agreement, it is likely that such important documents as the contract drawings bills of quantity or specification will be incorporated in this way. Indeed, the 1991 procedure for nomination of sub-contractors under JCT 80 provides for the parties to execute only the Articles of Agreement (NSC/A) and for the Conditions (NSC/C) to be kept 'on the shelf'.

The principle of the incorporation of terms by reference is also of great importance where (as happens all too often) the parties fail to execute a formal contract. For example, where the exchange of correspondence leading to an offer and acceptance stated 'assuming that we can agree a satisfactory contract price between us, the general conditions and terms will be subject to the normal standard form of RIBA contract', this was held to incorporate the RIBA contract then current (*Kilby & Gayford Ltd* v *Selincourt Ltd* (1973) 3 BLR 104). Indeed, the courts have on occasion gone a very long way to make sense of the true intentions of parties who have on the face of it agreed to incorporate contract forms which do not even exist! (See, for example, *Modern Building (Wales) Ltd* v *Limmer & Trinidad Co Ltd* [1975] 1 WLR 1281; *Brightside Kilpatrick Engineering Services* v *Mitchell Construction Ltd* (1973) 1 BLR 62.)

Notwithstanding such judicial generosity, the dangers of incorporation in this way should not be overlooked. Many of the conditions found in standard form contracts are meaningless unless and until an appropriate entry (such as a date for possession, or a rate for liquidated damages) has been made in the appendix to the contract. Without such an entry, the purported incorporation of the relevant condition will be of no effect, since the clause will have nothing on which to bite.

The problems surrounding the incorporation of contract terms by reference gain an additional dimension in relation to sub-contracts, which tend even more than main contracts to be entered into with a minimum of formality. The question which can arise in such circumstances is whether a sub-contractor's undertaking to carry out work in accordance with the terms of the main contract, or even an acknowledgment that he has notice of those terms, is sufficient to incorporate them into the sub-contract. The answer to this appears to be that, depending upon the precise wording of any undertaking, some but not all of the main contract terms will be incorporated. The sub-contractor is most likely to be bound by terms relating to quality of the work and payment for it (*Geary, Walker & Co Ltd* v *W Lawrence & Son* (1906) HBC (4th ed) Vol 2, p 382); on the other hand, the courts have refused to 'step down' an arbitration clause (*Goodwins, Jardine & Co* v *Brand* (1905) 7 F (Ct of Sess) 995) and a provision under which the employer could insist on the sub-contractor's removal from the site (*Chandler Bros Ltd* v *Boswell* [1936] 3 All ER 179).

4 Implied terms

In addition to those terms on which the parties have expressly agreed, building contracts may be subject to a range of implied terms, either by virtue of some statute (such as the Supply of Goods and Services Act 1982) or where a court seeks to give effect to the presumed intention of the parties. Such judicial implication may be further divided into two broad classes of case. First, there are those terms which are regarded as 'usual' for all building contracts and which will be readily implied into any such contract, provided that this would not be inconsistent with the express terms. Many of these implied terms are considered in Chapter 10, in conjunction with the kind of express terms which are usually found dealing with various aspects of the construction process.

The second type of judicial implication occurs where a court is persuaded that a particular contract will be altogether lacking in business efficacy unless a particular term is implied. Such creative intervention is not something in which the courts are eager to indulge—it is not to be done on the basis that the term in question would improve the contract or make it more reasonable, but only where, without such a term, the contract would be 'inefficacious, futile or absurd'. The strictness of this approach is illustrated by the well-known case of *Trollope & Colls Ltd* v *North West Metropolitan Regional Hospital Board* [1973] 2 All ER 260, where a contract for the construction of a hospital extension in phases provided that Phase III should commence six months after the issue of the certificate of practical completion of Phase I, but that Phase III should itself be completed by a fixed date. The late completion of Phase I (for which the contractors were given an extension of time) effectively halved the time remaining for Phase III, and the contractors argued for the implication of an 'obvious' term under which any extension of time for Phase I should have an equal knock-on effect on Phase III. The House of Lords refused to imply any such term, on the grounds that the express terms of the contract were perfectly clear and workable, and that the parties must be taken to have understood the risks which they were taking on.

Chapter 10

The Parties' Obligations

The previous two chapters dealt with the questions of how building contracts are created and how the terms of such contracts are identified. This chapter provides a general picture of what those terms (both express and implied) routinely involve. Such an overview is of course no substitute for a detailed scrutiny of particular contract documents; however, it may give the uninitiated some inkling of what they can expect to find there.

1 The site

(a) Possession and access

Most building contracts envisage work being carried out on the employer's land, and clearly the contractor will require possession of the site. It is usual for the contract to deal expressly with both the physical *extent* of possession (whether the contractor is to take over the entire site from the outset, or whether he is merely to have those parts which are necessary at any given stage) and also the *time* at which the site is to be handed over to the contractor. The latter may be a fixed date, or the employer may be given a period within which to comply, in which case the contractual completion date should be calculated from the moment of handover.

In the unlikely event that there are no express terms dealing with the site, it is implied that the contractor will have possession at a time sufficient to enable him to meet the contractual completion date (*Freeman* v *Hensler* (1900) 64 JP 260).

In addition to possession of the site itself (and of sufficient surrounding land to carry out the works), the contractor will require access to it. The contract should make a clear allocation of responsibility in respect of this matter since, while the employer will have an implied obligation to give access across his own land (though not necessarily by the route which the contractor prefers), this will not make him responsible for securing rights of access from third parties.

It may be that an obligation to give possession of the site will be interpreted more strictly than one to give access. The former has been held to have been breached where an employer took time to remove squatters from the site (*Rapid Building Group Ltd* v *Ealing Family Housing Association Ltd* (1985) 29 BLR 5). On the other hand, an obligation to afford access was not broken by the obstructive activities of unlawful pickets (*LRE Engineering Services Ltd* v *Otto Simon Carves Ltd* (1981) 24 BLR 127).

(b) Site conditions

It is in the nature of building work that unexpected site problems, especially those which relate to ground and subsoil conditions, may seriously affect the profitability or even the viability of an entire venture. Such problems are in principle a risk for the contractor to bear, for the courts have consistently refused to imply any warranty on the employer's part as to the feasibility of the project (*Bottoms* v *York Corporation* (1892) HBC 4th ed, ii, 208) or even as to the accuracy of the plans, drawings or other information which he provides (*Sharpe* v *San Paulo Brazilian Railway Co* (1873) LR 8 Ch App 597). However, some contracts (eg ICE 6 clause 12, GC/Works/1 clause 7) divert at least part of this risk on to the employer, by entitling the contractor to extra payment where adverse site conditions could not reasonably have been foreseen.

Apart from such express terms, contractors may seek compensation for unexpectedly difficult conditions in various ways. For instance, where a design and build contractor was positively instructed to design foundations on the basis of certain borehole data supplied by the employer, it was held that the latter must be taken to have assumed responsibility for these (*Bacal Construction (Midlands) Ltd* v *Northampton Development Corporation* (1975) 8 BLR 88). Again, where a contract was stated to be based on a Standard Method of Measurement which required excavation in rock to be a separate item in the bills of quantity, it was held that a contractor who unexpectedly encountered rock could treat this as extra work and claim additional payment for it (*Bryant & Sons Ltd* v *Birmingham Hospital Saturday Fund* [1938] 1 All ER 503). Furthermore, an employer might arguably owe a duty of care when supplying precontract information, though probably not in the face of express conditions to the effect that it is for the contractor to satisfy himself as to site conditions.

2 The contract work

Precisely what it is that a contractor undertakes to do depends upon the construction of the contract. If the description used connotes a complete building, such as a house fit for habitation, then it is implied that the contractor will provide everything which is indispensably necessary to achieve this result, whether or not it is expressly contained in the specification of works (*Williams* v *Fitzmaurice* (1858) 3 H & N 844). However, where the contract makes it clear that the works are exhaustively defined in the bills of quantity (eg under JCT 80 clause 14.1), the contractor's obligation is limited to providing what is in the bills; if this falls short of what is required to complete the building, the employer must pay for the extra work involved (*Patman & Fotheringham Ltd* v *Pilditch* (1904) HBC 4th ed, ii, 368).

3 Quality of work

The quality of work, like its quantity, is primarily to be defined by the contract documents. These may descend to considerable detail, by reference to performance specifications, codes of practice and the like, and there is frequently a requirement that work should be to the satisfaction of the contract administrator. In addition, this is an area in which implied terms, both statutory and common law, are well developed.

(a) Workmanship

An undertaking on the part of the contractor to use good workmanship (ie such care and skill as is reasonable) will readily be implied into any building contract, and will render the contractor responsible for his own work and for that of any sub-contractor, whether domestic or nominated. Whether this implied obligation refers only to the quality of the finished item, or whether it also requires the work to be carried out in a proper and workmanlike manner, is a matter of some debate. However, many contract provisions (eg JCT 80 clause 8) make it clear that both aspects of the obligation are imposed.

(b) Quality of materials

A term that all materials used by the contractor are of merchantable quality will be implied under s 4(2) of the Supply of Goods and Services Act 1982, confirming the common law position but apparently upgrading the term's status from warranty to condition (a difficult proposition, for it can surely not have been intended that a single defect should give the employer a right to terminate an entire building contract). It is important to note that a contractor will be liable on this basis even for materials in whose selection he has no choice, as where they are supplied by a sub-contractor, or even where they are selected by the employer (*Young & Marten Ltd* v *McManus Childs Ltd* [1969] 1 AC 454). However, where the employer insists (without any right of the contractor to object) that materials are obtained from a supplier who, to the employer's knowledge, excludes or limits liability for defects, the contractor will not be taken to warrant their quality (*Gloucestershire CC* v *Richardson* [1969] 1 AC 480).

(c) Fitness for purpose

Quite apart from the basic quality of materials, there may be an implied obligation governing the fitness of those materials for their intended purpose. Alternatively (or additionally), there may be an implied term to the effect that the entire building will be fit for its purpose on completion. In either case, 'fitness' involves both functional suitability and also compliance with any relevant legal requirements.

Unlike the obligation as to quality, terms of this nature are implied only where the employer has placed some reliance upon the skill and judgment of the contractor. In consequence, there will be no warranty of suitability in respect of materials selected by the employer, or by the architect on his behalf. As for the suitability of the building, a term to this effect will normally be implied only in design and build contracts (see Chapter 11).

(d) Testing and approval

The question of whether or not a contractor's work is up to the contractual standard may arise in arbitration or litigation, in the course of a claim for damages for breach of contract. More frequently, however, it will be something for the contract administrator to decide through the certification procedure. Where this is so, it is necessary to know (as a matter of construction of the contract) whether the requirement to satisfy the contract administrator replaces the more objective contractual standards described above, or whether it is an additional obligation upon the contractor. This question is of particular importance where (as under JCT contracts) the Final Certificate is expressed to be 'conclusive' evidence that the standard of workmanship or materials is to the contract administrator's satisfaction. In *Colbart* v *Kumar* [1992] CILL 752 it was held that this provision applied, not only to those items which the contract *expressly* reserved for the opinion of the contract administrator, but also to all those which were *inherently* for his opinion (a category which may well include most of the work). In consequence, the employer was not permitted to allege defects in the work after the expiry of the very short period within which a Final Certificate can be challenged.

The position of the contract administrator is the subject of very different traditions in building and civil engineering respectively. In the former, it is generally assumed (see for example JCT 80 clause 2.1) that, where any approval is left to the opinion of the architect, it must be to his *reasonable satisfaction*. By contrast, civil engineering work must *all* be to the satisfaction of the engineer and, further, there is no suggestion that the engineer must act reasonably.

The contract administrator's role in approving or disapproving the contractor's work is made easier under many contracts by specific provisions entitling him to order the contract to open up or uncover work for inspection or testing. Such clauses frequently make provision for the contractor to be paid compensation in the event that no defects are found.

(e) Rectification of defects

As a general principle, where defects of workmanship or materials are discovered in a building after practical completion has been achieved, the contractor may expect (subject to a 'conclusive' certificate, or to the expiry of a limitation period) to be liable for breach of contract. The principal remedy for such a breach is an award of damages; these should reflect the cost of restoring the building to its intended condition, plus any incidental losses suffered by the employer, such as relocation expenses while works of repair are carried out (*East Ham BC* v *Bernard Sunley & Sons Ltd* [1966] AC 406).

In addition to the above, many construction contracts make provision for something called a 'Defects Liability Period' or 'Defects Correction Period' (eg JCT 80 clause 17, ICE 6 clause 49), which begins on the date of practical completion and runs for whatever period is stated in the Appendix (typically six months). During this period, the contractor undertakes to rectify any defects which may emerge and, upon certification that this has been done, becomes entitled to the second half of the retention money (the first half having been handed over on practical completion). It is worth noting that some contracts (eg ICE 5) use the rather misleading term 'Maintenance Period' to describe this type of contractor's rectification duty.

A provision of this nature may be seen as creating a benefit as well as a burden for the contractor. Without it, he would be liable to the employer for the cost of having another contractor in to rectify defects, something which would in many cases be considerably more expensive than for the contractor who is already on site.

4 Working methods

Construction contracts vary widely as to the extent to which they subject the contractor's method of work to the control of the employer (through the contract administrator). ICE 6, for example, makes it clear in clauses 13 and 14 that the engineer has very substantial powers in this context—the contractor must produce a method statement at the outset and provide any further information which the engineer may from time to time require, and the engineer can insist that the proposed methods be altered. GC/Works/1 is rather less specific, but the areas in which the Project Manager is empowered to issue instructions certainly appear to extend to the way in which work is carried out.

By contrast with the above, JCT 80 adopts a strictly 'hands off' approach to questions of working method—the contract administrator, although empowered to inspect and approve each item of work as it is produced, has little or no authority as to the way in which the contractor chooses to produce it. Nor can such control come about through the contractor's undoubted duty to obey instructions; clause 4 makes it clear that this applies only to those matters about which the contract explicitly authorises instructions to be issued. The overall position under such a contract is that legal responsibility for any injury or damage caused by unsafe working methods is likely to rest with the contractor alone (*Clayton* v *Woodman & Son (Builders) Ltd* [1962] 2 All ER 33).

Closely allied to methods of work are questions of progress, programming and the sequencing of operations within a project.

Here the contract administrator under JCT 80 has rather more authority, since clause 23.2 empowers him to require the postponement of any of the contract work. Once again, however, ICE 6 and GC/Works/1 go further, by enabling their respective contract administrators to suspend the whole of the contract works for any reason whatsoever.

5 Progress

Where time is concerned, the major obligation imposed upon the contractor is to achieve practical completion of the works by whatever date, or within whatever period, the contract lays down. This obligation is discussed in some detail in Chapter 16.

In addition to *finishing* the work on time, many building contracts require the contractor to maintain a satisfactory rate of progress throughout the project. Such phrases as 'regularly and diligently proceed' (JCT 80 clause 23.1.1) and 'due expedition and without delay' (ICE 6 clause 41(2)) give an indication of the kind of obligation which is imposed in such cases. However, where a contract does not contain a provision of this kind, the courts will not readily imply one; the contractor's only obligation will be to complete on time (*GLC* v *Cleveland Bridge and Engineering Co Ltd* (1984) 34 BLR 50). Furthermore, while many contracts require the contract to submit a programme for the execution of the works, this in itself does not normally create a contractual obligation to adhere to the timetable set out therein (see *Kitsons Sheet Metal Ltd* v *Matthew Hall Mechanical and Electrical Engineers Ltd* (1989) 47 BLR 82).

6 Other obligations of the contractor

Depending on the type of work which is involved, a building contract may impose a host of detailed obligations upon the contractor, ranging from a requirement that a performance bond be provided (ICE 6 clause 10) to a prohibition against the taking of photographs of the site (GC/Works/1 clause 28). There would be little to gain from a long list of such provisions, but it is worth noting that most contracts deal expressly with the transfer of ownership in materials (in terms which seek to prevent both the contractor and any sub-contractor from subjecting goods to a retention of title clause). It is also common to impose some degree of control on the contractor's ability to assign his rights or to sub-contract his obligations, by means of either an absolute prohibition or a requirement that the employer's consent be obtained.

One very good reason for detailed drafting of this kind is the general reluctance of the courts to imply terms, other than those which define the contractor's basic obligations as to time and quality. Recent examples of this attitude may be seen in decisions that there is no *implied* obligation on the contractor to complete the work in stages (*Bruno Zornow (Builders) Ltd* v *Beechcroft Developments Ltd* (1989) 51 BLR 16), nor to guard on-site property of the employer against the possibility of theft (*Colbart* v *Kumar* [1992] CILL 752).

Judicial reluctance notwithstanding, there are some areas in which terms would almost certainly be implied, although direct authority is lacking (because in practice the point is invariably dealt with under an express provision). A good example concerns statutory requirements, such as the Building Regulations, which may apply to a project; there can be little doubt that the contractor, in addition to his statutory duty of compliance, is also under an implied contractual obligation to the employer to build in accordance with all relevant legal controls. More specifically, where a contractor works under a cost-based contract such as a management contract (in which the contractor is entitled to be paid whatever it costs him to have the works executed), there is surely an implication that the contractor will take all reasonable steps to keep those costs down and thus to avoid wasting the employer's money.

7 Payment

From a contractor's point of view, the most important obligation of the employer under a building contract is almost certainly that of paying what is due. This obligation will include, not only the agreed price for the works, but also other sums such as payment for extra work (variations) and compensation for loss and/or expense caused to the contractor by any disruption of the contract work for which the employer is responsible.

Contract terms dealing with various aspects of payment are considered in more detail in Chapters 13 and 14. At this stage it may simply be pointed out that, in the absence of any express contractual provision for payment, a contractor who carries out work at the request of another will be entitled to claim a reasonable sum for it. What is more, the courts have proved very willing to imply a term for interim payments on a regular basis (see, for example, *DR Bradley (Cable Jointing) Ltd* v *Jefco Mechanical Services Ltd* (1988) 6-CLD-07-19).

8 Other obligations of the employer

Building contracts tend on the whole to impose more in the way of specific obligations on the contractor than on the employer. In so far as the latter's duties are specifically mentioned, these may consist of little more than appointing an architect, giving possession of the site and making payments to the contractor as and when appropriate. Against such a background there is considerable scope for the implication of additional terms relating to the employer, and the relevant case law provides numerous examples of terms which the courts have been persuaded to imply. Nonetheless, when these detailed terms are examined, they all appear to be applications of a more general principle, namely, that the employer will not hinder or prevent the contractor from carrying out his obligations under the contract and, indeed, that he will positively co-operate with the contractor to bring about completion of the contract works.

(a) Non-hindrance and co-operation

This two-pronged obligation of non-hindrance and co-operation, recognised in *Merton LBC* v *Stanley Hugh Leach Ltd* (1985) 32 BLR 51, is of patent relevance in a number of situations. It will clearly be breached, for example, by failure to give the contractor necessary instructions or design information at a reasonably appropriate time. Again, the employer will be liable for any unreasonable delay in appointing or reappointing an architect if the contract requires one (*Hunt* v *Bishop* (1853) 8 Exch 675), or in nominating or renominating a sub-contractor (*North West Regional Hospital Board* v *TA Bickerton & Son Ltd* [1970] 1 All ER 1039; *Percy Bilton Ltd* v *GLC* [1982] 2 All ER 623). Less obviously, perhaps, it has been held that an employer cannot use a variations clause so as to omit work from the contract, in order to give it to another contractor; this would be preventing the original contractor from executing work in accordance with his contractual rights (*Commissioner for Main Roads* v *Reed & Stuart Pty Ltd* (1974) 12 BLR 55).

It should of course be emphasised that implied terms can only operate against the background of the express terms of a contract, and the employer's duty of co-operation does not extend to enabling the contractor to obtain anything more than his contractual entitlement. For example, while a contractor is perfectly entitled to programme his work so as to finish before the contractual completion date, he cannot compel the employer to assist him in such early completion (*Glenlion Construction Ltd* v *Guinness Trust* (1987) 39 BLR 89). Similarly, the fact that a pipe-laying contract requires the contractors to keep available a minimum number of gangs is no reason to imply an obligation on the employer to use them all (*Kelly Pipelines Ltd* v *British Gas plc* (1989) 48 BLR 126). And again, where a sub-contract requires work to be done 'at such time or times as the contractor shall direct or require', there is no room for any implication that the main contractor will programme so that sub-contractors can work in an efficient and economic manner (*Martin Grant & Co Ltd* v *Sir Lindsay Parkinson & Co Ltd* (1984) 29 BLR 31).

(b) Responsibility for others

A particularly interesting aspect of the employer's obligations discussed above concerns the extent to which he may be put in breach by other people who are involved in the project. Where there is more than one main contractor on site (as under a construction management arrangement), the employer will incur liability where one of them causes disruption to another (*Lawson* v *Wallasey Local Board* (1883) 11 QBD 229); likewise, if delays by a supplier mean that the employer is late with materials which he has specifically undertaken to provide. However, the employer will not in the absence of an express provision be held responsible for the acts or defaults of independent third parties such as statutory undertakers, nor (very importantly) for sub-contractors, even those whom he has nominated (*Leslie & Co Ltd* v *Metropolitan Asylum District Managers* (1901) 68 JP 86).

Most significantly, the employer may incur liability through what is done by the contract administrator, to whom many of the employer's duties and functions under the contract are delegated. However, it is necessary in this connection to distinguish between those matters in which the contract administrator is simply an agent of the employer (such as giving necessary information or instructions to the contractor) and those where he exercises an independent judgment, as when issuing certificates. In the former case, the employer is taken to guarantee that the contract administrator will act with reasonable diligence and with reasonable skill and care, and will thus be liable for any negligence on his part (*Merton LBC* v *Stanley Hugh Leach Ltd* (1985) 32 BLR 51).

The position in relation to the contract administrator's role as 'independent adjudicator' is more complicated. It was said in *Merton* v *Leach* that the employer is not taken to guarantee that these functions will be carried out with reasonable skill and care, but merely that he will not improperly interfere with the free exercise of the contract administrator's discretion. This statement, however, requires qualification. While an employer's obligations may indeed go no further than honest non-interference where the contractor has the opportunity to have a decision of the contract administrator overturned at arbitration (*Lubenham Fidelities and Investment Co Ltd* v *South Pembrokeshire DC* (1986) 33 BLR 39), the position is probably different where there is no applicable arbitration clause and where any decision would therefore be final. In such circumstances, it seems that an employer who becomes aware that the contract administrator is not applying the contract properly (for example by refusing altogether to deal with applications for extensions of time) must order him to carry out his duties and, if he does not, must dismiss him and appoint a substitute (*Perini Corporation* v *Commonwealth of Australia* (1969) 12 BLR 82).

9 Insurance obligations

It is highly unlikely that a court would recognise any *implied* obligation on either party to a building contract to take out insurance beyond what is required under the general law (eg for Employer's Liability). However, this is an area in which contracts usually impose express obligations—indeed, the insurance provisions of JCT 80 run to some five pages. The approach which is normally adopted is for the contract to identify various categories of risk, allocate these as between the contractor and the client and require the relevant risk-bearer to provide insurance cover to a specified level.

The topic of construction insurance is further considered in Chapter 12.

10 Determination

Any contract may be brought to a premature end under the general law, following either a serious 'repudiatory' breach by one of the parties or a neutral event which is sufficiently catastrophic to invoke the doctrine of frustration. In addition, a typical feature of construction contracts is the inclusion of express provisions enabling one or other of the parties to terminate the contract, or at least the contractor's involvement with it, if certain specified events occur. These commonly include various breaches of contract (such as late payment by the employer, or failure to rectify defective work by the contractor) which might not be sufficiently serious to justify termination at common law. They usually also include insolvency of a party, and some neutral disasters.

Determination provisions, which are further considered in Chapter 19, typically lay down strict implementation procedures; they also prescribe in detail the financial and other rights of the parties in the period between determination and the completion of the project.

Chapter 11

Liability for Defective Buildings

This chapter examines the legal remedies available to anyone with an interest in a building which is found to be defective. This person may be the original owner of the building, who will in all probability have been the employer under the building contract and the client of the designing architect and of any other consultants. On the other hand, in the case of a building with latent defects the claimant might well be a subsequent owner or tenant, or the lending institution responsible for funding the construction project.

The subject is one of considerable topical interest, due to the way in which recent decisions of the House of Lords have cut back the scope of the tort of negligence in this area. This retrenchment, which has of course been most deeply felt by parties other than the original building owner, has in turn led both to an investigation of other potential ways of securing redress (eg under various statutory provisions) and also to a growth in the use of devices such as collateral warranties, or the assignment by the original owner of rights of action, which are designed to offer protection in advance to those who acquire a building.

Much of what is said in the later parts of this chapter will apply with equal force, irrespective of whether the defects complained of are the result of poor design or poor construction. However, the issue of design raises a number of separate questions, not least that of identifying whose responsibility it is, and these are dealt with at the outset.

1 Responsibility for design

(a) Architect

Central to the traditional form of building procurement is the idea that the contractor merely builds what he is told to build, and that it is thus up to the employer to present the contractor with all the design information which is required. The responsibility for producing this design information has historically been that of an architect (or the engineer on civil engineering projects) and, while increasing technological complexity has led to the need to include specialist designers within the project team, the architect will normally remain responsible for the overall direction and co-ordination of their design elements.

The extent of an architect's legal responsibility for design will of course depend on the terms of the contract under which he is engaged but, unless that contract contains a fairly clear indication to the contrary, the courts appear to start from the premiss that he is entirely responsible. Thus if the architect, without the client's authorisation, delegates any part of the design work to another (who might be the contractor or a sub-contractor, or an independent consultant), he will be legally liable to the client for any design defects which result from the negligence of his appointee (*Moresk Cleaners Ltd* v *Hicks* [1966] 2 Lloyd's Rep 338).

The position where the architect is expressly permitted to delegate part of the design (or where authorisation can be implied, as in *Merton LBC* v *Lowe* (1981) 18 BLR 130) is rather more difficult. The RIBA Architect's Appointment states that, where the client employs other consultants, either directly or through the agency of the architect, the client 'will hold each consultant, and not the architect, responsible for the competence, general inspection and performance' of that consultant's work. The document also uses a similar form of words to cover cases where any design work is given to a contractor, sub-contractor or supplier. It might be argued that these clauses remove altogether the architect's responsibility in respect of such specialist elements of design; however, it is suggested that a court would still treat the architect's role as co-ordinator as sufficient to impose liability for any defects of specialist design which are sufficiently obvious that the (non-specialist) architect ought reasonably to have detected them (see *Investors in Industry Ltd* v *South Bedfordshire DC* [1986] QB 1034).

(b) Contractor

A contractor who operates under a design and build arrangement will, by definition, undertake legal responsibility for designing a building as well as constructing it. Indeed, as will be seen below, the contractor in such circumstances may (subject to the express terms of the contract) be deemed to warrant that the building will be fit for its intended purpose, an obligation rather stricter than a duty merely to design with reasonable care and skill. What remains unclear, since there are no reported cases on the point, is whether a design and build contractor who is in truth compelled to build to the employer's design (on the basis that this forms part of the Employer's Requirements) can nonetheless be held liable by the employer if this design proves in some way deficient.

Outside the design and build sphere, it is assumed that the contractor's duty is simply to build in accordance with the employer's design, and the courts will not readily interpret the contract documents in such a way as to impose any responsibility for design upon the contractor (*John Mowlem & Co Ltd* v *British Insulated Callenders Pension Trust Ltd* (1977) 3 Con LR 64). Nonetheless, it seems likely that a contractor who decides to exercise his own judgment in the face of a design problem, rather than insisting that the architect issue an instruction on the matter, may incur liability to the client for any defects which result. Furthermore, there is some authority for the view that a contractor who discovers flaws in the architect's design is under some legal obligation to draw these to the attention of the client, rather than simply continue to build something which he knows will be defective. The precise nature and extent of any such obligation is far from clear, but suggestions that it might be tort-based (*Equitable Debenture Assets Corporation* v *William Moss* (1984) 2 Con LR 1; *Victoria University of Manchester* v *Wilson & Womersley* (1984) 2 Con LR 43) appear to have given way to the idea that it rests upon an implied term in the building contract rather than upon the tort of negligence (*Duncan* v *Blundell* (1820) 3 Stark 6; *University Court of Glasgow* v *Whitfield* (1988) 42 BLR 66). In any event, the contractor does not owe any duty to the architect to warn him, although in practice it is to the architect that the contractor is likely to communicate his doubts about the design and thus fulfil his duty to the employer (*Southern Water Authority* v *Lewis & Duvivier (No 2)* (1985) 1 Const LJ 74).

(c) Sub-contractor

Advances in materials technology, and increasingly sophisticated production and installation processes, have led the construction industry to rely more and more heavily on specialist suppliers for the provision of such structural items as steel frames and cladding, as well as for more obviously specialist items like mechanical and electrical or heating and ventilation installations. What commonly occurs is that the specialist firm is brought into the project as a nominated sub-contractor, with specific responsibility for both design and construction of its part of the building.

The legal rights and duties arising under arrangements of this type will of course depend on the precise terms of the contracts concerned, but it is usual to find such a sub-contractor entering into a direct agreement with the employer. In the case of JCT 80, for example, the Employer/Nominated Sub-Contractor Agreement NSC/W contains a direct undertaking that reasonable skill and care has been and will be used in respect of design (though not in the execution of the work). It is also quite common to remove any responsibility from the main contractor for such design elements, as is done by clause 35.21 of JCT 80. ICE 6 clause 58(3), on the other hand, permits the main contractor to be made liable, but only where the design requirement is explicitly stated in both main contract and sub-contract, while GC/Works/1 clause 10 states expressly that the main contractor is responsible.

2 Liability for defects of design

Having identified the parties who bear responsibility for design, the next task is to discover just what that responsibility involves. In particular, the question arises whether a designer's duty is merely to use reasonable care and skill, or whether it extends to an implied warranty that the design will be fit for its purpose.

In dealing with this question, the courts have proved generally willing to imply a strict 'fitness for purpose' obligation into a design and build contract, on the basis that the position of one who supplies a physical building is analogous to that of a seller of goods (*Viking Grain Storage Ltd* v *TH White Installations Ltd* (1985) 33 BLR 103). However, such an implication is always subject to the express terms of the contract and it is worth noting that, while the ACA Form of Contract makes the contractor strictly liable in this respect, JCT design and build forms make it clear that the contractor's liability goes no further than that which would be incurred by 'an architect or ... other appropriate professional designer holding himself out as competent to take on work for such design'.

Even where the contract is silent on the issue, the law has always regarded the essence of a 'fitness for purpose' obligation as being the reliance which is placed by the client on the skill and judgment of the supplier. Where such reliance is clearly lacking, therefore, as where the contractor is contractually obliged to adopt the design of a nominated sub-contractor, there will be no implied term as to fitness for purpose in the main contract (*Norta Wallpapers (Ireland)* v *Sisk & Sons (Dublin)* [1978] IR 114).

By contrast with the position of a designer/builder, the courts have consistently treated the liability of a person who merely designs as resting upon professional negligence (*Hawkins* v *Chrysler (UK) Ltd and Burne Associates* (1986) 38 BLR 36). However, a designer may be induced to give an express warranty that his design will achieve its intended result (although, if he does so, it is unlikely that this warranty will have the backing of his professional indemnity insurers). Furthermore, in exceptional circumstances a court may find an implied warranty to this effect.

This last possibility is exemplified by the case of *Greaves & Co (Contractors) Ltd* v *Baynham Meikle and Partners* [1975] 3 All ER 99. The defendant structural engineers were appointed as consultants by the plaintiffs, a firm of design and build contractors who had undertaken a contract to design and build a warehouse. As the engineers knew, the warehouse was to be used for the storage of oil drums, which would be moved by fork-lift trucks, and it was therefore important that the floors should be strong enough to withstand the vibration of these trucks. When the engineers' design failed to meet this standard, they were held liable for professional negligence, but the Court of Appeal stated that they could in any event have been made liable on the basis of a 'fitness for purpose' warranty. Quite why this case justified the implication of such a warranty is not altogether clear, though it may have been important that the contractors' liability to their clients would in turn have been a strict one.

The duty of a designer involves him in giving attention, not only to the physical requirements of the building, but also to the relevant legal constraints, such as compliance with the Building Regulations or planning restrictions. In this respect, too, the standard of duty may vary; thus, while an architect need only exercise reasonable care and skill in avoiding any breach of the law (*BL Holdings Ltd* v *Robert J Wood & Partners* (1979) 12 BLR 1), a design and build contractor is more likely to be answerable to the client on a strict liability basis (*Newham LBC* v *Taylor Woodrow (Anglian) Ltd* (1981) 19 BLR 99).

It may finally be noted that, where a designer is also engaged on the project in a supervisory capacity (as where the architect is also the contract administrator), his duties may include not merely the exercise of care and skill in producing the original design, but keeping that design under review to see that it will actually work (*Brickfield Properties Ltd* v *Newton* [1971] 3 All ER 328; *Merton LBC* v *Lowe & Another* (1981) 18 BLR 130).

3 The position of the first owner

(a) Claims in contract

The person for whom a building is constructed will in many if not most cases have a contractual link with a number of those responsible for its design and construction. As the employer under the building contract itself, he has the right while work is in progress to demand full compliance with the drawings and specifications, if necessary by insisting (through the contract administrator) that any non-conforming work is removed and replaced. Furthermore, and despite the view expressed by Lord Diplock (in *P & M Kaye Ltd* v *Hosier & Dickinson Ltd* [1972] 1 All ER 121) that such 'temporary disconformity' in the work is not a breach of contract at all, it is suggested that the contractor will be liable in damages for any consequential loss caused to the employer (eg where the ensuing disruption entitles other contractors to make a loss/expense claim against the employer (see *Lintest Builders Ltd* v *Roberts* (1980) 13 BLR 39).

Where a contractor's breach is not discovered until after practical completion has been achieved, the employer is again in principle entitled to claim damages for breach of contract (provided of course that proceedings are commenced within the relevant limitation period). However, if the contract treats the issue of a Final Certificate as conclusive evidence that the work is up to the required contractual standard (either absolutely or, as under JCT contracts, subject to the employer's brief opportunity to challenge it in arbitration), a claim of this kind will be barred (*Colbart* v *Kumar* [1992] CILL 752). In any event, the discovery of such latent defects does not have the effect of invalidating the certificate of practical completion and thus making the contractor liable for delay as well as for defective work (*Westminster CC* v *Jarvis & Sons Ltd* [1970] 1 All ER 942).

It should not be overlooked that an employer may well have a direct contractual relationship with any nominated sub-contractors, on which an action in respect of defects in their work can be based. However, everything turns on the terms of such a collateral agreement which, if the JCT form NSC/W is typical, is likely to cover the *design* of the sub-contract works but not their *execution*.

As for any contractual claims against professional consultants, either for errors of design or, in the case of the contract administrator, for inadequate supervision of the contractor, these must depend upon the scope of the duties undertaken. This in turn requires an examination of the relevant terms of engagement, together with any terms which may be implied (eg under s 13 of the Supply of Goods and Services Act 1982).

(b) Claims in tort

As a general principle, an action based on the tort of negligence may offer an original building owner at least two advantages over one based on breach of contract. The first of these is that the limitation period applicable to tort claims (especially those falling within the Latent Damage Act 1986) is frequently far longer, since it refers to the date on which damage becomes discoverable, rather than that on which the relevant breach of contract took place. Secondly, as discussed below, there is some authority for the view that a right of action in tort can be assigned notwithstanding an express prohibition against the assignment of contractual rights.

The original owner of a defective building may therefore wish to proceed in the tort of negligence against whoever is responsible for its condition. However, before considering the potential liability of those various parties, there is a preliminary issue which must be addressed. This is the question of whether the law will permit an action between contracting parties to be framed in tort, or whether the contract will be treated as an exhaustive definition of those parties' rights.

For the moment at least it would appear that, notwithstanding occasional judicial criticisms of the practice (based on the views of Lord Scarman in *Tai Hing Cotton Mill Ltd* v *Liu Chong Hing Bank Ltd* [1985] 2 All ER 947), concurrent liability is acceptable. That at any rate was the view of the Court of Appeal in *Bell* v *Peter Browne & Co* [1990] 3 All ER 124, where a negligent solicitor was sued by a client in both contract and tort. However, it is worth noting that in *Hiron* v *Pynford South Ltd* [1992] CILL 716, which concerned a claim against structural engineers for their advice on underpinning work, it was held by an Official Referee that, although there was no rule of law which prevented concurrent liability, it would not be 'just and reasonable' to impose a duty of care in tort simply in order to secure a longer limitation period!

Even if a tort claim is in principle available, the current restrictive approach to negligence actions (discussed below) means that it will require proof that the relationship between plaintiff and defendant is a sufficiently 'proximate' one to justify the plaintiff in relying on the defendant's work. This requirement, which is based on the concepts of advice and reliance adopted by the House of Lords in *Hedley Byrne & Co Ltd* v *Heller & Partners Ltd* [1964] AC 465, is most likely to be satisfied in relation to professional consultants such as architects or consulting engineers. It seems unlikely that the courts will treat the relationship between employer and contractor in the same way (see *Nitrigin Eireann Teoranta* v *Inco Alloys Ltd* [1992] 1 All ER 854). Furthermore, and notwithstanding the apparent approval given to *Junior Books Ltd* v *Veitchi Co Ltd* [1983] 1 AC 520 by certain members of the House of Lords in *Murphy* v *Brentwood DC* [1990] 2 All ER 908, it would be an optimistic employer who attempted to bring an action against a nominated sub-contractor on the basis of *Junior Books*.

One final possibility, albeit a rather remote one, is that a local authority might be held to have assumed, in the exercise of its building control functions, a duty of care towards a 'do-it-yourself' house-builder. That such a claim could arise was recognised by the Court of Appeal in *Richardson* v *West Lindsey DC* [1990] 1 All ER 296 and, indeed, liability was actually imposed on this basis in the earlier case of *Dennis* v *Charnwood BC* [1982] 3 All ER 486. However, while the position of the original building owner was not discussed in *Murphy* v *Brentwood DC* [1990] 2 All ER 908, that decision must surely cast very severe doubts on the likelihood that such a claim could prove successful.

4 Subsequent owners and the tort of negligence

As mentioned earlier, the tort of negligence as applied to defective buildings has recently undergone drastic alteration at the hands of the House of Lords. Prior to these upheavals, while the governing principles were those laid down in *Anns* v *Merton LBC* [1978] AC 728, the second or subsequent owner of a defective building could successfully pursue a claim in negligence against anyone concerned in the construction process (eg architect, specialist engineer, contractor, sub-contractor or local authority), provided that the building was not merely 'defective' but a 'danger to health or safety'. Liability would then extend to the cost of restoring the building to a condition in which it was no longer dangerous.

The protection thus conferred upon remote owners lasted a mere decade. Then came *D & F Estates Ltd* v *Church Commissioners for England* [1988] 2 All ER 992, in which the House of Lords was highly critical of the principle laid down in *Anns* v *Merton*, followed shortly by *Murphy* v *Brentwood DC* [1990] 2 All ER 908, in which their lordships finally declared *Anns* to have been wrongly decided. The basis for this was that, in the eyes of the House of Lords, the loss suffered by the owner of a defective building (whether dangerous or not) must be perceived as pure economic loss, and such loss could only found an action in the tort of negligence if a proximate relationship of the *Hedley Byrne* v *Heller* type existed between plaintiff and defendant. And, of course, while the mere purchaser of a building might have such a relationship with his own surveyor (if he engaged one) or with a valuer who carried out an inspection of the property for mortgage purposes (*Smith* v *Eric S Bush; Harris* v *Wyre Forest DC* [1989] 2 All ER 514), he would probably have no relationship whatsoever with the original designers or constructors of the building.

In the light of *Murphy* v *Brentwood*, the general position, subject to one qualification dealt with below, is that a builder, architect or other construction participant can be liable in the tort of negligence to a remote owner only if the latter suffers personal injury or physical damage to some property *other than the defective building itself* (eg where a ceiling falls and damages furniture). The cost of restoring the building to its intended state, and any other losses which flow from this, are pure economic loss and thus irrecoverable (see *Department of the Environment* v *Thomas Bates & Son Ltd* [1990] 2 All ER 943).

The single qualification to this state of affairs lies in a suggestion by some members of the House of Lords in *Murphy* v *Brentwood* that, while damage to any part of the defective building itself could not normally be regarded as physical damage to 'other property', this might be possible if the defective part and the damaged part were the work of different contractors or sub-contractors! It was intimated that a remote owner would be able to claim in negligence on this basis against a central heating sub-contractor whose negligent installation of a boiler led to an explosion damaging the rest of the building. Whether this controversial suggestion (a revival of the discredited 'complex structure' argument which was floated in *D & F Estates*) will prove viable is open to considerable doubt; nonetheless, it appears highly likely to be tested in court before long.

Before leaving the tort of negligence, attention should be drawn to another part of the decision in *D & F Estates Ltd* v *Church Commissioners for England* [1988] 2 All ER 992 which has been rather overshadowed by the ruling on pure economic loss. The defects which occurred in that case were the result of negligent work, not by the main contractors who were sued, but by plastering sub-contractors who were described as 'not worth suing'. It was held by the House of Lords that the main contractors could not be held responsible for this, even on the basis of their own negligence in failing adequately to supervise the sub-contractors, since they owed no duty in tort to anyone to carry out such supervision. This somewhat surprising immunity of the main contractor is presumably still applicable in those situations where a negligent contractor might otherwise be liable (ie personal injury and damage to other property).

5 Subsequent owners and statutory protection

In the light of what was said above, it is hardly surprising that legal advisers are currently seeking alternative avenues by which to claim against negligent builders, architects and the like. We now consider three particular statutory provisions which may be of some assistance in this respect.

(a) Latent Damage Act 1986, s 3

When the principle laid down in *Anns* v *Merton LBC* [1978] AC 728 held sway, it operated to protect a person who purchased an apparently sound building, which then suffered 'damage' during his ownership. However, the *Anns* principle did not extend to cases where physical damage, albeit not yet discoverable, had already occurred at the time of purchase; in such circumstances the only cause of action in negligence would already have vested in the then owner.

The distinction thus drawn between cases where the physical damage occurred before purchase and those where it came afterwards appeared a quite unjustifiable one, and it was this anomaly which s 3 of the Latent Damage Act 1986 sought to rectify. This section provides in effect that, where a person X acquires an interest in a property which has already suffered damage (in such circumstances that the previous owner Y had a cause of action in negligence), X shall have an equivalent cause of action. This cause of action accrues on the date on which X acquires his interest in the property; however, the limitation period applicable to it is that which would have governed the original cause of action.

The main problem with this statutory provision is that, with the disapproval of *Anns* v *Merton*, the very reason for its existence has disappeared. Indeed, if it remains applicable, it creates an anomaly precisely equal and opposite to the one which it was enacted to remove, by giving an action to those who purchase already-damaged property but not to those where the damage occurs subsequent to the purchase! It seems likely that a court would wish to prevent such a conclusion, but it is rather less easy to see how the statutory provision could effectively be interpreted out of existence. A possible approach might be to argue that s 3 requires an 'original cause of action . . . in respect of negligence to which damage to any property . . . is attributable', and that this is not present in defective building cases, since the courts regard the building owner's loss as economic rather than property damage.

(b) Defective Premises Act 1972

In the case of defective *dwellings*, though not commercial buildings, an important remedy exists under s 1 of the Defective Premises Act 1972. This provides that any person 'taking on work for or in connection with the provision of a dwelling' owes a legal duty, not only to the person for whom the dwelling is originally built, but to anyone who acquires an interest in it within a certain period. This duty, which applies to dwellings provided by converting or enlarging existing buildings as well as to those newly erected, is 'to see that the work which he takes on is done in a workmanlike or, as the case may be, professional manner, with proper materials and so that as regards that work the dwelling will be fit for habitation when completed'.

An important feature of this provision is that it applies to every person who makes a contribution to the process of design or construction, including, by virtue of s 1(4), the property developer (or public sector equivalent). Each participant is then strictly liable in respect of his own contribution to the dwelling, and it has been held that this liability attaches as much to what a person fails to do as to what he does badly (*Andrews* v *Schooling* [1991] 3 All ER 723). However, it appears that the Act only applies to defects which are serious enough to make the dwelling 'unfit for habitation' (*Thompson* v *Clive Alexander & Partners* [1992] (CILL 755).

The main restriction upon this statutory duty lies in the fact that the limitation period for actions based on it is a mere six years from the date on which the dwelling is completed, save that, where a party who has done work which falls within the Act is called back to carry out further work of rectification, the six-year period only begins when that further work is finished.

Although, by virtue of s 6(3), any attempt to contract out of the Defective Premises Act is void, the Act is expressed not to apply to any dwelling which is subject to an 'approved scheme' (s 2). The original intention was to exempt all dwellings covered by a National House-Building Council guarantee (which would include the vast majority of new homes), and successive statutory instruments were duly passed to that effect. However, it appears that the relevant statutory instrument in 1979 was never effective and, in any event, the NHBC has not sought exemption for its 'Buildmark' scheme, which applies to houses and flats completed since 1 April 1988.

(c) Consumer Protection Act 1987

Enacted in order to give effect to an EEC directive, Part I of this Act imposes a form of strict liability (ie liability independent of negligence) upon manufacturers and other producers in respect of defective products which cause injury or damage. Space does not permit a detailed examination of the Act's provisions: the key concepts are those of a 'producer' (s 2); 'products' (s 1); 'defects' (s 3); 'damage' (s 5); and a number of specific defences (s 4).

That this Act applies in the context of construction is not in doubt; building materials (both raw components and preformed items such as radiators or double-glazed units) are clearly within the statutory definition of 'products', and it is specifically provided that the 'supply' of a product (which is a prerequisite of liability under the Act) includes its incorporation into a building or structure. However, the Act further provides that 'goods comprised in land' are not deemed to be 'supplied' by a transfer of the land itself, so that the vendor or landlord of a defective building will not incur liability in this way.

The combined effect of these definitions is that a person who constructs a building and then sells it, together with the land on which it stands, is outside the scope of the Act—he 'supplies' neither the building nor its component materials. Conversely, a building contractor who carries out work on someone else's land will be caught by the Act in respect of all goods and materials which he supplies. In either case, however, the Act will apply to subcontractors and suppliers of materials, since they undoubtedly supply products to the main contractor.

It should be borne in mind that the Consumer Protection Act is concerned solely with 'products' which contain a 'defect'. If damage results from an error of workmanship, rather than from a defect in the materials used, the present legislation is not applicable, although it may well be that a future statute will create a similar regime for the provision of services.

Where the 1987 Act applies, it enables an action for damages to be brought in respect of death or personal injury, and also for any loss of or damage to any property (including land). However, a claim for property damage is subject to two important limitations: the damaged property must be of a kind ordinarily intended for private occupation or use (and actually so intended by the plaintiff); and there can be no recovery in respect of damage to the defective item itself.

6 Assignment

One notable effect of those cutbacks in the tort of negligence which were described above has been a surge of interest in the possibility of protecting a person to whom a building is transferred by simultaneously assigning to that person any rights of action in respect of defects which the original owner may have. These could include not only the original owner's rights under a building contract, but also those based on consultants' terms of engagement, sub-contractors' warranties and any other relevant contractual relationships. It might also apply to any rights of action in tort which the original owner could establish against any of these parties.

It has been recognised for some time that an assignee of rights in this situation has a sufficient commercial interest in the property to be protected for the transaction not to offend the common law prohibition on 'trafficking in litigation' by assigning a bare right of action. In consequence, it has been generally accepted that rights are capable of either legal assignment (in accordance with s 136 of the Law of Property Act 1925) or equitable assignment (in cases where the strict statutory requirements are not satisfied). Nonetheless, the whole question has been bedevilled by other doubts and uncertainties, not least as to the nature of the assignee's rights and the principles on which the assignee's damages are to be assessed.

The whole question of assignment in the construction context has recently come under review by the Court of Appeal in the cases of *Linden Gardens Trust Ltd* v *Lenesta Sludge Disposals Ltd; St*

Martins Corporation Ltd v *Sir Robert McAlpine & Sons Ltd* (1992) 57 BLR 57 and, while a number of points will require further elucidation, the general picture which emerges is now a great deal clearer than it was.

The rules governing assignment which were laid down in these cases draw an important distinction between the right of an employer to enforce a building contract, in the sense of calling for its future performance, and the employer's right to claim damages in respect of any breach of the contract which has already taken place. However, this distinction (the significance of which is discussed below) does not affect the basic rule that, in principle at least, both categories of right are capable of assignment. What is more, there is no requirement that such an assignment takes place contemporaneously with the transfer of the building to the assignee (*GUS Property Management Ltd* v *Littlewoods Mail Order Stores Ltd* (1982) SLT 533).

The law has always refused to permit assignment under certain types of contract, notably those which involve personal characteristics or relationships. What is more, it is open to the original contracting parties to insert a term in their agreement which either prohibits assignment altogether or makes it conditional on the other party's consent. It is in this area that the distinction mentioned above becomes relevant, for the Court of Appeal stated that neither the 'personal' nature of a contract nor an express prohibition against assignment of 'this contract' (as in JCT 80 clause 19.1.1) would prevent a party from transferring an accrued right to claim damages for a prior breach; these bars would operate only on claims to enforce future performance. However, the assignment of accrued rights *would* be barred by a provision such as ICE 6 clause 3, which prohibits any assignment of 'the contract or any part thereof or any benefit or interest therein or thereunder' (*Helstan Securities Ltd* v *Hertfordshire CC* [1978] 3 All ER 262).

A point which emerged from the first instance decision in *Linden Gardens* v *Lenesta Sludge Disposals Ltd* (1990) 52 BLR 93, but which was not discussed in the Court of Appeal, was that an effective contractual prohibition against assignment does not in itself preclude the assignment of a right of action in tort. However, since rights in tort have no existence until damage is suffered, it follows that there can be no assignment of such rights unless damage to the property has already occurred (visibly or invisibly) at the time of assignment.

The doubts about assignment which remain are for the most part concerned with the way in which any damages awarded are to be assessed. Since the assignee's claim is based on legal rights obtained from the assignor, the Court of Appeal ruled (following *Dawson* v *Great Northern & City Railway Co* [1905] 1 KB 260) that he 'cannot enforce any claims, let alone under new heads of damage, which would not have been available to his assignor'. What is not clear from this ruling is whether the restriction applies only to the identification of heads of damage, or whether it also places a ceiling on the quantum of damages under each head. However, a defendant will not be able to escape by arguing that, since the assignor has sold the building at full market value and has therefore suffered no actual loss, the assignee in turn can claim only nominal damages (*GUS Property Management Ltd* v *Littlewoods Mail Order Stores Ltd* (1982) SLT 533).

The final question to be considered by the Court of Appeal was the precise effect of a contractual term which successfully prohibits assignment. It was held that the assignee in such circumstances receives no enforceable legal rights, but that these remain vested in the assignor. What is more, the assignor's claim for damages will not be defeated by the argument that, having transferred the building at full value, he has therefore suffered no loss.

7 Collateral warranties

A significant feature of the construction landscape in recent years has been the enormous proliferation of collateral warranties, as steps have been taken to bring remote owners into direct contractual relationships with those against whom they would previously have been able to claim in the tort of negligence. Such warranties are routinely sought from all the contractors, sub-contractors and consultants who are engaged on a construction project, and may be drafted in favour of the prospective purchasers or tenants of the completed building and/or the funding institution whose money is secured upon the property. The sheer number of possible relationships which may thus arise out of a single project has meant that the negotiating and drafting of collateral warranties frequently occupy a quite disproportionate amount of time for the parties and their solicitors. The problem was exacerbated by the fact that, until very recently, there were no standard forms of collateral warranty, so that each one was the product of individual negotiations. However, things may improve following the publication of warranties which have been jointly drafted by the British Property Federation, the Association of Consulting Engineers, the Royal Institution of British Architects and the Royal Institution of Chartered Surveyors. These come in two forms: CoWa/F for funding institutions and CoWa/P&T for potential purchasers and tenants. A standard form of warranty on behalf of contractors and sub-contractors is expected shortly from the Joint Contracts Tribunal.

One of the most important considerations in negotiating or drafting a collateral warranty is to seek to ensure that any liability which arises under it will have the backing of the warrantor's professional indemnity insurers. At the very least, this will involve checking that the policy covers all the relevant duties; some policies, for example, exclude all voluntarily assumed obligations, while few if any cover anything stricter than a duty to use reasonable skill and care. At worst, the warrantor may be required to submit any proposed warranty to the insurers, with the result that they too can sit at the negotiating table. One of the major advantages of the BPF forms is that, having been accepted by the insurers for the participating professional institutions, they can be used by members of the relevant institutional schemes without the need for such long-winded negotiations.

In the eyes of those who demand collateral warranties, the importance of insurance backing is such that many forms of agreement contain a specific undertaking by the warrantor to maintain an appropriate policy. While potential beneficiaries may feel more comfortable where such an undertaking has been given, it is important to appreciate that it is of very limited value; apart from the fact that PI insurance is an annual contract and there can be no guarantee of renewal, any legal action against a warrantor for wrongfully allowing his insurance to lapse will of course not be backed up by insurance!

Apart from insurance, there are three aspects of collateral warranties which tend to be especially contentious. The first of these is whether the warranty is to be assignable to future purchasers or tenants (as the law would normally permit) or whether it is to benefit only its original recipient, something which requires an express restriction. A compromise which is often found in practice, though somewhat lacking in logic, is to state the number of assignments which will be permitted.

The other two bones of contention concern attempts by warrantors to limit their exposure in some way. There is little that can be said about provisions which exclude liability for consequential loss;

whether this can be insisted upon depends simply upon the relative bargaining strengths of the parties (including of course the warrantor's insurers). However, more problematical are those clauses which attempt to mitigate the rule of English law under which any guilty defendant can be made to compensate the plaintiff in full for his losses, even though others are partly to blame. It is doubtful, to say the least, whether a 'net contribution' clause (under which the warrantor's liability is expressed to be no greater than what a court would assess as his contribution if all other participants in the project had signed equivalent warranties) will be legally effective, since it would require a court to make hypothetical allocations of responsibility against persons not party to the action. It therefore seems preferable to adopt the tactic of making it a condition precedent to the enforceability of every warranty, that warranties in similar form are obtained from every other member of the project team.

Chapter 12

Insurance and Bonds

1 Allocation of construction risks

In one sense it can be said that virtually every term of a contract operates to allocate risk. This is certainly true of all those provisions which specifically confer rights or impose obligations upon the parties. However, this chapter is concerned only with those risks arising out of construction activity which are commonly covered by insurance or by the provision of a bond or other guarantee. In relation to at least some of these risks, the contract may actually *require* insurance to be taken out or a guarantee to be provided. As for the others, the risk-bearer's decision on whether or not to take out insurance cover will be a matter of commercial judgment.

The risks with which we are concerned may be allocated by the contract to one or other of the parties in three main ways. First, the contract may expressly provide that, if a certain event occurs, then one party (A) is liable to indemnify the other (B) against any resulting loss or liability. Secondly, the contract may state that, in certain specified circumstances, A is *not* liable to indemnify B, thus clearly placing that risk on B. Thirdly, the contract may make no express provision either way about a particular risk, in which case any losses or liabilities will lie where general legal principles cause them to fall.

The major areas of concern in this chapter are those which arise out of the inherently dangerous nature of construction activity. First and foremost, there is the possibility that persons may be killed or injured, either by the way in which the work is carried out or by the defective nature of the finished product. People who are at risk in this way include those who work on the site, those who visit it and those who simply use or visit the finished building.

Similarly, though less seriously, property belonging to third parties may be damaged or destroyed by construction work, for example where excavation work causes adjoining land to subside. Damage to property of the employer or the contractor must also be considered, and this is an especially important factor where work is being carried out on existing buildings. Lastly, there is the risk of damage to the contract works themselves, something which has potentially serious repercussions in terms of delay in completion, disruption to other contractors and so on.

2 Construction insurance policies

Once risks have been identified and allocated, two main types of insurance policy may be used to provide protection against their consequences. The first of these is liability insurance, under which the insurer undertakes to provide an indemnity in respect of the insured person's legal liability to others. In the construction context, a contractor will carry such policies to cover potential liability to injured employees and also liability to members of the public who are injured or whose property is damaged. The professional indemnity insurance which is carried by designers and other consultants also falls into this category.

The second type of insurance is a 'loss' or 'material damage' policy. Under such a policy, the insurer undertakes to pay compensation if property in which the insured person has an insurable interest is damaged or destroyed. A 'contractor's all risks' (CAR) policy is primarily of this type, although such policies frequently also include sections which cover the contractor against employer's liability and public liability. Depending on the size of the contractor's organisation, the size of the particular project on which it is engaged and the state of the insurance market, a 'floating' CAR policy may be maintained; this will cover all work undertaken during the insurance period, thus obviating the need to seek separate cover for each project.

Some important features of these two types of insurance cover are discussed below.

3 Liability insurance

Perhaps the most significant feature of a liability insurance policy is that it is concerned to indemnify an insured person against legal liability to other parties, not to create any direct rights in those other parties. Assuming (as is commonly the case) that the policy prohibits the insured from accepting liability to a third party without the insurer's consent, this means that the insurer is not legally responsible until the insured person has actually been held liable to the victim by a court or arbitrator. Furthermore, where an insurer has some defence against the insured's claim (such as non-disclosure of a material fact before the policy was issued, or failure to give notice of claims as required), the third party will effectively lose the benefit of insurance backing for his claim against the insured. Indeed, the victim cannot even prevent the insured from reaching a settlement agreement with the insurer, unless there is evidence of fraud (*Normid Housing Association Ltd* v *Ralphs* (1988) 43 BLR 18).

There is a qualification to the principles described above by virtue of the Third Parties (Rights Against Insurers) Act 1930. Section 1(1) of that Act provides that, where a person or company becomes insolvent either before or after incurring a liability to a third party which is covered by the policy, that third party takes over the insured person's claim and may enforce it directly against the insurers.

While this statutory provision clearly improves the position of third parties, it should be noted that a victim acquires no greater rights against the insurer than would have been exercisable by the insured. Consequently, any defences which would have been available against the insured may equally operate to bar the third party's direct claim. Furthermore, since the insured has no rights against the insurer until liability to the third party has been established, a third party who is in no position to establish that liability (eg because the insured company no longer exists) cannot claim directly against the defunct company's liability insurers (*Bradley* v *Eagle Star Insurance Co Ltd* [1989] 1 All ER 961).

4 Loss insurance

Loss or 'first party' insurance is concerned, not with the insured party's legal liability to others, but with losses which fall directly upon the insured party. Subject to any specific conditions or exclusions in the policy, the cause of loss is irrelevant—it may be due to the fault of the insured or of a third party, or to some external force for which no human agency is responsible.

Where the loss *does* result from the fault (tort or breach of contract) of a third party, the legal principle of subrogation comes into play. Under this principle the indemnity insurer, having compensated the insured for the loss suffered, is entitled to take over any legal rights which the insured could have exercised against the third party in question. In consequence, many legal actions are in truth fought between the plaintiff's loss insurers and the defendant's liability insurers.

An important limitation upon subrogation is that it cannot be used by the insurer against anyone who is named as insured on the same policy. Thus, where contract works which are insured in the joint names of employer, contractor and all sub-contractors are damaged due to a sub-contractor's negligence, the insurers cannot take action against that sub-contractor to recover what they have paid out (*Petrofina (UK) Ltd* v *Magnaload Ltd* [1984] QB 127).

5 Liability and insurance under JCT 80

(a) Liability for injury or property damage

Clause 20.1 provides that the contractor 'shall be liable for and shall indemnify the employer against' any liability or loss which arises out of the injury to or death of any person, caused by the carrying out of the contract works. This liability is however reduced to the extent that the death or injury is due to any act or neglect of the employer, or that of anyone for whom the employer is responsible. Such persons include the employer's own employees, any other direct contractors and (presumably) consultants such as the architect or contract administrator; however, all sub-contractors (both domestic and nominated) are the contractor's responsibility under this clause.

Clause 20.2 similarly provides that the contractor shall be liable for and shall indemnify the employer against any liability or loss which arises out of damage to real or personal property. However, liability in this instance arises only in so far as the damage is due to negligence, breach of statutory duty, omission or default by the contractor or by someone for whom the contractor is responsible. It is further made clear (by clause 20.3) that damage to the contract works does not fall under this provision unless a certificate of practical completion has been issued, or the employer has taken early possession under clause 18, or the contractor's employment has been determined.

(b) Insurance for injury or property damage

Clause 21.1 requires the contractor to 'take out and maintain' insurance policies in respect of the types of liability imposed by clause 20. In the case of damage to property, the level of cover is prescribed by an entry in the Appendix. If the contractor fails in this obligation, the employer is entitled to take out loss insurance (at the contractor's expense) to cover the risk in question.

Where building works cause damage to neighbouring property, the employer may be held liable in nuisance whether or not the contractor has been negligent. If the contractor has not been negligent, the employer's loss may fall outside the scope of whatever insurance has been taken out by the contractor to satisfy clause 21.1 (*Gold* v *Patman & Fotheringham Ltd* [1958] 2 All ER 497). In order to close this gap in the employer's protection, clause 21.2 provides that, where the relevant part of the Appendix has been completed, the contractor may be instructed to take out a joint names policy to cover non-negligent damage to the property of both third parties and the employer. This policy, which is at the employer's expense, covers collapse, subsidence, heave, vibration, weakening or removal of support or lowering of ground water; however, it excludes both negligent design and also 'damage which can reasonably be foreseen to be inevitable'.

(c) Contract works in new buildings

Where the contract works consist of the erection of a new building, JCT 80 requires the parties to adopt either clause 22A or clause 22B. Their choice will determine whether it is for the contractor (clause 22A) or the employer (clause 22B) to take out a joint names policy for all risks insurance of the contract works, sufficient to cover their full reinstatement value. This cover is to be maintained until a certificate of practical completion has been issued, or the employer has taken early possession under clause 18, or the contractor's employment has been determined. Any failure by the contractor or by a private (though not a local authority) employer to maintain the required cover will entitle the other party to insure and charge the cost to the defaulter.

'All risks' insurance for this purpose is defined as providing cover against 'any physical loss or damage to work executed and site materials', subject to some specific exceptions such as wear and tear; obsolescence; defects of design, specification, workmanship or materials; radioactivity or other nuclear-linked damage; sonic booms; or enemy or terrorist action.

As mentioned, the policy required under this heading is to be in joint names, thus ensuring that there will be no subrogation claims by the insurer against a contractor who is guilty of negligence. Furthermore, the policy must also provide protection (either by naming them as insured or by a waiver of subrogation rights) for all sub-contractors, both nominated and domestic. However, this protection for sub-contractors is not on an 'all risks' basis, but only in respect of the 'specified perils', a somewhat narrower list of risks which includes damage from fire, lightning, explosion, storm, tempest, flood, burst water pipes, earthquake, aircraft and riot.

(d) Contract works in existing structures

Where the contract works consist of alterations of or extensions to existing structures, the appropriate provision is clause 22C. This deals with the contract works themselves in a similar fashion to clause 22B (ie it is for the employer to insure in joint names on an all risks basis). However, in relation to the existing structures, the employer's obligation to insure extends only to the 'specified perils'. Furthermore, while this policy too is to be in the joint names of employer and contractor, it is only nominated (and not domestic) sub-contractors who are to be protected from subrogation claims.

(e) Loss of liquidated damages

The insurance policy taken out under clause 22A, 22B or 22C (whichever is applicable) should cover the cost of reinstatement arising out of damage to the contract works. However, where such damage is caused by a 'specified peril', the contractor may be entitled to an extension of time for completion under clause 25.4.3, in which case the employer will have no claim for liquidated damages for the period of delay.

Some protection for the employer is found in clause 22D which provides that, so long as the relevant entry in the Appendix has been completed, the contractor may be required to obtain a quotation for insurance to cover the employer's loss of liquidated damages arising in this way. If the quotation is acceptable, the premiums are added to the contract sum, which leads one to wonder why, if the employer is paying for insurance to cover his own risk, it was thought necessary to involve the contractor at all.

6 Liability and insurance under ICE 6

Clauses 20 to 25 of ICE 6, like their counterparts in JCT 80, serve to allocate legal responsibility for a number of risks between the employer and the contractor. Where ICE 6 differs from the other contract, however, is that only the contractor is required to insure in order to cover these risks. As to the insurances required, clause 25 provides generally that, wherever the contractor fails to produce evidence that a satisfactory policy is in place, the employer is entitled to effect the necessary insurance at the contractor's expense.

(a) Damage to the contract works

Clause 20 provides in general that, until the issue of a certificate of substantial completion for the works or any section, the contractor shall 'take full responsibility for the care of the works and materials plant and equipment for incorporation therein'. Indeed, the duty is not merely one of taking care; the contractor's obligation (under clause 8) to complete the works effectively imposes the risk of damage on the contractor, who must repair and reinstate at his own expense.

The contractor's responsibility under clause 20 does not cover certain 'excepted risks' which are specifically allocated to the employer. These include the use or occupation of the works by the employer or his employees, agents and other direct contractors; design faults (other than those which lie within the contractor's own design); and the usual exclusions as to war, civil insurrection, nuclear accident and sonic booms. Specific provision is made for apportionment in cases where loss arises partly but not wholly from an excepted risk.

The risks having been thus defined, clause 21 requires the contractor to insure the permanent and temporary works in joint names for the full replacement cost plus 10 per cent. This insurance, which is to provide cover for loss or damage 'from whatsoever cause arising other than the excepted risks', must extend to loss or damage which results during the Defects Correction Period from a cause occurring prior to substantial completion.

(b) Damage to persons and property

Clause 22 provides that, with certain exceptions, the contractor must indemnify the employer against any loss or claim in respect of death, personal injury or damage to property (other than the works) arising out of or in consequence of the execution of the works. The main exceptions (in respect of which the employer must instead indemnify the contractor) are damage to crops on the site; any inevitable trespass to land, interference with easements or other damage; the right of the employer to construct the works; and any injury or damage resulting from the act, neglect or breach of statutory duty of the employer, his agents, employees or other direct contractors. Once again, specific provision is made for apportionment in cases where the loss arises partly but not wholly from one of these exceptions. By virtue of clause 23, it is the contractor's responsibility to insure in joint names against these liabilities, where they arise out of the execution of the contract. The insurance, which must provide cover to at least the amount stated in the Appendix to the Form of Tender, is to cover any liability which results from the fault of the employer and those for whom the employer is responsible; however, it need not cover the other exceptions mentioned in clause 22.

7 Liability and insurance under GC/Works/1

Risk allocation under GC/Works/1 is dealt with in clause 19, which applies to personal injury, sickness or death; loss or damage to property; loss or damage to the works; and consequential losses. All these risks, in so far as they arise out of or are in any way connected with the execution of the contract, are primarily borne by the contractor, who must indemnify the authority (employer) against any loss or claim. However, there are a number of exceptional cases, covering a wider area than either JCT 80 or ICE 6, in which it is the authority's responsibility to indemnify the contractor against any expense incurred. These exceptions include loss or damage which results from the neglect or default of the authority, its agents or direct contractors; 'accepted risks' (such as war, civil insurrection, nuclear accident and sonic booms); unforeseeable ground conditions; and 'any other circumstances which are outside the control of the contractor or of any of his sub-contractors or suppliers and which could not have been reasonably contemplated under the contract'.

The insurance provisions of GC/Works/1, which are much less specific than those of JCT 80 or ICE 6, are contained in clause 8. The contractor's basic obligation is to effect and keep in place until the end of the longest maintenance period insurance policies covering employers' liability; loss or damage to the works and 'things for which the contractor is responsible under the terms of the contract'; and liability for personal injury or loss or damage to property. These requirements may be met by either new or existing policies; as regards damage to the works, cover must be for the full reinstatement value.

Clause 8(3) provides two alternative provisions. One simply requires the contractor to effect the necessary insurance policies and send the authority a broker's certificate stating that this has been done. The other, which only applies where the Abstract of Particulars on which the contractor tenders so provides, requires the contractor to effect and maintain all risks insurance in the joint names of the authority, the contractor and all sub-contractors.

In all these cases it is specifically provided that, if the contractor fails to meet the insurance requirements, the authority may effect appropriate insurance cover and deduct the cost from any payment to which the contractor is otherwise entitled under the contract.

8 Professional indemnity insurance

Whether or not their terms of engagement actually require it, the professional members of the design team (and other project consultants) will invariably have indemnity insurance to cover their potential liability to both the employer and third parties. Many professional institutions operate indemnity insurance schemes for their own members, and the terms of such policies naturally vary considerably; however, some points of general application should be borne in mind.

First and foremost, a professional indemnity (PI) policy will normally contain a description of the 'business' in which the insured is engaged, and will only apply to work carried out in the course of that business. Within those bounds, the policy will normally provide the professional with an indemnity against liability, subject to a financial limit in respect of any one claim or in respect of all claims in any one year. The cover will usually apply to claims arising from negligence and possibly also from 'errors and omissions'; however, it is extremely unlikely that liability for breach of any strict warranty (whether express or implied) of 'fitness for the purpose' will be included, and indeed many policies explicitly exclude any liability which is voluntarily assumed by the insured. This point is obviously one of considerable practical importance to contractors operating under a design and build contract, where a fitness for purpose obligation will be readily implied by the courts.

It is worth noting that PI policies are normally written on a 'claims made' basis, under which the relevant policy is the one which is in force when the claim is made, rather than when the act of negligence occurs. In consequence, any failure by the consultant, when taking out or renewing a policy, to reveal that he knows of a pending claim may enable the current insurers to treat the policy as voidable and thus refuse payment.

It should also be remembered that PI policies are a category of liability insurance and thus, as mentioned earlier, are not concerned to confer any direct rights upon a victim of the insured person's negligence. In consequence, the victim may be left without any insurance backing for his claim against the consultant if the latter allows his policy to lapse, causes it to become unenforceable (eg by non-disclosure of a material fact) or reaches a *bona fide* settlement with the insurers in respect of the claim (*Normid Housing Association Ltd* v *Ralphs* (1988) 43 BLR 18).

9 Guarantees and bonds

A contract of guarantee is one by which the performance of a person's primary contractual obligations is backed up by another, frequently a financial institution. This backing up may amount to an undertaking actually to perform the contract in place of the defaulter, though it will normally consist of a promise to pay financial compensation for losses which are due to the default. Such an arrangement is frequently expressed in what is termed a 'bond', that is, a document whose form and content, though hallowed by long usage, may well be obscure and misleading.

Of the types of bond which are encountered in the construction context, by far the most common is that which guarantees the contractor's performance in general, up to stated financial limits (say 10 per cent of the contract sum). In other cases it is a single obligation which is guaranteed, such as a promise by a tenderer not to withdraw a bid for a specified time, or a contractor's duty to carry out necessary work during a maintenance period. A particular example of the latter type is a bond supporting a payment obligation, for instance where retention money is released to a contractor against his promise to repay it in case of default.

Recent years have seen an increasing use of 'unconditional' or 'on demand' bonds, a species imported from international trade, which entitle the employer to call for the specified sum without showing any default by the contractor. In the absence of fraud, such a bond must be honoured without question (*Edward Owen Engineering Ltd* v *Barclays Bank International Ltd* [1978] 1 All ER 976). What is not clear is whether, having made a call on an unconditional bond when the contractor is not guilty of any breach, the employer is *then under any* obligation to account to the contractor for the money. If not, then the bond must be seen as an effective 'discount' against the contractor's tender price, which should presumably be increased on the assumption that the bond will be called.

It is worth noting that, where a construction contract makes provision for the obtaining of a bond, this is regarded as an important matter. Failure by the contractor to have a required bond in place may well amount to a repudiatory breach (*Swartz & Son (Pty) Ltd* v *Wolmaranstadt Town Council* 1960 (2) SA 1), while an architect who fails to ensure that a contractor has obtained a promised bond may be liable to the client for negligence (*Convent Hospital* v *Eberlin & Partners* (1990) 14 Con LR 1).

10 Obligations of the guarantor

The precise obligations undertaken by a guarantor or 'bondsman' can only be found in the wording of the particular guarantee or bond, but it will usually be the case that liability depends upon proof by the employer that the contractor is in breach of his primary obligations under the contract and that loss has been suffered. Such proof may well take the form of a court judgment or an arbitration award. Since the employer is perfectly entitled to claim against the contractor for such losses, it is clear that what is in truth guaranteed is the contractor's continued solvency. Indeed, even if the employer prefers to claim against the guarantor, the latter may then seek indemnity from the contractor.

As mentioned earlier, a guarantor's liability is almost invariably subject to financial limits. It will frequently also be limited in terms of time (for example by expiring when practical completion is certified) since, if this is not done, it will continue for as long as the contractor remains potentially liable for breach (ie throughout the limitation period).

In addition to these restrictions, a contract of guarantee may require certain conditions to be satisfied, or procedures to be followed, in order for a valid claim to be made. If it is specifically stated that the employer must proceed against the contractor before turning to the guarantor, or that written notice must be given to the guarantor of any event which may lead to a claim, then failure to comply may well free the guarantor from his obligations (*Clydebank District Water Trustees* v *Fidelity Deposit of Maryland* 1916 SC (HL) 69).

11 Release of the guarantor

A contract of insurance is regarded in law as one requiring the utmost good faith, which in practical terms means that the insured is under a positive obligation to disclose all material facts before the policy is issued. Contracts of guarantee do not as a general rule impose any such obligation. Thus, where a civil engineering contract clearly required the contractor to inspect the site, failure by the employer to inform the contractor's bondsman that the contractor was taking a hopelessly optimistic view of ground conditions did not entitle the bondsman to be released (*Trade Indemnity* v *Workington Harbour & Docks Board* [1937] AC 1). However, the circumstances of a particular case may be sufficient to support a duty of disclosure, for example where a fidelity guarantee is issued in respect of someone whom the employer knows to have been dishonest in the past (*London General Omnibus Co Ltd* v *Holloway* [1912] 2 KB 72).

Once it is validly in place, an undertaking to guarantee a contractor's performance may be discharged by conduct of the employer which prejudices the guarantor. This would almost certainly apply if the employer were to act in bad faith towards the guarantor, for example by concealing or conniving at the contractor's default. It might also be the case where the employer fails to carry out a duty to supervise the contractor's work, though not where the employer merely chooses not to exercise an option to supervise (*Kingston-upon-Hull Corporation* v *Harding* [1892] 2 QB 494).

An important principle to note in relation to a guarantee is that it will be discharged by any material variation in the terms of the main contract, since this effectively alters the nature of what is guaranteed. This applies with equal force to variations or concessions which are for the contractor's benefit, since the contractor may thereby be relieved of pressure to comply with his obligations, which in turn makes it more likely that the guarantee will be called upon. In accordance with this approach, guarantors have been released where an employer has unilaterally waived late completion by a contractor (*Rees* v *Benington* (1795) 2 Ves Jun 540), or has knowingly overpaid the contractor (*General Steam Navigation Co* v *Rolt* (1858) 6 CBNS 550).

Chapter 13

Payment

The primary obligation of the employer is to pay the contractor for the work and materials supplied. This payment (which is more often than not made on an instalment basis) will consist of a sum of money known variously as the contract sum, tender sum or contract price. While the sum of money may be fixed from the outset, it rarely is; however, it is usually predictable within limits.

In order to achieve a full appreciation of construction contracts, it is necessary to understand the principles on which the sum due is calculated, and also the effect which different payment regimes have on the contractor's cash flow. Unfortunately, such understanding is made more difficult by the industry's use of terminology which is vague and often downright inaccurate. For example, 'fixed price' does not mean what it appears to mean, but merely that the *method of calculation* is fixed. Again, 'lump sum' does not mean that there will be only a single payment, but rather that all the specified work will be carried out for the quoted price. Nor does 'firm price' give any real guarantee to the employer that there will be no extras, only that there is no provision for the contractor to pass on increases in the costs of such items as labour and materials.

What follows is an attempt to clarify the meaning of some of the most important terms used in this context, and to explain the nature of different types of payment obligation.

1 Principles of calculation

What must be appreciated at the outset is that there are only two ways of calculating payment under a building contract. *All* items are paid for on one of these two bases: either 'fixed price' or 'cost reimbursement'. The difference between the two methods of calculation is as follows:

- *Fixed price* items are those paid for on the basis of a predetermined estimate of the cost of the work, adding an allowance for the risk involved as well as an allowance for the market situation in relation to the contractor's workload. What is paid by the client is an estimated price, irrespective of the actual cost incurred by the contractor.
- *Cost reimbursement* items are those paid for on the basis of the actual cost of the work to the contractor; if any prior estimate is given, it is for guidance only and does not form any commitment that no more (or less) will be charged.

It is obvious that the choice between these two methods of calculating price will have a fundamental effect upon the distribution of risks between employer and contractor. Under fixed price arrangements, the contractor agrees to stand by the judgments on which the estimate is based. Thus, any saving over the original estimate will be to the contractor's benefit, and any overspending will be the contractor's loss. Under cost reimbursement arrangements, the employer takes the risk of the final price being different from the estimate, keeping any savings and paying for any increases.

It should be appreciated that these two payment regimes are not entirely independent of each other, and indeed it would be very unusual to find a contract being discharged by one method alone. Normally a contract will employ both methods, to varying degrees, in combination. The contract will then be described as 'fixed price' or 'cost reimbursement' according to which method predominates.

Both JCT 80 and ICE 6 are examples of 'fixed price' contracts, in which the contractor in tendering states a rate for each category of work which may have everything or nothing to do with what it actually costs the contractor to carry out that work. Under a JCT 80 With Quantities contract, the employer is entitled to all the items specified in the bill of quantities, in return for the sum tendered. In effect, therefore, what the employer pays for each item is the rate in the bill multiplied by the *quantity in the bill*. Under an ICE 6 contract, on the other hand, the rate in the bill will be multiplied by the *actual quantity undertaken*. In both cases, however, the basis of payment is the contractor's estimate and the amount of money paid has no relationship with the contractor's costs, even if quantities are remeasured.

This type of contract is known as a fixed price contract, even though it may have some element which are cost reimbursable.

Such elements could include fluctuations, which are often related to actual changes in market prices.

By contrast, a fixed fee, prime cost contract (a category into which most management contracts fall) will lay down detailed provisions for payment, based largely upon the contractor's actual expenditure. Here again, however, there will be certain items which are calculated without any reference to actual costs and which are therefore of a fixed price nature. Most important among these are likely to be the contractor's attendance fee and profit margin, which are based on a predetermined proportion of the prime cost.

2 Status of contract price

'Fixed price' contracts, in the sense explained above, can be subdivided into 'lump sum' contracts on the one hand and 'remeasurement' or 'measure and value' contracts on the other. The former type of contract (typified by JCT 80 in both its With Quantities and Without Quantities versions) is one where the contractor's tender is based upon the work which is exhaustively described and quantified in the contract bills, or in an equivalent document such as a specification. If any quantities are altered because of variations in the client's requirements, then the contract sum too will be altered. If not, then the contractor can expect to be paid the amount of the tender.

This is by stark contrast with 'remeasurement', or 'measure and value' contracts, such as ICE 6 and also JCT 80 With Approximate Quantities. In these contracts, even though there may be quantities in the bills which the contractor prices, their purpose is purely for the tendering process, fixing rates of remuneration for every different element of the work. The contractor will be paid these rates, but payment will be based upon the actual quantity of work undertaken, not the predicted quantity. Quantities are included in these bills because the rate of payment depends upon the quantity, being affected, for example, by economies of scale. When the quantity departs significantly from that which was envisaged in the bills, new rates have to be negotiated, a process known as 'rate fixing'. Clearly, the price to be paid for the works will not be fully established until the works are complete. For this reason, ICE 6 refers to a 'tender sum' rather than a contract price.

These two types of contract are basic types, and naturally there are variations on these basic themes. The difference between them is of fundamental importance to any employer when considering which type of contract is appropriate for a particular project.

3 Contractor's cash flow

The true nature of construction contracting can only really be understood in terms of contractors' cash flow. Essentially, contractors earn their money by installing or assembling materials and components to meet a specification within a time period. Depending on what their outgoings are, these will have to be paid for at differing intervals. For example, it is quite usual in construction for suppliers of building materials to invoice contractors at the end of the month, for payment by the end of the following month. Reputable contractors are extended considerable amounts of credit by these suppliers, so materials are often not paid for until two or three months after they have been incorporated into the project. Sub-contractors also invoice the contractors for payment, and may have to wait two or three months. Contractors' directly employed labour must be paid weekly. On the other side of the balance sheet, contractors' income is based upon work certified to date, and most general contracts specify that certificates must be honoured by the employer within two weeks, or thereabouts. Therefore, contractors tend to be paid before they become liable to their own creditors, and the period for which they can hold on to money becomes a critical factor in their continued financial success. It is this which enables contractors to bid for work with little or no mark-up, yet still make satisfactory returns on capital employed—in fact in many cases they are employing no capital at all! This also explains why they are so sensitive to changes in the payment regimes on projects.

4 Final account

The final reckoning of the contractor's financial entitlement, known as 'final account', is a process which can take months or even years to reconcile. On many projects it is simply passed over and ignored, as the contractor loses interest in working for the last small payment, preferring instead more lucrative work on other contracts which are at an earlier stage. Similarly, many professional consultants lose interest in the final account. So, although the contract may envisage that the whole process will have been concluded within a few months, in practice it can drag on and may sometimes never reach a conclusion.

Whilst interim payments enable the contractor to maintain sufficient cash flow to keep the project moving, the final certificate releases the contractor from certain obligations, acknowledging, for example, that the contractor has rectified defects identified during the defects liability period. It also certifies the final settlement due to the contractor. Therefore, the final certificate cannot be issued until the final account has been agreed.

The final account in JCT 80 is an interesting example of the detail to which a contract may descend in laying down precisely how the final payment is to be calculated. Instead of simply instructing the employer to pay any remaining money outstanding, the clause provides that it is the whole contract sum which becomes payable, less amounts paid to date; it then contains a list of detailed instructions as to how the contract sum should be adjusted. For example, all variations valued to date have to be added to the contract sum, and all omissions deducted. The payments made on interim certificates to date have also to be deducted, and the balance paid one way or the other. The process begins with the contractor sending all necessary documents to the contract administrator within a certain time after practical completion. Older versions of the contract merely specified *a reasonable time*, but an amendment dated 1987 has specified six months as the maximum period. Within three months of receiving this information the contract administrator must ascertain the final account.

The ICE 6 contract, by comparison, arrives at the same position, but without the same degree of detail. It simply states that, within three months of the issue of the Defects Correction Certificate, the contractor will submit to the engineer a certificate which states the contractor's opinion of all sums due to him, along with supporting documentation. The engineer then has three further months within which to issue a certificate stating his opinion of how much is due (or owed). Such amount has to be paid within 28 days of the issue of the certificate. Thus, acting in accordance with this contract, the final account can take as long as seven months. Since the defects correction period is rarely less than six months, final account may not be finished until well over a year from substantial completion.

A final example is given by GC/Works/1, which allows six months from the date of completion of the works for the quantity surveyor to forward a draft final account to the contractor, who then has three months within which to disagree.

5 Payment on certification

(a) Interim certificates

The right of a contractor to receive payment is frequently expressly related by the contract to the issue of interim certificates. Under modern forms of contract it is very unlikely that these will represent anything more than the contract administrator's current views as to the value of work and materials supplied in accordance with the contract. Although this might seem to be an acknowledgment that the work has been properly done, it is in no sense conclusive; not only can an interim certificate be challenged at arbitration, it is subject to alteration by subsequent certificates, since each represents a valuation of all work done to date.

Notwithstanding their limitations, interim certificates do have an important role to play in determining the rights of the parties. It seems, for example, that (at least under JCT 80) an employer's basic obligation is to pay what is stated as due on the certificate, rather than what ought to have been so stated. In consequence, a contractor who claims that the work has been undervalued cannot exercise his normal contractual remedies for underpayment (such as a refusal to continue working); his remedy lies in seeking to have the certificate corrected, either by applying to the contract administrator or by going to arbitration (*Lubenham Fidelities & Investments* v *S Pembrokeshire DC* (1986) 33 BLR 39). However, an employer who claims that work has been *overvalued* in an interim certificate appears to be in a stronger position; he can resist a claim for summary judgment by raising sufficient doubts about the certificate in the court's mind, or by bringing evidence to support any other right of set off (*CM Pillings & Co Ltd* v *Kent Investments Ltd* (1985) 30 BLR 80; *RM Douglas Construction Ltd* v *Bass Leisure Ltd* (1990) 53 BLR 119).

Of course, an interim certificate will lose what limited binding force it possesses if it is open to challenge on any of the grounds considered in section (c) below.

(b) Conclusiveness of certification

The question of whether a certificate is 'conclusive', in the sense of binding the parties in law, arises most frequently in relation to final certificates. However, it should not be overlooked that a contract administrator's refusal to issue a certificate is as much a 'decision' as the issue of one, and thus the extent to which a contractor can recover payment without a certificate (either interim or final) is also one which, in the final analysis, depends upon whether the certificate in question is 'conclusive'.

The conclusiveness or otherwise of any given certificate depends upon the construction of the contract under which it is issued, and little general guidance can be given. However, it is worth noting that, while interim certificates are seldom of binding force (except in the limited sense described above), final certificates are frequently expressed to be conclusive on a number of issues, such as the standard of the contract works, the amount of money which is finally due to the contractor and any extensions of time to which he is entitled.

The well-known decision in *Northern Regional Health Authority* v *Derek Crouch Construction Co Ltd* [1984] QB 644 has had the effect in many cases of conferring a kind of 'limited conclusivity' upon certificates. This is because of the Court of Appeal's ruling that, where a contract contains an arbitration clause which enables the arbitrator to review certificates on their merits (for example by empowering him to 'open up, review and revise' any certificate), a court will have no equivalent power. The effect in such a case will therefore be that, where a final certificate is expressed to be conclusive unless challenged at arbitration within a short time limit (a mere 28 days under JCT 80), failure to start arbitration proceedings within that time will render the certificate immune from attack.

The implications of the *Crouch* case are further discussed in Chapter 20.

(c) Challenging a certificate

Assuming that a contract makes a certificate (or the absence of one) 'conclusive' in the sense described above, an issue which may arise is whether it is nonetheless possible to challenge it in some way. As to this, it appears that, while an attack on the merits of the contract administrator's decision is out of the question, evidence that the certification machinery itself has not been properly applied may enable that decision to be overturned.

There is a wealth of case law on these 'formal' challenges, from which a number of broad categories can be deduced. It seems that a certificate can be ignored (or a contractor may claim payment without a certificate) in the following circumstances:

(i) Where the certificate does not satisfy the contractual requirements of being issued by the correct person, in the correct form and at the correct time (*Lamprell* v *Billericay Union* (1849) 18 LJ Ex 282).

(ii) Where the contract administrator's decision is not within his jurisdiction. It appears that this will include cases where the contract administrator has mistakenly failed to address the question which he is required to address (*Panamena Europea Navegacion* v *Leyland & Co Ltd* [1947] AC 428), but not those where he has simply given the wrong answer to the right question, even if this is because he has made an error of law (*Jones* v *Sherwood Computer Services plc* [1992] 2 All ER 170).

(iii) Where there is fraud or collusion (*Sharpe* v *San Paulo Brazilian Railway Co* (1873) LR 8 Ch App 597).

(iv) Where the independence of the contract administrator is compromised by improper interference from the employer (*Hickman & Co* v *Roberts* [1913] AC 229).

(v) Where the contractual certification machinery has broken down, for example where the certifier has died, become incapable or is disqualified from continuing to act (*Croudace* v *Lambeth LBC* (1986) 33 BLR 20).

6 Set off, abatement and counter-claim

A question which frequently arises under building contracts (and even more frequently under sub-contracts) is whether and to what extent a claim for payment can be defended on the ground of some cross-claim which is alleged to reduce it or even to extinguish it altogether. Such a cross-claim is sometimes referred to as a right of set off, but this is not wholly accurate; as will be seen, there are three separate defences which may arise in this situation.

To begin with, much depends on what steps the contractor takes to enforce his claim to payment. If he takes the matter to arbitration, or if he issues a writ which results in a full trial, then the proceedings should deal with all the issues between the parties; in consequence, any counter-claim which the employer has can be set up against the contractor. It is for this reason that an application by the contractor for interim payment (under RSC Ord 29) may be defeated if the defendant can raise a 'mere' counter-claim, since the court in such proceedings is required to consider what would happen if the action proceeded to trial (*Smallman Construction Ltd* v *Redpath Dorman Long* (1988) 47 BLR 15).

In practice, however, contractors often seek to enforce a claim for payment by applying for summary judgment under RSC Ord 14, which requires the court to be satisfied that there is no arguable defence to the claim. If this tactic is adopted, it has the important consequence that a mere counter-claim by the employer is not in itself a defence; it will only defeat the contractor's claim if it fulfils the more limited definition of a set off (*Tubeworkers Ltd* v *Tilbury Construction Ltd* (1985) 30 BLR 67). According to the leading case of *Hanak* v *Green* [1958] 2 QB 9, this includes both legal set off (where both claims are for liquidated and ascertained amounts) and equitable set off (where the two claims are so closely connected that it would be unjust to deal with one without taking into account the other). In addition, a contract may expressly permit a defendant to set off cross-claims which do not fall into either of these categories, as under GC/Works/1 clause 51 (sums due under other contracts).

It is obvious from the above that the usefulness of set off as a defence depends to a great extent on how widely the courts define the equitable version, and the judicial approach to date has been a very liberal one. It is probably safe to assume that any cross-claim which is based on the building contract itself can be used in this way, and the Court of Appeal in *Hanak* v *Green* applied the same principle to tort claims arising out of the building works. However, it appears that claims based on other contracts between the parties are not normally close enough to found an equitable set off (*Anglian Building Products Ltd* v *W & C French (Construction) Ltd* (1972) 16 BLR 1; *B Hargreaves Ltd* v *Action 2000 Ltd* [1991] CILL 720), and this is even more strongly the case where the two contracts are not between the same parties (*George E Taylor & Co Ltd* v *G Percy Trentham Ltd* (1980) 16 BLR 15).

It was at one time thought that there could be no set off against sums which had been certified as due by the contract administrator (*Dawnays Ltd* v *FG Minter Ltd* [1971] 2 All ER 1389), in order to protect cash flow (the construction industry's 'life-blood'). However, this suggestion was strongly denied by the House of Lords in *Gilbert-Ash (Northern) Ltd* v *Modern Engineering (Bristol) Ltd* [1974] AC 689, where it was stated that the right of set off would only be excluded by a clear provision to that effect in the contract or, exceptionally, by other evidence that this was what the parties intended (as occurred in *Mottram Consultants Ltd* v *Bernard Sunley & Sons Ltd* (1974) 2 BLR 28). What is more, a provision in a supplier's standard terms of business which clearly *did* purport to exclude a client's right to set off claims for defects or other breaches of contract has recently been struck down by the Court of Appeal, on the ground that it failed the statutory requirement of reasonableness under the Unfair Contract Terms Act 1977 (*Stewart Gill Ltd* v *Horatio Myer & Co Ltd* [1992] 2 All ER 257).

The standard forms of building and civil engineering contract currently in use do not attempt to exclude or restrict the employer's right of set off. On the other hand, a number of standard form *sub-contracts* do just that, by laying down strict procedures which the main contractor must follow if he wishes to deny wholly or in part a sub-contractor's claim to be paid. Requirements of this kind are in principle effective, so that attempts by main contractors to exercise rights of set off have foundered, *inter alia*, for lack of an architect's certificate of delay (*Brightside Kilpatrick Engineering Services* v *Mitchell Construction (1973) Ltd* (1973) 1 BLR 62), failure to give the prescribed written notice (*Pillar PG Ltd* v *DJ Higgins Construction Ltd* (1986) 34 BLR 43), and failure to quantify the set off in sufficient detail (*BWP (Architectural) Ltd* v *Beaver Building Systems Ltd* (1988) 42 BLR 86). However, it is essential always to study the contract terms in detail, since a right of set off may arise under more than one clause, and they may not all be governed by the procedural conditions (*Mellowes PPG Ltd* v *Snelling Construction Ltd* (1989) 49 BLR 109; cf *Hermcrest plc* v *G Percy Trentham Ltd* (1991) 53 BLR 104).

Contract clauses which set out a specific set off procedure typically go on to provide that no other right of set off is to be implied in that contract. In recent years this has served to focus attention on a separate defence which may be raised against a claim for payment, that of 'abatement' (*Mondel* v *Steel* (1841) 8 M & W 858). Although sometimes loosely referred to as a set off, this defence is in truth a denial of the claim itself—the contractor responds to the sub-contractor by alleging that, owing to defects in the work, the money claimed is not in fact due.

The practical significance of this defence is that, since it is not the same thing as a set off, it is not subject to any restrictions on set off which the contract lays down. In consequence, main contractors who have failed to comply with sub-contract set off procedures may nonetheless avoid summary judgment by pleading abatement (*Acsim (Southern) Ltd* v *Danish Contracting and Development Co Ltd* (1989) 47 BLR 55).

The defence of abatement causes most difficulties in cases where the disputed claim rests, not upon a simple assertion that money is due, but rather on the decision of an independent third party operating under the contract in question. For example, where a contractor seeks summary judgment on the basis of an architect's certificate, the employer may argue that the architect was in error. The employer's task in such cases, though not impossible (*CM*

Pillings & Co Ltd v *Kent Investments Ltd* (1985) 30 BLR 80; *RM Douglas Construction Ltd* v *Bass Leisure Ltd* (1990) 53 BLR 119) is a difficult one—vague allegations of defective work will not suffice. Indeed, if the employer's evidence is less than compelling, the court may make leave to defend conditional on a payment into court of a substantial part of what is claimed.

Where third parties other than architects are concerned, it is important to examine closely the precise powers given to them by the relevant contract. Recent attempts to base summary judgment on the decision of an adjudicator under the DOM/1 form of sub-contract (*A Cameron Ltd* v *John Mowlem & Co plc* (1990) 52 BLR 24) and on that of a 'construction manager' on the Broadgate project (*Rosehaugh Stanhope (Broadgate Phase 6) plc* v *Redpath Dorman Long Ltd* (1990) 50 BLR 69) both failed; in neither case had the third party been given the power to decide on the validity of the basic claim.

7 Retention

Building contracts under which payments are made to the contractor as the work progresses commonly make provision for a small percentage of each payment to be retained by the employer, as some kind of security for the proper completion of the works and the rectification of any defects which appear. The rules governing retention naturally vary from one contract to another, but it is normal for the amount retained to be in the region of five per cent (with perhaps an overall ceiling); one-half of this fund will be released to the contractor when practical completion is achieved, with the rest following at the end of the Defects Liability Period provided that the contractor has duly made good any relevant defects.

Unless otherwise provided, the contractor's right to retention money is simply a matter of contract. However, some forms of contract, such as JCT 80 clause 30.5, designate the retention as a trust fund (albeit subject to the employer's right to make certain deductions from it), in an effort to give the contractor a priority claim to it in the event of the employer's insolvency. This is in principle an effective strategy, but only if the money is separately identifiable, which usually means that it is kept in a separate bank account. The contractor under JCT 80 has an express right to demand that this be done, and such a right would in any event be implied (*Rayack Construction Ltd* v *Lampeter Meat Co Ltd* (1979)

12 BLR 30); indeed, the Court of Appeal has upheld a contractor's demand that the employer put the money into a separate bank account, even where the relevant clause had been deleted from the standard form contract before it was executed (*Wates Construction (London) Ltd* v *Franthom Property Ltd* (1991) 53 BLR 23).

It is important to note that a contractor will not be entitled to an injunction to secure retention money in this way once insolvency proceedings against the employer have commenced (*Re Jartray Developments Ltd* (1982) 22 BLR 134). This is so, even where the bank which appointed receivers under a floating charge over the employer's assets had been given notice of the building contract terms at the time when the floating charge was granted (*MacJordan Construction Ltd* v *Brookmount Erostin Ltd* [1991] CILL 704). Furthermore, an employer will not be ordered to pay into a separate account money against which he is making a *bona fide* claim, such as for liquidated damages (*Henry Boot Building Ltd* v *Croydon Hotel & Leisure Co Ltd* (1985) 36 BLR 41), although unsubstantiated and speculative claims by the employer will not defeat the contractor's right (*Concorde Construction Co Ltd* v *Colgan Co Ltd* (1984) 29 BLR 120; *J. F. Finnegan Ltd* v *Ford Sellar Morris Redeployments Ltd* (1991) 53 BLR 38).

Chapter 14

Variations

As mentioned in the previous chapter, the contract sum may be changed for a variety of reasons. The contractor may require reimbursement for certain expense caused by the contract administrator, employer, or for certain events outside the control of the contractor. These matters are covered by clauses such as JCT 80 clause 26 under which the contractor can claim for 'loss and/or expense', and are considered in the next chapter. The contractor must be paid for extra work brought about by an instruction of the contract administrator, and finally there may be reimbursement for extra expense brought about by market fluctuations affecting the contractor's inputs. It is to these last two matters that we turn our attention in this chapter.

1 The need for variations

Because construction projects are so complex, changes are frequently made before they are completed. Further, it is rare for design to be completely detailed at the time of tender; a result of this is that changes have to be made in order simply to make the building work. If there were no provision in the contract for varying the work to be done, then any attempt by the employer to make changes would effectively enable the contractor to negotiate a new price for the whole contract. By inserting an express provision which allows for changes to be made to the works as they are being built, the employer, through the contract administrator, can alter the works as and when necessary. The purpose of the variation clause is to allow such changes to be made, and also to permit any consequential changes to be made to the contract sum.

It must be borne in mind that the existence of a variations clause does not entitle the employer to make large-scale and significant changes to the nature of the works, as these are defined in the Recitals to the contract. It was said in *Blue Circle Industries plc* v *Holland Dredging (UK) Ltd* (1987) 37 BLR 40 that a variation is something which bears some relationship to the work of which it is a variation. If the work could not have been in the contemplation of the parties at the time they made their contract, then it must fall outside the scope of a variations clause. Accordingly, it was held in that case that a variations clause in a dredging contract could not be used so as to require the contractor to construct an artifical island out of the dredged material.

A more liberal approach to the extent of permissible variations appears from *McAlpine Humberoak* v *McDermott International Inc* [1992] CILL 747, where the effect of a long series of design changes in a sub-contract for part of a drilling platform was to turn a contract based on 22 drawings into one based on 161 drawings. The trial judge held that the cumulative effect of all these changes was so extensive as to frustrate the original contract, but the Court of Appeal held that they fell within the contract's variations clause.

One possible disadvantage of a variation clause is that it may encourage the design team to be less than specific at the time of tendering, in terms of what is to be built. The fact that things may be varied as the contract proceeds means that the design team may not have to finalise their design until a very late stage. This is bad practice and should be discouraged, the intention of the variation clauses being for unforeseen changes.

2 Variations under JCT contracts

The following discussion concentrates on the principles contained in JCT 80 and IFC 84, which have very similar provisions for variations. Indeed, the definitions of 'variation' in the two contracts are identical, save that JCT 80 specifically excludes the nomination of sub-contractors for measured work already priced by the main contractor. Since IFC 84 is not intended for use where sub-contractors are nominated, this provision would be irrelevant and is therefore omitted.

The definition of variation in JCT 80 clause 13.1 is a wide one, applying to both the content of the work and the method of doing it. Indeed, at first glance the definition appears almost unlimited in scope, since it makes repeated reference to 'any' work. However, bearing in mind what was said earlier about the recitals, and not changing the nature of the contract, this is clearly not the true position.

We may now look in more detail at the JCT 80 provisions.

(a) Alteration of the work

The basic definition includes any 'alteration or modification of the design, quality or quantity of the works as shown on the contract drawings and described by or referred to in the contract bills'. The clause clarifies this further by stating that such alteration or modification includes additions, omissions or substitutions.

The inclusion of substitutions within the definition is somewhat strange, since a substitution normally involves omitting one thing and adding another. For this reason, it is by no means clear why the phrase 'substitution of any work' is there at all. However, it is possible that this refers to the situation where a thing is varied after it has been completely built.

This part of the definition of a variation specifically includes the alteration of the kind or standard of any of the materials or goods to be used in the works. Such changes necessarily involve the contractor's head office in expenditure, such as the additional time needed to cancel orders, find alternative suppliers and reorder materials and goods. Detailed records may be needed to prove this type of expenditure, or alternatively it may be calculated on a '*pro rata*' basis.

The third aspect of this part of the definition is the removal from the site of work or materials which are there for the proper purposes of the contract. This is by contrast with clause 8.4, which deals with the removal of things which are *not* in accordance with the conditions.

(b) Alteration of working methods

In addition to allowing the works themselves to be altered, clause 13.1 allows for variations in the means of achieving those works. The means available to the contractor may be seriously affected by access to the site, working space, hours of work or the sequence in which work is to be carried out. Unlike the permitted variations to the works, however, these definite and specific matters of working *method* are fairly limited in the way in which they can be varied. In particular, clause 13.1.2 (which is mirrored in clause 3.6.2 of IFC 84) provides that these things can only be changed where there are already restrictions on them in the contract bills (and not any other document). It must also be borne in mind that exercising further restrictions in these things could result in substantial money claims by the contractor under clause 26.1.

The final aspect of the definition, as briefly mentioned earlier, is that a variation under JCT 80 may not include the nomination of a sub-contractor for measured work already priced by the contractor. In accordance with the common law position, as stated in *North West Regional Hospital Board* v *TA Bickerton & Son Ltd* [1970] 1 All ER 1039, the contract provides specifically that none of the contractor's work can be taken away and given to others whilst the contract is current.

3 Variations under ICE 6

The ICE definition of a variation appears in clause 51. It includes additions, omissions, substitutions, alterations, changes in quality, form, character, kind, position, dimension, level or line, and changes in any specified sequence, method or timing of construction. This list, which contains a number of synonyms, means in effect that the engineer may issue variations about almost anything. The clause also makes it clear that a variation order need not be issued merely for the purposes of altering quantities in the bills. This is because the bills are not intended as a full description of the work, but only as a mechanism for selecting the contractor.

4 The issue of variations

In the JCT forms of contract, the definition of variations is distinct from the power to issue them. A variation for this purpose is an instruction issued by the contract administrator. Hence, in order for such an instruction to be valid under the contract, it must be issued in accordance with clause 4 (clause 3.5 of IFC 84). This means, for example, that it must be in writing. It also means that the contractor has the right to object on reasonable grounds to a variation.

As well as issuing an instruction which may require a variation, the contract administrator may sanction a variation that has been made by the contractor. The contractor normally has no authority whatsoever to vary anything (except for the execution of emergency work by clause 6.1). For example, the contractor cannot substitute higher quality work or materials than those specified. A contractor who *does* vary anything then can be instructed to remove it under clause 8.4 (*Simplex Concrete Piles Ltd* v *St Pancras MBC*

(1958) 14 BLR 80). This power for the contract administrator to sanction an unauthorised variation by the contractor is thus an important one, since it allows the contract administrator easily to pick up and deal with minor items which are varied by the contractor, or which are directed by the Clerk of Works and not confirmed by the contract administrator.

All the contract forms contain an express provision to the effect that 'no variation required by the architect/contract administrator or subsequently sanctioned by him shall vitiate this contract'. This in fact is an unnecessary and somewhat misleading statement, which adds nothing at all to the general legal position. Even without such a clause, an attempt by the employer to vary the contractor's obligations in a minor way would not 'vitiate the contract'; the contractor would simply be entitled to refuse. On the other hand, an alteration great enough to 'vitiate the contract' will continue to do so notwithstanding this clause, because such an alteration will go beyond the contractual definition of a 'variation'.

In JCT contracts, variations can only apply to firm quantities and to provisional sums; they cannot relate to approximate quantities. By amendment 7 to JCT 80, the With Quantities forms can now be used when some of the quantities are approximate. If this is done, the 'firming up' of those approximate quantities does not require the contract administrator to issue a variation instruction. Likewise, under ICE contracts, variations are not used to alter or firm up any of the quantities.

Both JCT forms contain a clause under which the contract administrator issues instructions as to the expenditure of provisional sums, and JCT 80 extends this to provisional sums in subcontracts (JCT 80 clause 13.3, IFC 84 clause 3.8). It should be noted that this is a *duty* of the contract administrator, as well as a power. Under JCT 80, such instructions may well consist of nominating a sub-contractor or supplier, but this is not necessarily the case. It will depend upon why the particular provisional sum was included in the contract bills.

5 Valuation of variations

(a) General principles

The basic underlying principle in valuing variations is to hold the contractor, as far as is reasonably practicable, to the terms of his original bargain. Thus, if the rates in the bills allow little or no profit, then the rates for varied work should also allow little or no profit. JCT 80 clause 13.5 and IFC 84 clause 3.7 each provide for certain work to be valued by the quantity surveyor in accordance with the valuation rules. The work in question includes any work executed as a result of a variation, work sanctioned as if it were a variation and work done as a consequence of an instruction on the expenditure of a provisional sum. In fact the use of the valuation rules is not compulsory; it is of course perfectly legitimate for the employer and the contractor to make a specific agreement about a price for the varied work. However, in the absence of such an agreement, each contract lays down a set of rules for calculating the value of the work. There is little difference between the two forms in this respect; what follows is based on JCT 80.

In considering the valuation of variations under JCT 80, two vital preliminary points must be made. First, clause 13.5.6 makes it clear that, if a particular case does not fit into any of the specific rules provided, then the contractor is entitled to 'a fair valuation'. This is very wide-ranging in scope, and is intended as a residual or 'catch-all' clause. Indeed, it may be noted that this provision is even wide enough to bring about a *reduction* in the contract price, if limitations on the contractor's working methods are removed under clauses 13.1.2.1 to 13.1.2.4. What constitutes a 'fair' valuation may be interpreted, in the context of the rest of the clause, as being related to the market conditions at which the tender was pitched, at the time of the tender. However, a contractor who finds that this would involve executing work at little or no profit may contend that 'fair' means that the valuation should relate to current market prices, at the time of the instructed variation.

The second preliminary point arises out of clause 13.5.5. This states that, if compliance with an instruction results in a consequential change to the conditions of any other work, then all that other work shall also be valued as if it were a variation. In other words, if the conditions of work are altered because the contractor has to comply with an instruction, then the provisions of clause 13 will apply to all that work as well.

(b) Valuation rules under JCT contracts

It will be seen that JCT 80 effectively divides work to be valued into three categories: work which can be valued by measurement, omitted work, and work which cannot be measured. We shall look at these categories in turn. First, however, attention should be given to three general points which are made in clause 13.5.3. These points relate to work which can be valued by measurement and to omitted work; they do *not* apply to work which cannot properly be valued by measurement.

The points in question are:

- In relation to measurable work and omitted work, any measurement is to be carried out in accordance with the same principles as those used for the preparation of the contract bills. This cross-refers to clause 2.2.2.1, which lays down which Standard Method of Measurement is to be used. The effect, therefore, is that all measurements taken to define the varied work must be taken in accordance with the relevant SMM.
- Allowance is to be made for any percentage or lump sum adjustments in contract bills. Such an allowance is necessary because it is common practice for contractors when tendering to allow for overheads and profit by a lump sum or percentage addition to the sum of the preliminaries, instead of allowing a proportion in each and every measured item. This provision allows the lump sum to be adjusted in line with the variation.
- An appropriate allowance is to be made in respect of certain preliminary items, the use of which would not be attributable in whole to the varied item, but which would be needed in a different way if items are varied. For example, changing the way in which brickwork is to be finished may involve keeping scaffolding on site for an extra period. The Standard Method of Measurement contains further examples of preliminary items which may be affected in this way.

We may now turn to the three categories of work to be valued which were identified above.

Measured work The basic rule applying to 'additional or substituted work which can properly be valued by measurement' is that the rates and prices in the contract bills shall apply. However, this only applies to work which is of similar character, is executed under similar conditions, and does not significantly change the quantity given in the bills. There is of course room for argument over exactly what is meant by such words as 'similar' and 'character'; nonetheless, most variations would be expected to fall within this principle. If the varied work is of a similar character to work already in the contract bills, but is executed under different conditions and/or there is a significant change in the quantity, a different method of valuation must be used. Once again, the rates in the bills must be used as a basis, but here the valuation must include 'a fair allowance' for the difference in conditions and/or quantity. The new rate, which is thus derived from a bill rate by making this fair allowance, is known as a 'star rate'.

Examples of 'different conditions' under this clause would include winter instead of summer working; night instead of day working; differences in levels (such as storey heights etc) at which work is carried out; and the discovery of antiquities under clause 34. It is also worth making the point that changes in quantity alone must be 'significant' in order to justify the adoption of 'star rates'.

Work which does not fit into either of the previous two categories, because it is *not* of a similar character to work priced in the bills, is to be valued at 'fair rates and prices'. It is not easy for a contractor to invoke this clause after the work has been done. The contractor should make clear to the contract administrator, before undertaking the work, his assertion that it should be valued under this rule. If this is not done, the contract administrator can claim that the contractor's lack of protest shows that the work falls into one of the previous two categories, so that no further allowance need be made.

Omitted work The position regarding the omission of work set out in the contract bills is simple. Clause 13.5.2 provides that the bill rates can and should be used for valuing the work. Once again, however, account should be taken of any 'knock-on' effect on other work.

Unmeasurable work In respect of 'additional or substituted work which cannot properly be valued by measurement', valuation may be on a 'dayworks' basis. It is important to note that a decision as to whether or not this method should be adopted is for the quantity surveyor to make; it is not for the contractor to insist on valuation according to dayworks.

The clause lays down details as to how the dayworks items are to be calculated, both for the main contractor and for specialists. Certain 'official' definitions are used to determine the prime cost, and to this is added the relevant profit percentages set out in the bills. There are strict procedures requiring the contractor to produce vouchers specifying the time spent each day on the work, the names of the workers employed on it, and details of the plant and materials used. All these vouchers must be given to the contract administrator by the end of the week following that in which the work was executed. If these administrative procedures are not followed to the letter by the contractor, the claim for valuation on a dayworks basis will probably fail.

(c) Valuation rules under ICE 6

Under ICE 6, the rules for the valuation are very much more straightforward, yet seem to arrive at a very similar position as JCT. The rates in the bill will be used where possible, otherwise, they will form a basis for calculation. If this is not possible, then a rate will be negotiated between the engineer and the contractor. If they fail to reach an agreement, the engineer will simply decide how much to pay.

6 Fluctuations

We may now look briefly at fluctuations, which are the third mechanism by which the contract sum may validly be adjusted. The purpose of a 'fluctuations clause' is to provide a mechanism for reimbursing contractors for changes in input prices over which they have no control at all. The JCT 80 fluctuations provisions are printed in a separate booklet from the main form of contract, because these clauses are to an extent optional. The appendix must state which of the fluctuations clauses apply.

In JCT 80, clause 37 (which is part of the main form) simply brings into operation the fluctuations clauses. It does this by stating that fluctuations shall be dealt with according to whichever of three alternatives is identified in the appendix. These alternatives are clauses 38, 39 and 40. In the absence of any entry in the appendix, the basic minimum provision for fluctuations contained in clause 38 is stated to apply.

The three fluctuation schemes are as follows:

- *Clause 38*: Contributions, levy and tax fluctuations. This clause applies to items which are affected by the government and are thus completely beyond both the control and the prediction of the contractor. The elements to which the clause applies fluctuations are labour, materials and goods, electricity and fuels, but only to the extent that they are affected by tax etc. In some cases they are only covered as far as they have been listed in the contract documents. There are no methods for calculation set out in the clause, but obviously it would be necessary to take into account man-hours, quantities of materials and other directly ascertained costs. It is not intended that this clause should change the amount of contractor's profit.

- *Clause 39*: Labour and materials cost and tax fluctuations. This clause includes all the government-related items that are covered by clause 38; it adds in labour and materials fluctuations. This covers the market costs of input, such as wage rates and prices of materials.
- *Clause 40*: Use of price adjustment formulae. This is a completely different type of calculation. It incorporates by reference a set of formula rules which define a technical financial calculation based on a wide variety of categories. The whole of the works is divided up into financial categories and a monthly published bulletin gives indices by which each sum should be multiplied. In order for this to work, it is necessary for the contract bills to reflect the categories used by the fluctuation categories. Since the index numbers reflect the market situation each month, they are deemed to include the matters covered by clauses 38 and 39, and so only one of the clauses has to apply. The purpose of this method is to reduce the amount of calculation which has to be undertaken by the project team.

These different types of fluctuations are referred to as 'limited fluctuations' (clause 38) and 'full fluctuations' (clauses 39 and 40). In addition, it is of course possible to have no fluctuations provisions at all, by crossing out clause 37. Such a procedure would however only be suitable for a small project under steady conditions.

ICE 6 approaches the question of fluctuations in a similar way to JCT 80. Again the fluctuations clauses are optional, are printed separately from the remainder of the contract and are based on published *indices*. However, to bring them into force requires a Special Condition in the contract, rather than an entry in the appendix.

Chapter 15

Contractors' Money Claims

The previous two chapters have considered the contractor's right to be paid for whatever work is executed under the contract, including that which is added during the course of the project under a variations clause. However, such payments will not necessarily compensate the contractor for various losses and expenses which may be incurred in carrying out the contract work, and there are several ways in which claims for additional sums of money can arise. This chapter is largely concerned with one of these sources of extra money, namely, the contractual claim for 'loss and/or expense' (the term used in JCT 80).

Such claims are of considerable practical importance, not least because their 'creative' use by an experienced consultant can sometimes rescue a contractor who has seriously underpriced a job. On the other hand, contractors who are overly claims-conscious have done much to tarnish the image of the construction industry. They have also led many regular employers to appreciate that what appears an attractively low tender may ultimately be paid for through the back door in this way.

1 Meaning of claims

For the purposes of this chapter, a contractor's claim may arise in one of three ways. First, and most important, there are those entitlements given to the contractor by specific provisions of the contract in question. Secondly, and mainly for the purpose of comparison, there is the possibility of seeking compensation by means of an action against the employer for breach of contract. Thirdly, there are certain situations in which a contractor may seek through the doctrine of *quantum meruit* to recover, not damages, but the reasonable value of work done.

It may be noted that *ex gratia* claims, under which an employer may be prepared to pay the contractor something to which there is no legal entitlement, are not further considered here, since they raise no legal issues.

(a) Contractual claims

Most of the standard form construction contracts and sub-contracts currently in use contain provisions under which the contractor can recover compensation from the employer (or the sub-contractor from the contractor) for various losses suffered where the project is prolonged or disrupted by certain specified causes. Most, that is, but not all—some minor works contracts (such as MW 80 and GC/Works/2) make no express provision for compensation to be paid, in which case the contractor is thrown back on to his common law rights.

When a contractual claims provision is examined, it will frequently be found to bear a close resemblance to the term in the same contract which deals with extensions of time. However, any such resemblance should not be allowed to obscure the fact that these are entirely separate issues, and that (contrary to an apparently widespread belief in the construction industry) a contractor's right to one of these benefits in no way confers entitlement to the other.

To illustrate this point, it will commonly be the case that extra time for completion may be granted in respect of delays caused by events (eg adverse weather) which are the fault of neither party. However, it is far less usual for such neutral events to give the contractor any *financial* entitlements. Likewise, it is clear that an extension of time can only be granted where the relevant delay will result in late completion of the contract works. A financial claim, by contrast, relates to *disruption* of the work, which may or may not affect the completion date—whether it will do so depends on such factors as whether the disrupted work lies on the critical path and whether the contractor can 'accelerate' in order to make up the time lost.

In seeking to make a claim under the contract, a contractor must be able to show that losses of the kind specified have been suffered; that these were the result of some qualifying event; and that there has been compliance with whatever procedures (as to giving notice, keeping records etc) are prescribed by the contract. These matters are considered in more detail below.

(b) Claims for breach of contract

Since many, if not most, of the causes of disruption supporting a contractor's claim for loss and/or expense are things for which the employer (or the contract administrator on his behalf) may be regarded as responsible, they will frequently also permit the contractor to maintain an action for damages for breach of contract. Where this is so, the contractor has a free choice as to which remedy to pursue, unless the contract itself clearly provides otherwise. This would be very unusual; if a contract refers to the point at all, it is normally in order specifically to preserve the contractor's common law rights.

In cases where a contractor has a choice of remedy, practical considerations may well lead him to favour making a claim under the contract. Such a claim can in most cases be made as soon as the relevant event occurs and the loss is suffered (or even earlier, so long as it can be shown that loss is likely). By contrast, a contractor's action for breach of contract, at least where it falls within the scope of an arbitration clause, will normally have to wait until practical completion of the works is achieved before proceedings can be commenced.

Not only can a contractual claim be *made* sooner; it is also likely to result in much earlier payment. This is because claims are normally a matter for the contract administrator to decide and, once an award has been made, this will result in an adjustment to the contract sum which will be reflected in the next interim certificate. The contrast with the time necessary to secure and enforce a court judgment or an arbitrator's award is only too obvious.

The price to be paid for the advantages offered by the contractual claims machinery often lies in the tightly drawn procedural restrictions by which it is governed. Naturally, a contractor who fails to comply with stated requirements, for example as to when notice of disruption must be given, or what records must be shown to the contract administrator, will be forced to pursue his claims through arbitration or litigation.

Actions for damages for breach of contract are discussed further in Chapter 19.

(c) Quantum meruit *claims*

A contractor who carries out work for an employer will expect to be paid for that work in accordance with the terms of a contract between them. In normal circumstances this will indeed be the case, but there are some situations in which, for one reason or another, there is no express contractual entitlement. In such circumstances the contractor may seek instead to recover a 'reasonable sum', basing his claim either on an implied term or on a quasi-contractual entitlement to payment for benefits conferred.

The situations in which *quantum meruit* claims are most likely to arise in the construction context are as follows:

(*a*) where work is requested but no price is agreed (eg under a 'letter of intent', considered in Chapter 8);

(*b*) where a price fixing clause in a contract fails to operate;

(*c*) where so-called 'variations' in fact go beyond the scope of the contract altogether (*Sir Lindsay Parkinson & Co* v *Commissioners of Works* [1949] 2 KB 632);

(*d*) where the 'contract' is void.

In assessing the 'reasonable sum' in a *quantum meruit* claim, a court is likely to consider both the value to the employer of the work done and the cost to the contractor in doing it. Where the reason why the claim has arisen is because there is no contract between the parties, there can of course be no counter-claim by the employer in respect of alleged delays or deficiencies (*British Steel Corporation* v *Cleveland Bridge & Engineering Co Ltd* [1984] 1 All ER 504). Whether such matters can nonetheless affect the sum awarded is a very interesting question; unfortunately, it is one which the Court of Appeal has refused to answer in Order 14 proceedings (*Crown House Engineering Ltd* v *Amec Projects Ltd* (1989) 48 BLR 32).

2 Basis of contractual claims

(*a*) *General*

The essence of a claim of this nature is that it is based upon some specific entitlement given by the contract in question. As a general rule, such claims are expressed to arise where certain specified events materially affect the progress of the works, and where this disruption in turn causes the contractor to incur extra expense for which the contract does not otherwise offer reimbursement. It is emphatically not enough for the contractor simply to show that, for reasons beyond his control, the project has proved unexpectedly difficult or expensive, nor that he has been deluged by variation instructions from the contract administrator. He must be able to identify the cause of his loss and relate this to an express term of the contract.

A crucial element which a contractor must prove, in respect of each and every part of his claim, is that the loss in question was *caused*, both factually and legally, by a qualifying event. Suppose, for example, that a contract administrator's delay in providing the contractor with necessary information means that a contract which should have been completed in September in fact drags on until December. Winter working is in general terms more expensive than summer working and so, if the contractor can identify increased costs, these will be recoverable from the employer. However, suppose further that, in November, a totally unforeseeable strike takes place which keeps the contractor on site for an extra month. Can it really be said that the employer has 'caused' this strike to happen, and should therefore be held responsible for its effects? A *dictum* in *Fairweather (H) & Co Ltd* v *Wandsworth LBC* (1987) 39 BLR 106 suggests that the employer would indeed be liable in such circumstances, but this seems debatable, to put it no higher.

One aspect of causation which has given rise to problems in practice is the question of multiple causes. As to this, the courts have accepted in principle that a 'global' claim (ie one which does not seek to apportion each item of loss to a single identifiable cause) may succeed (*J Crosby & Sons Ltd* v *Portland UDC* (1967) 5 BLR 126; *Merton LBC* v *Stanley Hugh Leach Ltd* (1985) 32 BLR 51). However, this will only be permitted where *all* the causes are qualifying events under the contract, and where the impossibility of separating them is not itself due to the contractor's delay in claiming (see *Wharf Properties Ltd* v *Eric Cumine Associates (No 2)* (1991) 52 BLR 1; *Mid-Glamorgan CC* v *J Devonald Williams & Partner* [1991] CILL 722).

(b) Standard form contracts

JCT 80 clause 26 requires a contractor who claims under the contract to show that he has incurred or is likely to incur direct loss and/or expense for which he would not otherwise be reimbursed under the contract. He must further prove that this loss arises either from deferred possession of the site (where provision for this has been made in the Appendix) or 'because the regular progress of the Works or of any part thereof has been or is likely to be materially affected by any one or more of' certain specified matters. These consist mainly of things which would also amount to a breach of contract by the employer (late information, discrepancies in contract documents, failure to supply materials or give access to the site etc). Also included are matters which the employer has a *right* to order, such as variations, postponement of work, or the inspection or testing of work which turns out to be satisfactory.

ICE 6 adopts a rather different approach to this question, in that clause 52(4) deals only with claims *procedures*; the *grounds* on which the contractor may be entitled to additional payment are to be found scattered throughout the conditions. As to what these grounds cover, it may be noted that they appear to stretch somewhat wider than most of the other standard forms; however, a number of the provisions restrict claims to things 'which could not reasonably have been foreseen by an experienced contractor'.

The general wording used in GC/Works/1 clause 46 is not dissimilar to that in JCT 80, since it refers to 'the regular progress of the works or any part of them being materially disrupted or prolonged' in such a way that 'the contractor properly and directly incurs any expense'. However, the qualifying events listed in this clause are considerably narrower in scope than those found in JCT 80, covering mainly defaults of the employer which cause delay. On the other hand, the contractor under this form of contract is given a separate entitlement to claim where 'unforeseeable ground conditions' involve him in additional work (clause 7).

In this context it is perhaps worth mentioning the ACA form of contract, simply because of the different way in which it approaches the problem. Rather than set down a detailed list of qualifying events, clause 7 of that contract entitles the contractor to claim in respect of any 'damage, loss and/or expense' suffered when 'any act, omission or default or negligence of the employer or of the architect disrupts the regular progress of the Works or of any Section or delays the execution of them in accordance with the dates stated in the Time Schedule'.

3 Contractual claims procedures

As mentioned above, contract provisions under which a contractor may claim for loss/expense almost invariably lay down a particular procedure which must be followed. These procedures naturally vary from one form of contract to another, but they usually involve the contractor in giving notice (often in writing) to the contract administrator. The precise form which such a notice must take is seldom specified; all that matters is that it should sufficiently identify the issue on which the architect's decision is required (*Merton LBC* v *Stanley Hugh Leach Ltd* (1985) 32 BLR 51). As to the *time* at which notice must be given, provisions in the standard forms range from 'as soon as may be reasonable' after the events causing disruption to 'as soon as it has become, or should reasonably have become, apparent' to the contractor that disruption is likely to occur.

Apart from giving this initial notice, the contractor will be required under most forms of contract to furnish the contract administrator with details of the claim, sometimes accompanied by documentary evidence in support. Some contracts make this an automatic obligation (with its own time limits); others require no more of the contractor than compliance with any reasonable request for information which the contract administrator may make.

The effect on a contractor's claim of failure to comply with whatever procedure is set down will depend on the terms of the contract in question. At one extreme, GC/Works/1 makes clear that strict compliance is a condition precedent to obtaining an increase in the contract sum. JCT 80, while not so explicit, effectively arrives at the same conclusion, since it appears that the contract administrator may simply ignore any application from the contractor which does not satisfy the conditions laid down (see *Merton LBC* v *Stanley Hugh Leach Ltd* (1985) 32 BLR 51).

The ACA form, which sets up a complicated procedure of estimates, negotiation and adjudication, is slightly less severe upon contractors who fail to follow it. The contract merely provides that there will be no entitlement to any adjustment of the contract sum until final certificate and that, even if an adjustment is made at that stage, it will not include any interest or financing charges for the intervening period.

The most liberal of all the major standard form contracts in this respect appears to be ICE 6, which (perhaps in reaction to its Draconian previous editions) contains two important provisions which serve to alleviate the consequences of non-compliance by the contractor with the prescribed procedure. First, it is provided that the engineer may uphold a claim 'to the extent that the engineer has not been prevented from or substantially prejudiced by such failure in investigating the said claim'. Secondly, it is made clear that, where the contractor seeks *interim* payment on a claim but has submitted insufficient particulars, the engineer may nonetheless authorise payment 'of such part of the claim as the particulars may substantiate to the satisfaction of the engineer'.

4 Assessment of claims

(a) Loss, expense and cost

Assuming that a contractor's work has been delayed by some qualifying event, and that he has complied with the contractual procedures for making a claim, the final question to be addressed is how the claim is to be quantified in financial terms. This must of course depend primarily upon the wording of the particular contract, but the courts have made it clear that terms such as 'expense' (GC/Works/1) and 'direct loss and/or expense' (JCT 80) provide an entitlement which is equivalent to an award of damages for breach of contract (*Wraight Ltd* v *P H & T (Holdings) Ltd* (1968) 13 BLR 26; *FG Minter Ltd* v *Welsh Health Technical Services Organisation* (1980) 13 BLR 1). This interpretation has the important consequence that, notwithstanding the use of words such as 'loss' and 'expense', the contractor will also be able to recover for *loss of profit*.

It is of course open to a draftsman to avoid the normal judicial interpretation by the use of clear words in the contract, and this is done by ICE 6. A number of conditions in that form of contract provide for the contractor to claim his 'cost', which is defined by clause 1 to include overhead finance but *not* profit. As a result, the contractor will only be entitled to his profit margin under those clauses which expressly provide for this (as many do).

The equiparation of loss/expense with damages for breach of contract has the further effect of bringing into play such contractual rules as those governing remoteness which, in construction cases, have proved fairly liberal. It has for instance been held (in the face of a clause excluding liability for 'consequential loss or damage') that a contractor's damages from a supplier of defective materials should nonetheless include loss of productivity, inflation costs resulting from delay and the cost of meeting a claim brought against the contractor by sub-contractors.

It is perhaps hardly necessary to point out that a contractor who claims in respect of some loss must be able to prove that he has actually incurred it. Where a project is prolonged over a considerable period, for example, one might reasonably expect the contractor to suffer increased costs of both labour and materials as a result of inflation. Such increases are in principle recoverable, but not in so far as the contractor is insulated against them by a fluctuations clause in the contract. Only to the extent that the increases exceed what that clause provides can the contractor show loss/expense.

A particularly knotty problem of loss-proving concerns the contractor who is ahead of schedule and expecting to finish the work early when he is delayed by the employer; as a result, the contractor's 'slack' is taken up. The question which then arises is whether the contractor can claim for the expenses of prolongation, or whether it can be said that he had in any event priced on the assumption of remaining on site for the whole contract period. This matter, which has provoked debate and divided commentators, has not yet been authoritatively settled by the courts, although the case of *Glenlion Construction Ltd* v *Guinness Trust* (1987) 39 BLR 89 appears to run counter to the contractor's claim.

Before turning to three heads of claim which raise particular difficulties, it may be as well to note the kinds of item which appear almost as a matter of course in claims for prolongation and disruption. As far as the *prolongation* of a contract is concerned, it is self-evident that this will lead to an increase in 'site overheads' such as accommodation and services, insurance and staff costs, and highly likely that there will also be extra costs in relation to plant (which, if it is the contractor's own, will be valued on the basis of maintenance and depreciation—*B Sunley Ltd & Co* v *Cunard White Star Ltd* [1940] 1 KB 740). Losses attributable to *disruption* without prolongation are often more difficult to quantify, but extra labour charges due to 'uneconomic working' frequently appear.

(b) Off-site overheads and profit

Where disruption or prolongation is caused by something which justifies the contractor in making a claim, he may be entitled to recover any extra administrative costs incurred at head office (*Tate & Lyle Food and Distribution Co Ltd* v *GLC* [1981] 3 All ER 716). However, any such costs must be detailed and supported by evidence (eg as to extra staff taken on), and this will seldom be an easy task.

A separate issue arises from the fact that, where any contract is prolonged, the contribution made by that contract to the contractor's general overheads and/or profits will be less than expected. These losses are in principle recoverable as part of a claim, but this is subject to a very important proviso—the contractor must produce satisfactory evidence to the effect that he could, if not tied up on site, have been profitably engaged on other work (*Peak Construction (Liverpool) Ltd* v *McKinney Foundations Ltd* (1970) 1 BLR 111). Such evidence may of course be difficult to come by in times of recession, where many contractors are competing for a relatively small number of contracts.

Assuming that this basic evidential hurdle is overcome, the task of quantifying the missing contribution may yet raise formidable difficulties. In order to assist, the courts have on the whole proved receptive to claims based on a 'formula' approach, in which a notional daily or weekly contribution from the contract in question is identified, and then multiplied by the number of days or weeks for which the contractor is entitled to claim (*Whittall Builders Co Ltd* v *Chester-le-Street DC* (1985, unreported; *JF Finnegan Ltd* v *Sheffield CC* (1988) 43 BLR 124). The best known of these calculations, the 'Hudson formula', takes as its starting point that percentage for overheads and profit which has actually been used by the contractor in making up his tender. However, the more acceptable approach seems to be that adopted by the 'Emden formula', which derives a notional overall percentage from a study of the contracting organisation's annual accounts over the last few years. In either case, it is important that adherence to a predetermined formula should not be allowed to mask the realities of the situation, and thus to achieve figures which are completely out of keeping with common sense.

(c) Financing charges

A contractor who makes a claim under the contract is in most cases seeking reimbursement for expenses which have actually been incurred, and for which the contractor will therefore have been out of pocket for a period. Not surprisingly, therefore, many contractors seek to include in their claim a sum in respect of interest paid on their overdraft, or interest which their tied-up capital could otherwise have earned. It might be thought that to award such sums would be inconsistent with the common law's refusal to award interest on debts paid late but before proceedings commenced (*President of India* v *La Pintada Cia Navegacion SA* [1985] AC 104; cf Supreme Court Act 1981, s 35A and Arbitration Act 1950, s 19A). However, such doubts notwithstanding, the Court of Appeal has permitted the recovery of 'financing charges' as part of a contractor's loss/expense claim (*FG Minter Ltd* v *Welsh Health Technical Services Organisation* (1980) 13 BLR 1). Assuming that the contractor is operating on an overdraft, this head of claim will represent the actual cost to him of the amount laid out, including the compound interest charged by the bank (*Rees & Kirby Ltd* v *Swansea CC* (1985) 30 BLR 1). If the contractor is in fact using his own capital, then he should be entitled to a reasonable sum to reflect the interest which he is not free to earn.

It should be noted that GC/Works/1 clause 47 provides that finance charges shall be payable to the contractor only in certain specified (and very limited) circumstances. Furthermore, the ACA form of contract precludes the payment of such amounts to a contractor who has failed to follow the prescribed claims procedure.

(d) Preparation costs

The preparation and presentation of a claim by a contractor is something on which a great deal of time and money may be expended, and a question which has arisen is whether the costs incurred may themselves be added to the substantive claim. The answer to this is probably that, since the contractor is under no obligation to present a formal claim in this manner, the costs of so doing cannot be recovered. This, at any rate, was the decision reached in *James Longley & Co Ltd* v *South West Thames RHA* (1983) 25 BLR 56, where a contractor was denied the fees paid to a quantity surveyor for preparing documents for a Final Account, but was allowed those fees which related to the preparation of similar material for arbitration. On the other hand, if the contractor's expense results from unusually onerous demands for information from the contract administrator, this may well be recoverable (see *Tate & Lyle Food and Distribution Co Ltd* v *GLC* [1983] 2 AC 509).

Chapter 16

Delay and Liquidated Damages

1 The contractor's obligation to complete the works

The carrying out and completion of the contract works is the very essence of the contractor's obligation to the employer. Indeed, a building contract is presumed to be an 'entire' contract, in the sense that a contractor who abandons the work when it is partly performed is not entitled to any payment for what has been achieved (*Hoenig* v *Isaacs* [1952] 2 All ER 176). Of course, this principle cannot apply in full where, as is frequently the case, the contract makes express provision for interim payments, or where such provision can be implied (as in *DR Bradley (Cable Jointing) Ltd* v *Jefco Mechanical Services Ltd* (1988) 6-CLD-07–19). Even here, however, it will continue to govern the earning of each instalment of the total contract sum.

(a) The meaning of completion

The designation of a contractual obligation as 'entire', in the sense described above, does not mean that a contractor will forfeit all entitlement to be paid whenever there is a single defect in the work. The doctrine of substantial performance, which is strongly presumed to apply to building contracts, means that he will normally be entitled to the agreed price less an amount to reflect the defects or omissions (*Hoenig* v *Isaacs* [1952] 2 All ER 176). Only in exceptional cases will the courts take a more drastic line, such as perhaps where defects in work mean that a consumer has not received the basic thing for which he contracted (see *Bolton* v *Mahadeva* [1972] 2 All ER 1322).

The position thus taken under the general law of contract is largely reflected by the meaning which is given to 'completion' in most standard form contracts. That something less than perfection is envisaged often appears from the contract wording: 'practical completion' in JCT 80, 'substantial completion' in ICE 6. Even without such qualifying adjectives, however, it is unlikely that a court would impose any more stringent obligation on the contractor than to achieve practical completion as that term is now understood.

As to precisely what practical completion requires, judicial *dicta* range between two extremes. In *Westminster CC* v *Jarvis & Sons Ltd* [1969] 3 All ER 1025, Salmon LJ adopted a very functional (and liberal) approach, defining it as 'completion for all practical purposes, that is to say for the purpose of allowing the employers to take possession of the works and use them as intended'. However, when the case reached the House of Lords ([1970] 1 All ER 943), Lord Dilhorne took the much stricter line that 'what is meant is the completion of all the construction work that has to be done'. The current judicial view, which lies somewhere between these poles, appears to be that a contract administrator may certify practical completion where defects or omissions are '*de minimis*', but not where there are patent defects in the work which exceed that margin (see *HW Nevill (Sunblest) Ltd* v *William Press & Sons Ltd* (1982) 20 BLR 78; *Emson Eastern Ltd* v *EME Developments Ltd* (1991) 55 BLR 114).

(b) The time for completion

The vast majority of building contracts contain a clear statement as to the time by which the contractor must complete the works. This may be done in either of two ways. First, the contract may specify the completion date itself, albeit with provision for that date to be altered if an extension of time is awarded. This method is adopted by JCT 80, where the Date for Completion appears in the Appendix. Secondly, where it is not certain exactly when the contractor will commence the works, the contract may specify the length of time required to complete the works, and provide that this shall run from the date on which the contractor is instructed or permitted to begin work. This method is used in both ICE 6 (clauses 41 and 43) and GC/Works/1 (clause 34).

In the rare event that no completion date has been expressly set, it is of course possible to fall back on an implied term for completion in a reasonable time. However, the courts will strain to avoid this (on the basis that commercial parties invariably require more certainty in their affairs); hence, if an intended date can be deduced from extra-contractual correspondence, the court may well imply a term for completion on or before that date (*Bruno Zornow (Builders) Ltd* v *Beechcroft Developments Ltd* (1989) 51 BLR 16).

(c) Sectional completion

If an employer requires a project to be completed in stages by specified dates, the contract should identify separate sections of the work, attaching to each a completion date and liability to pay liquidated damages for delay. Both ICE 6 and GC/Works/1 make provision for this to be done; JCT 80 does not, but can be easily amended by using the Sectional Completion Supplement.

If the contract is not carefully drafted, the employer's wishes are likely to be frustrated, for the courts will not imply a term for sectional completion (*Bruno Zornow (Builders) Ltd* v *Beechcroft Developments Ltd* (1989) 51 BLR 16). Nor is it safe to assume that provisions as to staged handover in the contract bills will have the desired effect, since many building contracts, such as JCT 80, do not permit the contract conditions (which stipulate a single completion date) to be modified by what is in the bills (see *MJ Gleeson (Contractors) Ltd* v *Hillingdon London Borough* (1970) 215 EG 165).

2 The effects of completion

Once the contract administrator certifies that the contractor has achieved completion, as defined by the particular form of contract, the employer takes possession of and responsibility for the contract works and any liability of the contrator to pay liquidated damages for delay comes to an end. What is more, that liability will not be revived if the work is later found to contain defects; such a discovery does not retrospectively invalidate the certificate (*Westminster CC* v *Jarvis & Sons Ltd* [1970] 1 All ER 942).

A second effect of achieving completion of the works is that it marks the commencement of what is variously known as the Defects Liability Period (JCT 80), Defects Correction Period (ICE 6) or Maintenance Period (GC/Works/1). The last of these titles is perhaps misleading, since what is involved is not really 'maintenance'. That is, the contractor's obligation is not to maintain the finished work in pristine condition for the duration of the period, but rather to correct certain defects.

The precise details of these provisions naturally vary from one form of contract to another, but the general principle is that during the specified period (which may be of any length but which in building contracts is commonly six months), any defect which appears and which is due to the contractor's default is to be made good by the contractor. Indeed, to carry out such work is arguably the contractor's right as well as his obligation; an employer who chooses to have it executed by someone else, and then claims the cost incurred from the original contractor as damages for breach of contract, may well find his claim defeated on the ground that he has unreasonably failed to mitigate his losses (see *William Tompkinson* v *The Parochial Church Council of St Michael* (1990) 6 Const LJ 319).

Thirdly, it is usual to find that, upon achieving completion of the works, the contractor becomes entitled to the release of one-half of the accumulated retention fund. The balance will normally be released when all Defects Liability Periods have expired and all defects appearing during these have been made good.

3 Liquidated damages

As mentioned earlier, potentially the most significant effect of a contractor's failure to complete on time is that it triggers his liability to pay (or, more commonly, to suffer deduction of) liquidated damages to the employer. These damages (which are sometimes called 'liquidated and ascertained damages' or 'LADs') are a pre-determined sum which, if certain conditions are satisfied, will replace the normal liability to pay general damages measured by the amount of the employer's loss.

In some cases (depending on market conditions and the relative bargaining strengths of the parties), a building contract may set a level of liquidated damages which is *lower* than any loss which the employer is likely to suffer. Where this occurs, the provision is in effect a limitation clause, and it will be construed in the restrictive manner in which the courts habitually approach such contract terms. However, the traditional attitude of the courts towards liquidated damages provisions is based on the suspicion that they are set at an artifically *high* level, as a threat to induce timely completion by the contractor. This underlying judicial belief explains why such clauses are normally subjected to close scrutiny, construed strictly against the employer in case of ambiguity (see for example *Bramall & Ogden Ltd* v *Sheffield CC* (1983) 29 BLR 73), and struck down altogether if they fail to meet the following conditions.

(a) Requirements of a valid claim

In order to claim or deduct *liquidated* damages (as opposed to damages based on actual loss), the employer must of course be able to point to a specific provision in the contract. What is more, liquidated damages for delay must be expressed to run from a fixed or ascertainable date, which will be either the original completion date or one properly substituted under an extension of time clause. A court will not award liquidated damages for breach of the more vague obligation to complete 'within a reasonable time'.

This last point also serves to explain why an employer's claim to liquidated damages will be defeated where any part of a delay in completion can be attributed to the employer. It is well settled that this is so, both where the employer is guilty of a breach of contract (*Holme* v *Guppy* (1838) 3 M & W 387) and where the delay arises from things which the employer is entitled to do under the contract, such as to order extra work (*Dodd* v *Churton* [1897] 1 QB 562). Unless the contract enables time to be extended for such matters (and an ascertained completion date to be thereby preserved), the contractor's obligation will become that of completing within a reasonable time and the liquidated damages clause will fall.

Even where the above conditions are satisfied, a contractual provision will be struck down as unconscionable if, on a true construction, it is a 'penalty' rather than liquidated damages. The distinction between these two concepts is one of degree rather than of kind; a court faced with the problem of classification will usually refer to the guidelines laid down by Lord Dunedin in *Dunlop Pneumatic Tyre Co Ltd* v *New Garage & Motor Co Ltd* [1915] AC 79. Of these, the most relevant in building contract cases appear to be the following:

(i) Unlike a penalty, liquidated damages represent a genuine attempt at a pre-estimate of likely damage. Thus, if the sum stipulated is 'extravagant and unconscionable' compared with the greatest amount of loss which could be caused, it is a penalty.

(ii) Notwithstanding the previous point, the fact that an accurate pre-estimation of the likely damage is almost impossible to achieve (eg in respect of public buildings, housing associations and other non-profit-making ventures) does not prevent a stipulation from being classed as liquidated damages. In such cases the court is likely to look instead at the 'reasonableness' in general terms of what is stipulated. For example, a figure based on capital tied up at current interest rates will probably qualify as liquidated damages, as will an estimate of the cost of alternative accommodation.

(iii) The terms actually used in the contract (as in ICE 6 clause 47), are by no means conclusive, although they may be persuasive on the question.

(iv) The question whether a contract term is a penalty or liquidated damages is to be decided in the light of circumstances at the time of making the contract, not at the time of breach. Thus, the fact that a provision *might* have operated harshly and oppressively is enough to make it a penalty, even though as things have turned out it has not done so. It was on this ground that clauses which provided for liquidated damages on a reducing basis as parts of the work were taken over, but which contained a minimum figure below which there would be no reduction, were struck down in *Arnhold & Co Ltd* v *A-G of Hong Kong* (1989) 47 BLR 129 and *Philips Hong Kong Ltd* v *A-G of Hong Kong* (1990) 50 BLR 122.

In addition to the conditions described above, it is not unusual for a contract to specify certain procedures which must be followed in order for liquidated damages to be validly claimed. The two conditions most frequently found (eg under JCT 80 clause 24) are the need for the contract administrator to issue a certificate of non-completion, and a requirement that the employer give the contractor notice in writing of his intention to deduct liquidated damages. In *A Bell & Son (Paddington) Ltd* v *CBF Residential Care & Housing Association* (1989) 46 BLR 102 it was held that any extension of time which is subsequently granted would require these procedures to be carried out again. However, JCT 80 as amended now requires only a fresh certificate; the employer's written notice of intention to deduct, once given, remains in force until expressly revoked.

(b) Effects of a liquidated damages provision

Where all these conditions are fulfilled, the employer is entitled to claim or deduct liquidated damages at whatever rate is stated in the contract (usually in the Appendix). This right may be exercised where the sum stipulated is in excess of the employer's actual loss, or even where the employer has suffered no loss at all (*BFI Group of Companies Ltd* v *DCB Integration Systems Ltd* [1987] CILL 348).

Where a provision for liquidated damages is in operation, it is not open to the employer to waive the clause in order to claim unliquidated damages at common law. Thus, it has been held that a contractor guilty of delay may nonetheless be entitled to reimbursement under a 'fluctuations' clause for the increased costs of labour and materials; the liquidated damages provision in the contract represents the employer's sole remedy for the delay (*Peak Construction (Liverpool) Ltd* v *McKinney Foundations Ltd* (1970) 1 BLR 111). (It may be noted that this situation should not normally occur, since most fluctuations clauses are so expressed as to become inapplicable once the contractor is in delay.) Even more extremely, where an employer had inserted '£nil' in the Appendix as the rate for liquidated damages, it was held by the Court of Appeal in *Temloc Ltd* v *Errill Properties Ltd* (1987) 39 BLR 30 that he could recover nothing at all for a delay in completion. However, an Australian court has since refused to follow this decision (*Baese Pty Ltd* v *RA Bracken Building Pty Ltd* (1990) 6 B & CL 137).

This 'all-embracing' nature of liquidated damages is one reason why it may be dangerous to insert such a provision into a sub-contract. It is all too easy to fall into the trap of repeating the figure stated in the main contract; however, delay by a sub-contractor may well cause the main contractor losses in excess of what he in turn has to pay the employer, and a liquidated damages clause which used the main contract figure would effectively deprive the main contractor of compensation for those other losses (see *MJ Gleeson Construction plc* v *Taylor Woodrow Construction plc* (1989) 49 BLR 95).

It should be noted that, in the unreported case of *E Turner & Sons Ltd* v *Mathind Ltd* (1986), the Court of Appeal suggested that the presence of a provision for liquidated damages on completion of a whole project might not rule out the recovery of *unliquidated* damages for late completion of designated phases. However, the possibility of dual recovery in such a case was regarded as very doubtful in *Bruno Zornow (Builders) Ltd* v *Beechcroft Developments Ltd* (1989) 51 BLR 16.

Although an operative liquidated damages provision will bar any other claim for delay, one which is *ineffective* will leave it open for the employer to claim other remedies (*Rapid Building Group Ltd* v *Ealing Family Housing Association Ltd* (1985) 29 BLR 5). However, if it is due to the employer's own acts that the clause has become ineffective, it seems unlikely that he will be permitted to recover more as general damages than he would have received under the liquidated damages provision, since this would in effect permit the employer to profit from his own breach.

4 Extension of time

Most building contracts contain express provisions enabling the contract administrator to grant the contractor additional time in which to complete the contract works. The effect of taking such action is that the contractor is then under no liability to pay liquidated damages for delay during the period of extension. However, contrary to what many in the construction industry appear to believe, the grant of additional time gives the contractor no right to claim monetary compensation for his prolongation costs; if these are to be recovered, the contractor must satisfy whatever provisions the contract contains regarding 'loss/expense' claims.

Contract terms for extending time fulfil two rather different purposes. In the first place, where the timely completion of a project is delayed by some neutral cause (or, exceptionally, by some cause which is the contractor's fault—see *Surrey Heath BC* v *Lovell Construction Ltd* (1988) BLR 25), the contractor benefits by being relieved of his strict obligation to complete on time. Without such a provision, a contractor delayed by such matters as adverse weather, strikes, unavailability of essential materials, or inevitable delay in replacing a defaulting sub-contractor would have to pay liquidated damages for non-completion (*Percy Bilton Ltd* v *GLC* [1982] 2 All ER 623).

The second purpose of an extension of time clause is to protect the employer's position in respect of delays for which he is partly responsible. As already noted, an employer cannot recover liquidated damages for any delay which he has caused, whether by ordering extra work or by some breach of contract (*Holme* v *Guppy* (1838) 3 M & W 387; *Dodd* v *Churton* [1897] 1 QB 562). Hence, by granting an extension of time for any employer-caused delays, the employer preserves the right to claim liquidated damages for any other delays which are the fault of the contractor.

It is worth noting that an extension of time clause may not always be effective in cases of extreme delay. For example, where the probable delay resulting from some neutral event is so great that to continue with the contract would result in something radically different from what the parties intended, the contract may be discharged under the doctrine of frustration (*Metropolitan Water Board* v *Dick, Kerr & Co Ltd* [1918] AC 119). However, it is quite likely that, before that stage is reached, one or both of the parties will have been able to invoke an express power of determination under the contract (see Chapter 19).

(a) Grounds for extending time

(i) General A point which is sometimes overlooked is that extension of time provisions are concerned, not with all the events which may cause disruption to a project (even if that disruption proves costly to the contractor), but only with those events which delay or are likely to delay *completion*. It follows that where delayed work is not on the critical path, or where a contractor is actually ahead of schedule and can take up the slack, no extension of time should be granted at that stage (*Hounslow BC* v *Twickenham Garden Developments Ltd* [1971] Ch 253). Of course, the contract may make provision for the contract administrator to review the whole question of time after practical completion has been achieved (see JCT 80 clause 25.3.3; ICE 6 clause 47(5); GC/Works/1 clause 36(4)). If so, then hindsight may well lead the contract administrator to take a different view of the causes of delay, in which case a retrospective adjustment can be made.

The task of establishing the cause or causes of delay in completion of a construction project is a difficult and complex operation, since it almost always appears that a number of potential causes were in operation at the same time. Assuming that these embrace both 'qualifying' and 'non-qualifying' events, the question which arises is how a court should allocate responsibility. It has been said that the contract administrator should not seek to identify one of the causes as 'dominant' and to attribute the whole of the delay to that cause (*H Fairweather & Co Ltd* v *Wandsworth LBC* (1987) 39 BLR 106). On the other hand, it would seem logically incorrect to conclude that, if two concurrent causes have resulted in six weeks' delay, each of them has 'caused' three weeks of that delay. The correct answer, it is suggested, lies in the burden of proof. The contractor is *prima facie* liable for late completion unless he can positively prove that he was delayed by a qualifying cause. Hence, if a non-qualifying cause is operating concurrently, the contractor will fail unless the contribution made by that cause can be dismissed as '*de minimis*'.

(ii) Standard form contracts In laying down the grounds on which a contractor may be granted an extension of time for completion, two very different approaches are found in the main standard form building contracts. At one extreme (exemplified by JCT 80 clause

25), the contract will contain an exhaustive list of qualifying events, defining each of those events in more or less detail. At the other extreme (of which the JCT Agreement for Minor Building Works MW 80 clause 2.2 is typical), the contract merely refers to 'reasons beyond the control of the contractor'—such general phrases may then be qualified in some way. Of course, many contracts (such as ICE 6 clause 44(1)) adopt an approach which lies somewhere between these extreme points, by adding a general 'catch all' provision to a list of specified matters. However, almost all add the caveat that the contractor shall not be granted an extension of time for delays which he could have avoided by taking reasonable steps.

One very important point, which appears to have been overlooked by some draftsmen, is the ruling of the Court of Appeal in *Peak Construction (Liverpool) Ltd* v *McKinney Foundations Ltd* (1970) 1 BLR 111). It was there held that general words such as 'other unavoidable circumstances' do not cover delays which are caused by the employer. Hence, if an employer is responsible for a delay which is not covered by some specific provision, there will be no power to extend time and the employer's right to claim liquidated damages for the *contractor's* delay will be lost.

Turning to the grounds for extension of time which are laid down in standard form contracts, it has already been noted that JCT 80 clause 25 contains a long list of 'relevant events'. This includes a number of neutral causes of delay:

— *force majeure* (which has a restricted meaning in this clause, since many of the things which it would normally cover appear as separate items);
— exceptionally adverse weather conditions;
— loss or damage resulting from the 'Specified Perils' (certain matters set out in the insurance clauses, including fire, storm, flood etc);
— strike action;
— delay on the part of nominated sub-contractors or nominated suppliers:
— government action;
— unforeseeable inability to obtain essential labour or materials;
— work carried out by a local authority or statutory undertaker.

The clause also includes a number of matters which could be regarded as the employer's responsibility:

— compliance with various instructions of the contract administrator;

— opening up and testing work which is then found to be in accordance with the contract;
— late drawings, details, instructions etc from the contract administrator;
— work carried out by the employer or by his direct contractors;
— late supply of materials by the employer;
— failure by the employer to provide access to the site;
— delay by the employer in giving possession of the site (beyond any right to defer possession which may have been entered in the Appendix).

The list of delaying events for which a contractor under ICE 6 may qualify for an extension of time is rather shorter. It includes:
— variations;
— increased quantities;
— causes referred to specifically in other clauses (including late information from the engineer, adverse physical conditions or artificial obstructions, facilities for other direct contractors, a suspension order and failure by the employer to give possession of the site);
— exeptional adverse weather conditions;
— 'other special circumstances of any kind whatsoever which may occur'.

GC/Works/1 (which, notably, excludes weather conditions) is briefer still:
— the execution of modified or additional work;
— the act, neglect or default of the employer or the PM;— strike action;
— certain risks (such as sonic booms, radioactive contamination or war);
— unforeseeable ground conditions;
— any other unforeseeable conditions (other than weather conditions) beyond the control of the contractor or sub-contractors.

(b) Operation of extension of time provisions

(i) Procedures Most contracts lay down specific procedures to be followed by a contractor who seeks an extension of time. These naturally vary greatly in detail, but their general approach is to require the contractor to give notice to the contract administrator as soon as a potential cause of delay arises, and therafter to furnish the contract administrator with whatever information the latter may reasonably require to monitor the continuing effect on progress.

An important question is whether any failure by the contractor to adhere to these procedural requirements will destroy the right to an extension of time. This will only be so where the specific procedure is regarded as a condition precedent to the grant of an extension, and the courts have for the most part proved reluctant to interpret contracts in this way (see for example *London Borough of Merton* v *Stanley Hugh Leach* (1985) 32 BLR 55 on the construction of JCT 63). It seems likely that a contractor's request is a condition precedent under GC/Works/1 clause 36, but it is certainly not so under ICE 6 clause 44; under JCT 80 clause 25 it appears that a contractor who does not give notice at the right time will lose the right to any extension prior to practical completion, but that a subsequent review may retrospectively grant an extension. It has further been held that failure by a contract administrator to give a decision on a contractor's application for an extension within the 12 weeks stipulated by JCT 80 does not render a later decision invalid (*Temloc Ltd* v *Errill Properties Ltd* (1987) 39 BLR 30).

(ii) Retrospective extensions A question which has occasionally troubled the courts is whether it is possible to extend the time for completion *after* practical completion has already been achieved. Such an extension would not of course have the effect of giving the contractor a date to work towards (which led the Court of Appeal in *Miller* v *LCC* (1934) 50 TLR 479 to deny that a retrospective extension could be granted). However, it would have the important effect of reducing the period for which the contractor would be liable to pay liquidated damages, and the courts in more recent cases seem to assume that it is possible (see *Amalgamated Building Contractors Ltd* v *Waltham Holy Cross UDC* [1952] 2 All ER 452). In any event, post-completion adjustments to the completion date are expressly envisaged by JCT 80, ICE 6 and GC/Works/1.

Where a retrospective extension is granted in this way, it may result in a contractor having paid liquidated damages for too long a period. In such circumstances the damages must be repaid to the contractor (although GC/Works/1 does not expressly say so); however, what is not always clear is whether the repayment should carry interest. ICE 6 clause 47(5) provides specifically that interest is payable, but JCT 80 does not deal with the point. It has been held in Northern Ireland (in *Department of the Environment for Northern Ireland* v *Farrans Construction Ltd* (1981) 19 BLR 1) that the employer is liable for interest anyway, but the court's reasoning (that the subsequent extension means that the original deduction of liquidated damages was in breach of contract) appears highly dubious.

(iii) Extensions during an overrun period An important question which, though much debated, has not yet been settled by the courts, concerns the effect of a 'qualifying' event which occurs at a time when the contractor is already in culpable delay (and thus already liable to pay liquidated damages). Assuming that the contract does not deal specifically with the issue, what falls to be decided is whether it is possible to operate an extension of time clause at all and, if so, what extension of time should be awarded.

Although Denning LJ in *Amalgamated Building Contractors Ltd* v *Waltham Holy Cross UDC* [1952] 2 All ER 452 could see no problem in retrospectively awarding a 'net' extension of time (ie adjusting the completion date by whatever amount of time the latest delay has caused to the project), it is suggested that this may not be always be possible. Under contracts such as JCT 80 which refer, not to 'extending time', but rather to 'fixing a new completion date', it is difficult to see how a contract administrator's opinion as to when the works *should* have been completed can logically be affected by events taking place at some later date. If this argument is accepted, it leads to the conclusion that any extension of time must be 'gross' (ie it must cover the whole period until the new cause of delay ceases to operate), which would in turn wipe out the contractor's accrued liability to pay liquidated damages!

It is suggested that the best solution to this problem (which was effectively accepted by an Australian court in *SMK Cabinets* v *Hili Modern Electrics Pty* [1984] VR 391) is, where possible, to regard a contractual extension of time as inapplicable to events which occur during a period of overrun, but then to treat any employer-caused delay in that period as suspending the employer's right to liquidated damages, perhaps on the basis of an implied waiver.

Until recently, the only standard form of contract which even began to address this issue was IFC 84 which, although conferring a power to extend time for certain specified events causing delay during a period of overrun (in clause 2.3), did not indicate whether the extension so awarded should be net or gross. However, ICE 6 clause 47(6) has now expressly adopted the approach suggested in the previous paragraph, but only in respect of *some* qualifying causes. How a court would treat a case concerning one of the other qualifying events is a matter for speculation.

Chapter 17

Sub-contracts

The UK construction industry is characterised by the prevalence of sub-contracts. Main contractors are, to an ever-increasing extent, reducing their dependence on directly employed labour. In consequence, most if not all projects involve some degree of sub-contracting, and in many cases the whole of the actual construction work will be carried out in this way.

1 Reasons for the prevalence of sub-contracting

Sub-contracting as a phenomenon is not unique to the construction industry. Indeed, practice in the construction industry seems to be following in the footsteps of many other non-construction businesses. There are many influences on a business which encourage sub-contracting, and it is useful to distinguish those pressures which are general (affecting all businesses), and those which are specific (affecting the unique position of construction). The general pressures for sub-contracting include the following:

(*a*) non-wage costs of employment, such as training, pension rights, redundancy payments and sick pay;
(*b*) the increasingly diverse skill base required for the growth in complexity;
(*c*) the rising expectations of workers and a concomitant shift to free-lancing;
(*d*) the choice every firm faces between diversifying and contracting out;
(*e*) the perceived threat posed by trade unionisation of permanently employed labour;
(*f*) offsetting the risks associated with responsibility by transferring them;

(*g*) the need to employ specialists of proven reliability and repute.

The specific pressures for sub-contracting in construction combine in such a way as to make the idea of a general contractor (employing directly all of the labour) a thing of the past.

The factors which affect a contractor's decision to employ permanently or to sublet are numerous, but are rarely directly considered as specific choices over whether to sublet. In fact, contractors respond to the pressures on their businesses in the most appropriate way, and the increasing prevalence of sub-contracting is merely a symptom of these phenomena, each of which is dealt with below.

The nature of construction dictates that sites are geographically dispersed, meaning that some workers will be better placed for some sites than for others. Since an itinerant workforce is a thing of the past, the travelling time to the site from home will mean that employers are more inclined to employ local workers. Associated with the general pressure to specialise, mentioned above, is the fact that different types of project call for different types of skill. The pattern of required skill combinations is different for each project. Combined with the geographical constraints, it clearly makes little sense for contractors to keep permanently employed craftsmen in all of the necessary trades within each region of activity. This situation is tempered when the skill needed is specific to the firm itself, such as many middle-management roles, because in this instance the training overhead is high. Therefore, it is more economical to employ such specialists permanently, even if they are not fully utilised.

There was a time when a large proportion of the construction workforce was permanently employed, and the trade union movement had a great deal of influence and power. The 1972 building strike was a watershed for industrial relations in the UK construction scene. This fuelled the growing wish by employers to curb the power of the unions. Trade unions have little effect upon a temporary and intermittent workforce, so employers were well disposed to labour-only sub-contractors who supplied labour simply when it was needed. In this way, workers were no longer dependent upon large employers but became largely transient. At around the same time, the government introduced the Selective Employment Tax, which was designed to force employers to pay a tax on their payroll. Predictably, every time a tax is introduced, people adjust their *modus operandi* so that they can minimise their tax liability. The immediate consequence of SET was that employers sought alternatives to directly employed labour. Coupled with the bad feeling after the building strike, sub-contracting enjoyed a tremendous surge in popularity.

As a consequence of the increasing technical complexity identified earlier, there are ever-increasing numbers of specialist inputs into the building and construction processes. These take place because the more complex technologies need highly developed skills and expertise to apply them. Indeed, in many cases the increasing sophistication of the technology is a direct result of the increasing specialisation of those who deal with it. Clients and designers frequently have no choice but to harness these new technologies; even if they are not particularly well disposed towards the implementation of new technologies, economic exigencies often force them into it. In this way, the construction process, which is essentially an assembly process dominated by a site-based labour force, becomes dominated by the need to specify 'high-tech' equipment at an early stage. Particularly for developers, failure to do so will result in eventual difficulty in letting the facility. This new equipment frequently takes a long time to procure, longer than the design and fabrication cycle for the whole building. One of the best ways to cope with this is to specify the installer of the equipment, leaving the main contractor no choice in the matter, so that the installer can initiate the process of getting the equipment ready by the time it is needed for installation. This obviates delays on the building site whilst the equipment is procured. This practice is one of the main reasons for the existence of nominated sub-contracting in particular, and for the continuing growth of sub-contracting in general.

2 The legal basis of sub-contracting

As a general principle, while the benefit of a contract can be transferred by one person to another (subject to any restriction on assignment in the contract itself), the burden is not freely transferable. To pass a contractual burden to a substitute, in such a way that the original party ceases to be liable on the contract, requires a novation agreement entered into by all three participants (the original contracting parties and the substitute).

Not to be confused with novation is the doctrine of vicarious performance, under which a party may have his contractual duties carried out by someone else, while remaining legally responsible for the proper performance of those duties. This is what is meant by 'sub-contracting', and whether or not it is available depends on the contract concerned. The question is expressly dealt with by most modern standard form construction contracts, which provide widely differing answers. ICE 6 clause 4, for instance, prohibits the contractor from sub-contracting the whole of the works without the written consent of the employer, but otherwise permits the sub-contracting of any part of the works or their design. By contrast, GC/Works/1 provides in clause 62 that the contractor shall not sub-let any part of the contract without the prior consent of the PM.

An intermediate position is taken by the JCT family of contracts, of which JCT 80 clause 19.2 is typical. This clause requires a contractor who wishes to sublet any portion of the works to obtain the written consent of the contract administrator, but provides that such consent shall not be unreasonably withheld. Unauthorised sub-letting is a ground for the employer to determine the contractor's employment. The restriction on subletting is reinforced by clause 19.4, which requires any sub-contract to contain certain terms (governing the circumstances in which it will be determined and the ownership of materials supplied). These terms are designed to protect the employer's position *vis-à-vis* the sub-contractor, but it should be remembered that the obligation to include them is merely placed upon the contractor in the *main* contract. Should he fail to do so, the employer's only remedy lies against the contractor; he is left unprotected as against the sub-contractor.

Where there are no terms dealing explicitly with the issue of sub-contracting, the contract must be construed in the light of its subject matter and all the surrounding circumstances (*Davies* v *Collins* [1945] 1 All ER 247). Permission will readily be implied in the case of non-specialist work (*British Waggon Co* v *Lea* (1880) 5 QBD 149); conversely, an employer who had relied on the personal skill and experience of a small firm of designers and developers was held to be entitled to insist that a refurbishment contract was actually carried out by that firm (*Southway Group Ltd* v *Wolff* (1991) 57 BLR 33).

It is worth noting that the principles outlined above, which govern both 'labour and materials' and 'labour only' sub-contracts, have not been applied by the courts to those 'sub-contracts' which consist merely of the supply of materials. This is perhaps because it is common knowledge that contractors who undertake to supply materials (and who will be responsible for their quality) will almost always obtain those materials from suppliers—whatever the reason, it is clear that main contract clauses which place restrictions upon sub-contracting do not in themselves apply to 'supply only' sub-contracts.

Of course, a main contract may impose specific restrictions on the sources from which materials are to be obtained, in which case those restrictions must be observed. In this connection it has been held that a contractual identification of a particular supplier, followed by the phrase 'or other approved firm', does not entitle the contractor to choose a substitute of equivalent quality (*Leedsford Ltd* v *Bradford Corp* (1956) 24 BLR 49). The employer, through the contract administrator, has an absolute right to insist on the original selection and to refuse any alternative put forward.

3 Domestic sub-contractors

The term 'domestic sub-contractor' is used in the construction industry to describe those whose selection and appointment is entirely a matter for the main contractor (though subject, in some cases, to the employer's consent). This is 'vicarious performance' at its simplest, under which the main contractor may be placed in breach of his obligations to the employer by some default of the sub-contractor. Privity of contract means that the employer can take action *only* against the main contractor in this situation; if the sub-contractor is to be made answerable for his default, it will be by the main contractor and not directly by the employer. Conversely, the sub-contractor's right to be paid for his work lies exclusively against the main contractor, who must claim in turn from the employer.

Although the usual meaning of domestic sub-contractor is that given above, JCT 80 also uses the term to describe those selected under a procedure contained in clause 19.3. This permits the contract bills to specify that certain work, although priced by the main contractor, is to be carried out by a person selected by the contractor from a list annexed to the bills. The idea is that the list (which must contain at least three names) will represent the employer's choice. However, since the clause permits either party to add names to this list, subject to the consent of the other (which is not to be unreasonably withheld), the employer's control over selection may be easily reduced if not altogether defeated.

4 Sub-contract terms

Where domestic sub-contracts are concerned, the picture is very much that of a chain of contracts, up and down which rights and liabilities flow. This image shows how important it is to ensure that the terms of main contract and sub-contract are consistent, so that a main contractor does not incur some liability (to either the employer or the sub-contractor) which he is unable to pass on. For example, a sub-contract should always provide for its own automatic determination in circumstances where the main contract, or the contractor's employment under it, comes to an end. Similarly, any provision in the main contract for the employer or contract administrator to suspend the works should be mirrored by a provision in the sub-contract. If this is not so, then a suspension order may put the contractor in breach of the sub-contract (*Smith and Montgomery* v *Johnson Bros* [1954] 1 DLR 392).

The range of 'negotiated' standard form main contracts in the construction industry is by no means matched at sub-contract level. However, the BEC/FASS/CASEC form of sub-contract known as DOM/1, designed for use with JCT 80, has achieved widespread acceptance, as has the FCEC form of sub-contract for use with the ICE Conditions. Furthermore, JCT itself has published IN/SC, to be used where the main contract is IFC 84, and the Government form GC/Works/1 comes with a sub-contract GW/S.

These examples apart, the terms of domestic sub-contracts are the result either of individual negotiation or, commonly, of imposition by one side or the other (which could well subject them to control under the Unfair Contract Terms Act 1977). As a generalisation, it seems that firms who merely supply materials are more likely to have their own standard terms than those who also carry out work; the latter may well be employed on standard terms drafted by the larger main contractors. Such contracts have provoked fierce criticism from trade associations representing sub-contractors, as being one-sided to the point of unfairness. Common complaints relate to such matters as 'pay when paid' clauses, wide-ranging provisions under which the contractor may deduct from monies due in respect of cross-claims, requirements that all work be done to the main contractor's satisfaction, and the absence of any guarantee that the sub-contractor's work will be allowed to proceed in a regular and ordered manner.

In the absence of a formally drafted and signed sub-contract (and domestic sub-contracts are frequently entered into on the most informal basis), parties sometimes attempt to incorporate terms by reference to other documents, such as a standard form of sub-contract with which they are familiar (see *Modern Building (Wales) Ltd* v *Limmer & Trinidad Co Ltd* [1975] 1 WLR 1281). More dangerously, the reference may be to the *main* contract (*Brightside Kilpatrick Engineering Services* v *Mitchell Construction Ltd* (1973) 1 BLR 62). If this practice (which is not to be recommended) is adopted, careful wording is necessary to ensure that all the required terms and only those terms are caught. For example, it has been held that a mere undertaking by a sub-contractor to carry out the work in accordance with the terms of the main contract is not enough to incorporate into the sub-contract either an arbitration clause (*Goodwins, Jardine & Co* v *Brand* (1905) 7 F (Ct of Sess) 995; cf *Aughton Ltd* v *MF Kent Services Ltd* (1991) 57 BLR 2) or a power to remove a sub-contractor on grounds of delay (*Chandler Bros Ltd* v *Boswell* [1936] 3 All ER 179).

In some instances it is impossible, even with the aid of incorporation, to identify the express terms of a sub-contract in any detail. In such cases much will depend on what terms a court is prepared to imply. Some terms are readily implied, such as an undertaking by the main contractor that he will not cause the main contract to be determined and thus deprive the sub-contractor of the benefits of the sub-contract (*ER Dyer Ltd* v *Simon Build/Peter Lind Partnership* (1982) 23 BLR 23). Indeed, this is an area where the courts, especially Official Referees, have proved willing to imply quite detailed terms (eg as to interim payments) which will meet the normal expectations of the construction industry (see *DR Bradley (Cable Jointing) Ltd* v *Jefco Mechanical Services Ltd* (1988) 6-CLD-07-19).

However, it must always be borne in mind that there can be no implication of a term where there is an express term dealing with the matter in question. This is of particular importance as regards the timing of sub-contract works, a matter on which sub-contracts are often rather vague. For example, where a sub-contract stipulated that the work was to be carried out 'at such time or times as the contractor shall direct or require', it was held by the Court of Appeal that there could be no implied term that the main contractors would make sufficient work available to the sub-contractors to enable them to work in an efficient and economic manner (*Martin Grant & Co Ltd* v *Sir Lindsay Parkinson & Co Ltd* (1984) 29 BLR 31).

5 Defaults of domestic sub-contractors

As has already been emphasised in this chapter, the view which the law takes of domestic sub-contracts is that these are entered into by the main contractor for his own benefit, in order to secure the performance of his own contractual obligations to the employer. It follows that any failure of performance by the sub-contractor will render him liable for breach of contract to the main contractor; the damages payable will reflect both the main contractor's own losses (such as disruption costs or compensation which he has to pay to other sub-contractors) and also the amount which the contractor in turn has to pay to the employer.

In this connection one must be careful to identify the precise nature of the main contractor's obligations. It is clear, for example, that his duty in respect of materials used amounts to a strict guarantee of their quality, and that it is not enough to use reasonable care and skill in selecting them from a supplier (*Lee* v *West* [1989] EGCS 160). Furthermore, such liability will be imposed even where the defect in question springs from a faulty *design* by a supplier. However, where there is a 'design fault' in *work* carried out by a domestic sub-contractor, the main contractor cannot be held responsible unless he has actually undertaken to design, something which will not normally be the case under a traditional procurement method.

As well as incurring liability for the defaults of a domestic sub-contractor, a main contractor will in general have no claim against the employer for either time or money arising out of such defaults. However, regard must always be had to the terms of the particular contract. In this respect it is worth noting that clause 25.4.10 of JCT 80 makes provision for the contractor to be granted an extension of time on the grounds of inability for reasons beyond his control and which he could not reasonably have foreseen at the outset to secure necessary labour or materials. Such inability could of course very easily result from sub-contractor default. Furthermore, the House of Lords in *Scott Lithgow Ltd* v *Secretary of State for Defence* 1989 SLT 236 construed the phrase 'matters beyond the contractor's control', in a loss/expense clause in a shipbuilding contract, so as to include latent defects in materials obtained for use in the work. The supplier in that case was in fact nominated, but the way in which the House of Lords expressed its decision would appear equally applicable to 'domestic' cases.

A final point is that, while a domestic sub-contractor will not normally incur any direct contractual liability to the employer (since the possibilities for construing a collateral contract between them are much more limited than in the case of nominated sub-contractors), there are suggestions of possible liability in the tort of negligence. This, it appears, would occur where defects in the sub-contractor's work, such as a negligently installed boiler or electrical wiring, cause physical damage to other parts of the structure (*Murphy* v *Brentwood DC* [1990] 2 All ER 908; see Chapter 11).

6 Payment of sub-contractors

A sub-contractor's right to be paid is primarily a matter for the sub-contract so that, even if a sub-contract is prohibited by the terms of the main contract, the contractor must pay the sub-contractor for work done under it. In addition, there may very occasionally be an opportunity for the sub-contractor to pursue a claim directly against the employer.

(a) Payment by the main contractor

This depends on the terms of the sub-contract, which may well include detailed provisions governing interim valuations, the main contractor's rights of set off and so on. In addition, many domestic sub-contracts which have been drafted by main contractors (though not as yet any of the UK standard forms) include a 'pay when paid' clause, which seeks to make the main contractor's payment obligation dependent upon having actually received the money from the employer. Clauses of this type have in other jurisdictions been interpreted quite literally, so that a main contractor may avoid paying a sub-contractor even where the reason why the main contractor has not been paid is because the employer is exercising a right of set off in respect of his own defective work (*Schindler Lifts (Hong Kong) Ltd* v *Shui On Construction Co Ltd* (1984) 29 BLR 95; *Nin Hing Electronic Engineering Ltd* v *Aoki Corporation* (1987) 40 BLR 107; *Brightside Mechanical & Electrical Services Group Ltd* v *Hyundai Engineering & Construction Co Ltd* (1988) 41 BLR 110).

Such an interpretation seems tantamount to allowing the main contractor to benefit from his own breach of contract, a result which the law normally strives to avoid. It has accordingly been suggested by some commentators that a clause of this nature, if imposed as part of a main contractor's standard terms, might be struck down under s 3 of the Unfair Contract Terms Act 1977.

However, the most that can be said at present is that the English courts seem disposed to interpret 'pay when paid' clauses in a restrictive manner, for example by holding that they do not continue to govern a sub-contractor's entitlement after the contracts have been determined (*Rushpass Ltd* v *G Percy Trentham Ltd* (1991, unreported)).

It should be appreciated that, in addition to protecting the main contractor's cash flow, a 'pay when paid' clause may have the effect of making the sub-contractor bear the risk of the employer becoming insolvent. In the United States it has been held that, since this is not what these clauses are designed to achieve, they may be interpreted as not having such an effect (*Thomas J Dyer Co* v *Bishop International Engineering Co* 303 F 2d 655 (1962)). However, it seems unlikely that an English court would be prepared to interpret a clear contract term in so robust a manner.

(b) Payment by the employer

As mentioned above, it is possible, though highly unusual, for an employer to become directly responsible for paying a domestic sub-contractor. Such liability will not arise merely because the employer permits the main contractor to sublet (indeed, even the *nomination* of a sub-contractor carries no such implication). If any liability is to be incurred, it will be on the basis of some direct dealing between employer and sub-contractor, in which the employer (perhaps to induce sub-contractors to keep working when the main contractor is close to insolvency) undertakes to see that they will be paid. Even where such negotiations have taken place, the courts are slow to infer a binding promise of payment (*Victorian Railway Commissioners* v *James L Williams Pty Ltd* (1969) 44 ALJR 32). Furthermore, where the negotiations are conducted by a contract administrator on the employer's behalf, that person's implied authority does not usually extend to giving any commitment binding upon the employer (*Vigers Sons & Co Ltd* v *Swindell* [1939] 3 All ER 590).

7 Retention of title by sub-contractors and suppliers

Building contracts often make provision for the value of materials delivered to the site but not yet fixed to be included in interim certificates. Where this is done, it is usual for the contract to state further that property in those materials shall pass to the employer as soon as the contractor is paid what is due on the relevant certificate.

A provision of this kind can cause problems where the materials in question have been supplied by a sub-contractor, whose terms of supply include a 'retention of title' clause. The House of Lords has recently confirmed the legal effectiveness of such clauses, apparently even where they reserve the seller's title to goods until the whole balance of account between seller and buyer has been settled (*Armour* v *Thyssen Edelstahlwerke AG* [1990] 3 All ER 481). The question which can arise is therefore: If the employer duly pays the main contractor, but the main contractor fails to pay the sub-contractor in his turn, whose claims to the materials will prevail?

Before seeking to answer this question, it may be noted that the problem should not arise in respect of nominated sub-contractors; here the employer is likely to be in a position to control the sub-contract terms, and can accordingly ensure that they do not provide for reservation of title. However, the employer's situation is much more difficult where *domestic* sub-contracts are concerned. The employer may attempt to prescribe in the main contract the terms on which these can be made (as is done for example in clause 19.4 of JCT 80) but, if the main contractor enters into a sub-contract in contravention of such a provision, what is the remedy? Clearly the main contractor is liable to the employer, but can the sub-contractor be bound by provisions in a contract to which he is not party?

The answer to this last question was given in *Dawber Williamson Roofing Ltd* v *Humberside CC* (1979) 14 BLR 70 where a main contractor, who had been paid for materials delivered to the site by a sub-contractor, went into liquidation without paying the sub-contractor. It was held that a retention of title clause in the sub-contract prevailed over the title-passing provisions of the main contract, so that the employer's refusal to release the materials to the sub-contractor was an act of conversion.

Although this decision appears to give primacy to retention of title provisions, it should be noted that a *pure* supply of materials (ie with no labour involved) falls within the Sale of Goods Act 1979. As a result, the main contractor will be a 'buyer in possession' of the materials and, if his purported transfer of ownership to the employer constitutes a 'disposition' of those materials, the employer will acquire title under s 25 of the Act (*Archivent Sales and Developments Ltd* v *Strathclyde Regional Council* (1984) 27 BLR 98). As to whether there is indeed a disposition by the main contractor to the employer, it appears that this will be so only where the main contract contains express provisions dealing with the transfer of ownership on the basis of interim payments. Without such provisions, the mere fact that payments are made will not attract the operation of s 25 (*W Hanson (Harrow) Ltd* v *Rapid Civil Engineering Ltd and Usborne Developments Ltd* (1987) 38 BLR 106).

Chapter 18

Nomination of Sub-contractors and Suppliers

Sub-contracting, in the context of the previous chapter, may have appeared to be something which main contractors enter into entirely at their own choice in order to secure the vicarious performance of their obligations. However, there is another aspect of sub-contracting which has become dominant in modern times, due largely to the enormous increase in the use of specialised techniques and materials in construction. This is the practice of 'nomination', whereby the employer selects specialists who then contract, not with the employer directly, but instead with the main contractor.

Nomination enables the employer to exercise control over both the quality of the relevant work and also its cost (since it is the employer who decides which sub-contractor's tender the main contractor is to accept). It can also help to reduce the overall time required for a project, by enabling tenders for items with a long lead time to be obtained and evaluated from specialist suppliers before the main contract is let, and perhaps even for off-site work to begin at that stage under cover of a letter of intent.

Notwithstanding its attractions to employers, the system of nominating sub-contractors and suppliers of materials has certain drawbacks. Both contract draftsmen and judges have shown some reluctance to maintain the basic position, that of a main contractor being fully responsible for the defaults of a sub-contractor, in circumstances where the choice of that sub-contractor is entirely the employer's. In consequence there has been a tendency, in both the drafting and the interpretation of contracts, to shift at least part of the risk of nominated sub-contractor default on to the employer. This has in turn resulted in an extremely complex legal situation, as employers unable to take action against main contractors have sought direct warranties from the sub-contractors themselves. The overall complexity is further increased because many specialist sub-contractors undertake design obligations beyond those contained in the main contract; in respect of such obligations they can hardly be described as 'sub-contractors' at all.

Before considering the web of legal responsibilities which nomination creates, a brief account may be given of the procedures by which it is effected under some of the standard forms of contract. It is worth noting in each case that the contractual consequences which flow from nomination are expressed to apply only where the prescribed procedure has been used. If it has not, then the mere fact that the contractor is forced by other means into obtaining labour or materials from a particular source will not constitute 'nomination'. It is difficult if not impossible to predict how a court would define the rights and duties of the parties in a case of 'nomination by another name'.

1 Nomination procedures

(a) Nominated sub-contractors under JCT 80

The nomination of sub-contractors under JCT 80 is governed by clause 35. As originally drafted, this clause provided two alternative procedures, and two sets of prescribed documents, for nomination. However, following sustained criticism of these procedures as unnecessarily complex and cumbersome, they were replaced by a single procedure, which was introduced in March 1991 by Amendment 10.

Use of the prescribed procedure is compulsory for any true 'nomination' under JCT 80, which will occur wherever the contract bills either name a sub-contractor or contain a prime cost sum. It will also apply where an instruction as to the expenditure of a provisional sum is used to name a sub-contractor; in respect of certain variations; and finally where the contractor and the contract administrator agree.

Although it is fundamental to the idea of nomination that the main contractor has neither the right nor any obligation to carry out the work himself, a limited exception to this principle is contained in clause 35.2. This permits the contractor to tender for work which has been designated as nominated sub-contract work, provided that it is work of a kind which he carries out in the ordinary course of business and that the Appendix indicates that the contract administrator will be prepared to receive such a tender. The employer in these circumstances is under no obligation to accept the main contractor's tender, even if it is the lowest; if he does accept it, the contractor may not then sublet the work to a domestic sub-contractor without the contract administrator's consent.

The 1991 procedure for nomination under JCT 80 requires the contract administrator to invite tenders from potential sub-contractors on form NSC/T Part I. This document is accompanied by the standard form of employer/nominated sub-contractor agreement NSC/W, which the sub-contractor executes and returns with his completed tender (on form NSC/T Part 2). When the employer has decided that a particular tender is to be accepted, he too executes NSC/W; the contract administrator thereupon issues a nomination instruction to the contractor (on form NSC/N), sending a copy to the sub-contractor. At this point the sub-contractor is also sent a copy of the Appendix to the main contract (which may not even have been let when sub-contract tenders were first invited).

Having received these documents, it is then up to the contractor and sub-contractor (subject to a right of reasonable objection when each discovers the other's identity) to complete NSC/T Part 3, entitled 'Particular Conditions'; this is in effect the Appendix to the sub-contract. Once these have been agreed, the contractor and sub-contractor execute the Articles of Nominated Sub-Contract Agreement (NSC/A). This creates a sub-contract and incorporates by reference a document NSC/C, a set of standard form conditions based on the earlier form of sub-contract NSC/4.

It seems clear that the prescribed procedure may run into problems at the point when the contractor and sub-contractor are seeking to agree the particular conditions of their sub-contract, for example because the main contract when let differs from what the sub-contractor was led to expect at tender stage. If this happens, the contract administrator may seek, by issuing instructions, to remove the obstacles to agreement. Should it prove impossible to do so, there must be either a renomination or an instruction omitting the work from the contract altogether. Whichever path is chosen by the contract administrator, any delay to the project may entitle the contractor to an extension of time for completion. However, only an instruction to omit the work will carry with it also a right to claim compensation for loss/expense.

(b) *Nominated suppliers under JCT 80*

A person is not to be regarded as a 'nominated supplier' under clause 36 of JCT 80 merely because the intended source of materials is expressly identified, nor because there is only one source of supply for a specified item. Clause 36 is expressed to apply only where the goods or materials to be supplied are the subject of a prime cost sum. This may be contained in the original bills, it may arise from the conversion of a provisional sum in the original bills, or it may be included in a contract administrator's instruction requiring a variation.

Where there is a nomination within the above definition, clause 36.4 provides that the contract administrator cannot force the contractor to deal with a nominated supplier unless the supply contract contains certain terms. These terms are largely concerned to ensure that any liability which the contractor incurs in respect of defective materials or delay can be passed on to the supplier. They also make provision for title in the materials supplied to pass to the contractor on delivery, and allow the contractor a discount of five per cent for prompt payment. It should be noted that this discount represents the contractor's sole 'profit' on nominated suppliers, since clause 36.3 makes it clear that the employer is to pay the contractor only the *net cost* of obtaining the materials.

There is no compulsory form of contract for use by nominated suppliers under JCT 80. However, the Joint Contracts Tribunal publishes a form of tender (TNS/1) for nominated suppliers, the use of which is strongly recommended. This document contains all the terms specified in clause 36.4, and also provides an optional warranty agreement TNS/2. When TNS/2 is used, the supplier guarantees to the employer that design, selection of materials and satisfaction of performance specifications have been and will be carried out with care and skill. The supplier also undertakes to indemnify the employer if any default on his part entitles the contractor to an extension of time or to claim loss/expense under the main contract.

(c) *Nomination under ICE 6*

Clauses 58 and 59 provide in effect that, in respect of 'Provisional Sums' or 'Prime Cost Items', the engineer may either nominate a sub-contractor to supply the work and/or materials or may instruct the contractor to supply it himself. In the case of a Prime Cost item, the latter option is subject to the contractor's agreement.

In the event of nomination by the engineer, the contractor has a right of objection on any reasonable grounds and, in addition, clause 59(1) lists a number of terms which the contractor can insist on having in the sub-contract. These terms are designed to ensure that the contractor is indemnified for any liability incurred because of the acts or defaults of the sub-contractor. They also require the sub-contractor to give security for due performance, and seek to provide for determination of the sub-contract if the contractor is expelled from the site under clause 63.

If the contractor exercises his right of objection to a particular nomination, clause 59(2) gives the engineer a wide range of powers to deal with the situation. The engineer may renominate, vary or omit the works in question, instruct the contractor to quote for having the work carried out by a domestic sub-contractor or invite the contractor to execute the work himself.

(d) Nomination under GC/Works/1

Clause 63(1) reserves the title of 'nominated' sub-contractor or supplier for those persons from whom the contractor is required, either in the contract itself or in any subsequent instruction, to obtain work or materials designated as 'Prime Cost' or 'PC' items. The contractor may not supply such items himself, nor place orders for them, without the written consent of the PM; however, the employer may choose to pay for such items directly, in which case the contractor is nonetheless entitled to his profit margin.

As with other forms of contract, the contractor may object on reasonable grounds to any nomination, except where the identity of the nominee was contained in the invitation to tender. However, it is worth noting that the 'reasonableness' of any such objection is a matter for the employer to decide!

2 Responsibility for workmanship, materials and design

(a) The general position

Apart from any express terms in a building contract, the contractor is normally under an implied obligation to build in a workmanlike manner, with materials which are of good quality and fit for their intended purpose. The 'fitness for purpose' obligation depends upon evidence that the employer has relied on the skill and judgment of the contractor, and will accordingly not be implied where a sub-contractor or supplier is nominated. However, exclusion of the implied warranty as to *quality* of materials requires more than the mere fact of nomination (*Young & Marten Ltd* v *McManus Childs Ltd* [1969] 1 AC 454). That warranty will only be excluded by special circumstances, such as the nomination of a supplier who excludes or restricts his own liability, and to whose nomination the contractor has no right of objection (*Gloucestershire CC* v *Richardson* [1969] 1 AC 480).

A main contractor's responsibility for the quality of materials will effectively render him liable for any which prove faulty, irrespective whether this arises from manufacturing or design defects on the part of a nominated *supplier*. By contrast, a main contractor under a traditional procurement system cannot be held liable for design errors by a nominated *sub-contractor*, since design of the contract works is not part of his own contractual responsibility.

(b) Responsibility under standard form contracts

The position under JCT 80 and its supporting documentation largely follows the common law position described above. Clause 35.21 of the main contract confirms the contractor's basic responsibility in respect of defective workmanship or materials supplied by a nominated sub-contractor. However, it goes on to provide that, whether or not the sub-contractor has given a direct warranty to the employer as to design, selection of materials and satisfaction of performance specifications (as he should have done under NSC/W), the main contractor is not liable to the employer for anything which that warranty would cover.

Although it thus appears that design faults in nominated sub-contract work are a risk for the employer, the limited extent of that risk should be noted. If losses (eg through disruption) are caused directly to the contractor, the sole remedy is against the sub-contractor—the employer is under no obligation to compensate for loss/expense suffered in this way.

In relation to nominated suppliers, it has already been noted that the contractor can refuse a nomination unless the supply contract contains specified terms for his protection. Clause 36.5 of JCT 80 further provides that, if any other terms in that contract exclude or restrict the supplier's liability, the contractor can seek the written approval of the contract administrator, following which his own liability to the employer will be similarly excluded or restricted. Once again, however, it should be appreciated that this will not render the employer liable to compensate the contractor for any losses suffered.

The position under ICE 6 is far more straightforward than that under JCT 80. Clause 58(3) provides that if any Provisional Sum or Prime Cost Item includes an element of design, this requirement must be expressly stated in both the contract and nominated sub-contract, and the contractor's liability is limited by what is so stated. Subject to this, the contractor is fully responsible for whatever is done by a nominated sub-contractor (clause 59(3)).

GC/Works/1 does not appear to deal specifically with this problem at all. However, the inference from clauses 62 and 63 is clearly that the main contractor is entirely responsible for all work done by sub-contractors, whether domestic or nominated.

3 Responsibility for delay

The most drastic possible effect of delay under JCT 80 is that of leading to determination of the contractor's employment. Clause 28.1 (amended to give effect to the Court of Appeal's ruling in *John Jarvis* v *Rockdale Housing Association Ltd* (1986) 36 BLR 48) entitles the contractor to take this step if the carrying out of the contract works is suspended by the contract administrator for whatever period is stated in the Appendix (usually one month) for one of a number of specified reasons. In the present context, what is important is that these reasons include the defaults of a nominated (though not a domestic) sub-contractor.

Apart from the possibility of determination, a contractor is entitled under JCT 80 clause 25.4.7 to an extension of time in respect of 'delay on the part of nominated sub-contractors or nominated suppliers which the contractor has taken all practicable steps to avoid or reduce'. In such circumstances the employer will be deprived of his claim for liquidated damages for the period of extension, and must claim the equivalent amount directly from the nominated sub-contractor (under NSC/W) or supplier (*if* there is a direct warranty in place). However, the employer is under no obligation to compensate the contractor for financial losses arising out of disruption, since sub-contractor delay is not a qualifying matter under clause 26.2.

It should be noted that the wording used in clause 25 was restrictively interpreted by the House of Lords in *Westminster CC* v *Jarvis & Sons Ltd* [1970] 1 All ER 942. It was there held that 'delay on the part of' (which also appeared in JCT 63) does not cover all delays which are *caused* by a nominated sub-contractor or supplier, but only those resulting from their failure to complete their own work on time. Thus, for example, where a certificate of practical completion has been issued in respect of nominated sub-contract work, defects subsequently discovered will not entitle the main contractor to an extension of time, however great the delay which they cause to the project.

Once again, the complexities of JCT 80 do not appear to affect other forms of contract. True, the phrase 'other special circumstances of any kind whatsoever which may occur', which appears in clause 44 of ICE 6 as a ground for an extension of time, might be thought sufficient to encompass delays caused by nominated sub-contractors. Indeed, such a view might also gain some support from the decision of the House of Lords in *Scott Lithgow Ltd* v *Secretary of State for Defence* 1989 SLT 236. However, to allow the contractor an extension on this ground would seem inconsistent with the clear statement in clause 59(3) of his total responsibility for a nominated sub-contractor's work.

As for GC/Works/1, the position is even clearer. Extensions of time are to be granted under clause 36 only where the 'other circumstances' are 'outside the control of the contractor or any of his sub-contractors'.

4 Repudiation by nominated sub-contractors

Although the allocation of responsibility for defective work and delay may be somewhat complex, it does not cause too many serious practical problems so long as the defaulting sub-contractor remains solvent. The employer will either make a direct claim on the basis of a collateral agreement, or proceed against the main contractor who will pass on liability to the sub-contractor. However, where a sub-contractor becomes insolvent before completing the work, the allocation of risk between employer and main contractor becomes crucially important.

This problem was considered in a series of important decisions on the JCT 63 form of contract, in which the House of Lords and Court of Appeal came to the following conclusions:

(i) Where the main contract provides that certain work is to be executed by a nominated sub-contractor, the main contractor has neither the right nor the obligation to carry out that work. Hence, if the nominated sub-contractor 'drops out' (ie repudiates the sub-contract), it is the employer's responsibility to nominate a substitute (*North West Regional Hospital Board* v *TA Bickerton & Son Ltd* [1970] 1 All ER 1039).

(ii) The employer's responsibility extends only to renominating within a reasonable time. Any delay which *inevitably* results from the sub-contractor's repudiation is a risk which the contractor must bear, so that he can claim neither an extension of time nor compensation for disruption (*Percy Bilton Ltd* v *GLC* [1982] 2 All ER 623).

(iii) If the effects of delay are such that the proposed substitute sub-contractor cannot undertake to complete his work by the main contract completion date, the contractor is entitled to refuse the nomination (*Fairclough Building Ltd* v *Rhuddlan BC* (1985) 30 BLR 26). If this happens, then the contract administrator appears to have no option but to omit the work from the contract (something which must be treated as a variation).

(iv) If the original sub-contractor has been paid for work which is defective, the overpayment is recoverable by the employer from the main contractor. However, the employer must then pay the full cost of renomination, including whatever remedial work is necessary (*Fairclough Building Ltd* v *Rhuddlan BC* (1985) 30 BLR 26).

It is of course dangerous to attempt to derive principles of general application from judicial decisions based on a particular form of contract, but it is thought that these propositions will be applied by the courts where they are not inconsistent with the express terms of the contract before them. However, an unresolved issue is whether they will govern cases arising under the procedure laid down in JCT 80 clause 19.3, whereby the contractor selects a sub-contractor from a list in the contract bills. Here the contract states that the work in question must be carried out by a person named in that list, which might suggest a 'renaming' obligation on the employer if the original selection drops out. On the other hand, clause 19.3 specifically states that the person selected shall be a domestic sub-contractor. It is unfortunately very difficult to predict the likely answer of a court to this important practical problem.

The case law summarised above shows clearly that, where a nominated sub-contract is determined and the sub-contractor is insolvent, most of the resulting financial damage will fall upon the employer. It is for this reason that many building contracts prohibit the main contractor from terminating a nominated sub-contract without first obtaining the consent of the contract administrator.

As to the way in which the current versions of the major standard form contracts deal with the insolvency of a nominated sub-contractor, the legal position outlined above is closely followed by the express terms of JCT 80. However, this is subject to the qualification that, where a nominated sub-contractor has received final payment for his work but then fails to remedy defects which appear in it, it is the main contractor who bears the cost of the necessary remedial work.

The complexities of JCT 80 are largely avoided by both ICE 6 and GC/Works/1 although, interestingly, the allocation of risk between employer and main contractor is much the same. Both these contracts provide that, where a nominated sub-contractor drops out, the main contractor is responsible for completing the works (including whatever remedial work may be necessary). The main contractor must then pursue the defaulting sub-contractor for compensation *but*, if he fails to recover this (because the sub-contractor is insolvent), the employer is to reimburse the contractor for the shortfall.

5 Direct liability to the employer

It is clear from what has been said above that a main contractor's liability to the employer for the defaults of a nominated sub-contractor or supplier will often be limited. In such circumstances it is important to know whether the employer can seek a direct remedy and, as has been seen, it is not uncommon for an express collateral agreement to be entered into. As to these agreements, all that need be said is that it is important to ensure that they cover all the potential defaults in respect of which the employer might otherwise be left unprotected.

Even without a specific agreement, the courts have on occasion inferred a collateral contract between an employer and a nominated supplier, where the supplier has made specific claims about the product in order to secure nomination (eg *Shanklin Pier Co Ltd* v *Detel Products Ltd* [1951] 2 KB 854). It is even possible that liability might be imposed on this basis in respect of extravagant claims contained in advertising literature, where these are relied on in selecting materials (*GLC* v *Ryarsh Brick Co Ltd* [1985] CILL 200).

The employer's 'reliance' on a nominated sub-contractor was held in the notorious case of *Junior Books Ltd* v *Veitchi Co Ltd* [1983] 1 AC 520 to impose on the sub-contractor a duty of care *in tort* as to the execution of the works. However, notwithstanding certain remarks of the House of Lords in *Murphy* v *Brentwood DC* [1990] 2 All ER 908, it appears highly unlikely that this decision will be followed (see, for instance, *Simaan General Contracting Co* v

Pilkington Glass Ltd (No 2) [1988] 1 All ER 791; *Nitrigin Eireann Teoranta* v *Inco Alloys Ltd* [1992] 1 All ER 854).

6 Payment of nominated sub-contractors

In general, the fact of nomination makes no difference to the basic principle that a sub-contractor's payment rights are contained in the sub-contract and are therefore exercisable only against the main contractor. Indeed, attempts by sub-contractors to enforce such claims (eg by refusing to continue work until they are met), and the counter-arguments of main contractors seeking to set off cross-claims, represent a sizeable proportion of all building contract litigation. These matters are dealt with in Chapters 13 and 19.

A nominated sub-contractor's entitlement to be paid is frequently linked to certification by the architect under the main contract (as is the position in NSC/C, the sub-contract conditions used under JCT 80). However, such a provision does not govern the sub-contractor's rights following determination of the contracts—he will then be entitled to claim for work done, even though no certificates have been issued (*Scobie & McIntosh Ltd* v *Clayton Bowmore Ltd* (1990) 49 BLR 119).

A further aspect of the payment of nominated sub-contractors which is closely linked to main contract provisions is that of the retention. Since a retention fund is, it appears, held by the employer on trust, the question which arises is whether the separate identification of 'Nominated Sub-contract retention' (as is done under JCT 80, for example) means that there are two or more separate trusts. If so, then it would mean that the employer could not have recourse to the nominated sub-contractor's retention fund in order to satisfy his claims against the main contractor.

The 'separate trusts' argument was accepted in *Re Arthur Sanders Ltd* (1981) 17 BLR 125, but convincingly criticised in the Hong Kong case of *Hsin Chong Construction Co Ltd* v *Yaton Realty Co Ltd* (1986) 40 BLR 119, on the ground that *all* retention money has to be paid to the main contractor (who may indeed have his own right of recourse against it). In consequence, it appears that the sub-contractor has no enforceable right to this money until it reaches the main contractor.

An employer is not liable to pay a sub-contractor directly merely because he has selected him, nor because he has accepted the benefit of his work (*Hampton* v *Glamorgan CC* [1917] AC 13). Nor, without clear evidence of authorisation, will the employer be bound by assurances of payment given by the architect to nominated sub-contractors (*Vigers Sons & Co Ltd* v *Swindell* [1939] 3 All ER 590). However, there is nothing to prevent an employer from expressly agreeing with a nominated sub-contractor that he will pay directly if the main contractor fails to do so, and both JCT 80 (clause 35.13) and ICE 6 (clause 59(7)) enable this to be done.

The procedure under each of these clauses (and most others like them) is that, if the contractor cannot produce evidence that payments due to nominated sub-contractors have been duly discharged, the employer may deduct the relevant amounts from future sums due to the main contractor and instead pay them directly to the sub-contractors. It is clear therefore that the employer is not risking his own money under this provision, but rather diverting what would otherwise be paid to the main contractor. Nor do these clauses in themselves *require* the employer to pay directly—an obligation to this effect will only arise out of a direct agreement between employer and sub-contractor (such as is contained in NSC/W under JCT 80).

It is important to note that 'direct payment' provisions are of somewhat doubtful effectiveness in precisely the situation in which they are most useful, namely, when the main contractor becomes insolvent. This is because of fears that they offend against the general principle of insolvency law, that all unsecured creditors are to be treated on an equal footing. It is argued, on the basis of this principle, that for an employer to pay a sub-contractor directly and in full would put that sub-contractor in an unfairly preferential position as against the main contractor's other creditors, who will receive at best only a part of what they are owed.

Whether this argument invalidates direct payment clauses is not at all clear, in the current state of the law. Certainly an employer who pays a sub-contractor directly *without* an express provision in the main contract will be liable to pay the sum again to the liquidator (*Re Holt, ex p Gray* (1888) 58 LJQB 5). On the other hand, it has twice been held that a direct payment clause makes all the difference—the contract administrator, in refusing to certify in the contractor's favour, is not dealing with the contractor's property and thus not infringing insolvency principles (*Re Wilkinson, ex p Fowler* [1905] 2 KB 713; *Re Tout and Finch Ltd* [1954] 1 All ER 127). However, over these cases hangs the shadow of *British Eagle International Airlines Ltd* v *Compagnie Nationale Air France* [1975] 2 All ER 390. This decision of the House of Lords, although set in a quite different context, casts serious doubt on the continued validity of direct payment clauses. Whether or not this doubt is justified, it has led the draftsmen of JCT 80 to provide specifically that the direct payment provisions of clause 35.13 shall cease to operate at the moment of the contractor's insolvency.

Chapter 19

Remedies for Breach of Contract

It should be acknowledged at the outset that the title of this chapter is not entirely accurate. While all the topics discussed are undoubtedly 'remedies', in the sense that they can arise where there has been a breach of contract, this is not a sufficient reflection of *quantum meruit* claims, which may also arise in a variety of situations not involving any breach. A similar point may be made in relation to those contractual provisions which can lead to determination of the contractor's employment. Such clauses are frequently expressed to operate in the event of a party's insolvency. Furthermore, under some contracts they may apply to certain supervening events which are undeniably 'neutral' in origin.

The scheme of this chapter is to consider the various remedies in ascending order of severity; from claims for the payment of money, through self-help (which may take the form of refusal to pay or refusal to work), to the ultimate step of bringing to an end altogether the contract, or at least the contractor's involvement in it.

1 Damages

An award of damages is the one remedy which, subject to any express terms excluding or restricting liability, is always available for a breach of contract. Where the contract itself specifies the amount to be awarded for a particular breach, these are known as 'liquidated damages'. Such a provision is commonly found in building contracts to cover the contractor's liability for late completion, and is dealt with in Chapter 16.

As to the amount which should be awarded as *unliquidated* damages, this is based upon the law's objective of placing the innocent party, in so far as money can do this, in the position in which he would have been had the contract been properly performed (*Robinson* v *Harman* (1848) 1 Ex 850). It follows therefore that the award will be concerned, not merely to replace out-of-pocket losses, but also to compensate the plaintiff for any profits which he should have been able to earn.

This basic principle is of course subject to a number of specific qualifications, notably that no compensation will be payable in respect of losses which are 'too remote'. In contract cases, this effectively means that damages will cover those consequences which a reasonable man, at the time of making the contract, would have regarded as likely to result in the usual run of things from a breach. They will also cover consequences which, given any *special* knowledge of the parties at the time of contracting, would have been regarded as likely (*Hadley* v *Baxendale* (1854) 9 Ex 341; *Victoria Laundry (Windsor) Ltd* v *Newman Industries Ltd* [1949] 2 KB 528; *Koufos* v *Czarnikow Ltd* [1969] 1 AC 350).

This is not the place for a detailed discussion of damages for breach of contract, but two of the general principles which govern their award are worth bearing in mind in the context of construction. First, the doctrine of mitigation of loss means that a plaintiff cannot recover damages for any part of his loss which he could have avoided by taking reasonable steps (*British Westinghouse Electric Co Ltd* v *Underground Electric Railways* [1912] AC 673). Thus, for example, an employer cannot hold an architect liable for rental income lost due to his negligent supervision of a conversion project, where the evidence shows that the employer could easily have done what was required to render the premises lettable (*Hutchinson* v *Harris* (1978) 10 BLR 19). Secondly, a plaintiff cannot normally recover damages in respect of loss suffered by a third party (*Woodar Investment Development Ltd* v *Wimpey Construction UK Ltd* [1980] 1 All ER 571), even where the plaintiff and third party are two companies within the same group (*Richard Roberts Holdings Ltd* v *Douglas Smith Stimson Partnership* (1988) 46 BLR 50).

(a) Breach by the contractor

As a general principle, a contractor who fails to complete the contract works (either because he abandons the contract or because the employer is justified in terminating it) will be liable to reimburse the employer for the full cost of having the work completed by another contractor, less the unpaid balance of the contract price (*Mertens* v *Home Freeholds Co Ltd* [1921] 2 KB 526).

Where a contractor's work, although defective, is nonetheless sufficient to achieve practical or substantial completion, the amount of damages payable to the employer might logically be assessed on either one of two bases: the amount which the necessary remedial work will cost or the amount by which the value of the employer's property is reduced on account of the defects. It now appears settled that, in normal circumstances, the appropriate measure will be the cost of reinstatement (*East Ham BC* v *Bernard Sunley & Sons Ltd* [1966] AC 406), assessed at the date when repairs ought reasonably to have been put in hand (*Dodd Properties (Kent) Ltd* v *Canterbury CC* [1980] 1 All ER 928). However, if the employer has no intention of repairing (or if it would be wholly unreasonable to do so), then the award will be based on diminution in value (*CR Taylor (Wholesale) Ltd* v *Hepworths Ltd* [1977] 2 All ER 784).

Where defects in building work render the employer's residence unhealthy or uncomfortable, a claim may be made in respect of what has been termed 'distress and inconvenience'. Such claims have often proved successful, against both builders (*Batty* v *Metropolitan Property Realisations Ltd* [1978] QB 554) and negligent surveyors (*Perry* v *Sidney Phillips & Son* [1982] 3 All ER 705), although two qualifications should be noted. First, it has been made clear that, since these damages are primarily concerned to compensate the plaintiff for the *physical* discomfort involved, they will not be awarded where the contract work is a business venture (*Hutchinson* v *Harris* (1978) 10 BLR 19). Secondly, damages under this head should in any event be at a 'modest' level (in *Watts* v *Morrow* [1991] 4 All ER 937 a married couple's award was reduced by the Court of Appeal from £8,000 to £1,500).

(b) Breach by the employer

Where an employer is guilty of a repudiatory breach of contract, and the contractor duly terminates the contract, the contractor's damages will reflect everything which he should have received under the contract, less what it would have cost him to complete the work. The importance of this formulation is that it clearly includes the profit element on work which the contractor will not now carry out (*Wraight Ltd* v *P H & T (Holdings) Ltd* (1968) 13 BLR 26). It also follows that, where a contractor has so underpriced the work that he is actually carrying it out at a loss, he should receive no more than nominal damages for wrongful termination. This is because it is not the function of an award of damages to rescue the plaintiff from a bad bargain (see *C & P Haulage* v *Middleton* [1983] 3 All ER 94).

In cases where the employer's breach is not sufficiently serious to justify termination of the contract, the contractor will nonetheless be entitled to claim compensation for whatever losses he can establish and which fall within the normal rules of remoteness of damage. Some idea of the kind of losses which are likely to arise may be gained from Chapter 15, since contractors' claims for loss/expense under express contractual provisions cover substantially the same area as their claims for damages.

2 *Quantum meruit* claims

A *quantum meruit* claim, in which the contractor seeks the reasonable value of work done for the employer, arises in a variety of situations where there is either no contractual entitlement to payment or at least no contractual assessment of the amount due (see Chapter 15). To take the latter point first, it is clear that a request by one person for professional or trade services to be performed by another normally raises the implication that they are to be paid for; if no specific rates or prices are agreed, then a reasonable sum is payable (Supply of Goods and Services Act 1982, s 15).

Cases where there is no contractual entitlement at all include those where a 'contract' under which work is done turns out to be void, for example because of mistake. Of more importance in the context of construction, this category also covers the situation where preliminary work is done (often under a 'letter of intent') in expectation of a contract which does not materialise. As discussed in Chapter 8, the contractor in such circumstances will be entitled to recover a reasonable price for the work.

One area of difficulty, which has generated considerable academic debate, concerns the use of a *quantum meruit* claim against an employer who is guilty of a repudiatory breach of contract. There is some authority (notably the decision of the Privy Council in *Lodder* v *Slowey* [1904] AC 442) for the view that the contractor in such circumstances can ignore the contract and claim a reasonable sum for all the work done, even if he thereby recovers more than he would have been paid under the contract. However, there is a strong counter-argument (see *Keating on Building Contracts*, 5th edn (Sweet & Maxwell), p 208) to the effect that this remedy should not extend to rescuing the contractor from a bad bargain.

3 Non-payment as an employer's remedy

In practical terms, one of the most potent weapons which an employer may use against a contractor is refusal to pay some or all of what appears to be owing to him. Even if the contract administrator has certified that a particular interim payment is due, the employer may seek to set against the stated sum a claim in respect of defects or delay. As to the validity of such an action, it appears that a mere counter-claim will not suffice to prevent the contractor from obtaining summary judgment on an interim certificate. However, the employer is undoubtedly entitled to use the defences of abatement (a claim that the work is defective and thus not worth the amount stated) or set off (a cross-claim so closely linked to the contractor's claim that the law will not enforce one without taking the other into account).

The whole question of justified non-payment is dealt with in Chapter 13.

4 Suspension of work as a contractor's remedy

If non-payment is a powerful self-help remedy for employers, its counterpart for contractors must surely lie in the suspension of work. It is not uncommon for a contractor to react to an alleged underpayment or late payment by withdrawing his labour from the site, or at least threatening to do so. And, since such direct action all too frequently leads to an escalation of the dispute, with the employer perhaps claiming to terminate the contract altogether on the ground that the contractor has repudiated it, it is very important to know whether it is justified in law.

As to this, much depends on whether the building contract requires the contractor to proceed regularly and diligently with the work (as the vast majority of contracts do, although a term to this effect will not be implied—*GLC* v *Cleveland Bridge and Engineering Co Ltd* (1986) 34 BLR 50). If there is such a term, then a contractor who stops work temporarily in order to exert pressure on the employer will thereby commit a breach of it (*Canterbury Pipe Lines Ltd* v *Christchurch Drainage Board* (1979) 16 BLR 76; *Lubenham Fidelities and Investment Co Ltd* v *South Pembrokeshire DC* (1986) 33 BLR 39). However, it appears that a breach of this particular obligation will not usually be treated by the courts as repudiatory (see *below*), and thus the employer cannot safely rely on it as a ground for termination (*JM Hill & Sons Ltd* v *Camden*

LBC (1980) 18 BLR 31; *F Treliving & Co Ltd* v *Simplex Time Recorder Co (UK) Ltd* (1981, unreported)).

This discussion of the legal position naturally assumes that the contract does not itself give the contractor a right of suspension for non-payment or other defaults of the employer. None of the standard forms of main contract appear to confer such a remedy, but it is worth noting that both NSC/C and DOM/1 permit a *sub-contractor* to suspend execution of the work, after giving written notice of his intention, where any payment from the main contractor is overdue.

5 Termination for repudiatory breach

Where a contracting party is guilty of a 'repudiatory breach' of that contract, the other party has in principle an election to make. He may choose to *affirm* the contract, in which case both parties remain fully bound by its terms; or he may *accept the repudiation*, in which case all the outstanding primary obligations of both parties come to an end. However, the acceptance of a repudiatory breach does not prevent the enforcement of any obligations which have already accrued; nor does it destroy the binding effect of such contract terms as exemption clauses, liquidated damages provisions or arbitration clauses. Whichever option the innocent party selects, it should always be borne in mind that damages may be claimed in respect of the breach.

Although it is sometimes said that repudiation by itself can never bring a contract to an end (since the innocent party may always refuse to accept the repudiation), it seems that this proposition requires some qualification. Even in *White & Carter (Councils) Ltd* v *McGregor* [1962] AC 413, where a bare majority of the House of Lords accepted the basic principle, it was recognised that the innocent party would need to show some legitimate interest in continuing with the contract. Furthermore, where the continued performance of the contract requires the co-operation of the guilty party, he can by refusing this co-operation effectively deprive the innocent party of his election. Thus in *Hounslow LBC* v *Twickenham Garden Developments Ltd* [1971] Ch 233 it was held that, if an employer refused to allow the contractor on to his land, the contractor would have no option but to treat the contract as terminated. (It also appears that the employer can reinforce his wrongful repudiation by obtaining an injunction to eject the contractor from the site—*Tara Civil Engineering Ltd* v *Moorfield*

Developments Ltd (1989) 46 BLR 72, refusing to follow the *Hounslow* v *Twickenham* case.)

A decision to affirm or terminate the contract is irrevocable once it has been communicated to the other side. What is more, failure to take prompt action to exercise a right of termination may lead to the conclusion, at least where work is continuing, that the contract has been affirmed; if this is so, the right to terminate will be lost (see *Pigott Construction* v *WJ Crowe Ltd* (1961) 27 DLR (2d) 258).

(a) Repudiation in general

A breach of contract will be treated as 'repudiatory', in the sense described above, in two situations. First, and most obviously, one of the parties may clearly and explicitly renounce any intention of continuing with the contract. Secondly, a party may be guilty of some other breach which 'goes to the root' of the contract. This in turn may be because the particular term broken has been given the status of a 'condition' of the contract (in which case any breach, however minor, will be treated as repudiatory), or because an 'innominate term' has been breached to a sufficiently serious extent.

'Renunciation' can cause immense practical difficulties in construction disputes. These difficulties arise from the tendency of employers to react to alleged breaches of contract by refusing to pay, and contractors to react to non-payment by refusing to work. Such self-help by either side may subsequently be held to have been an over-reaction, on the ground that the other party's breach of contract was not sufficiently serious to justify it. If this happens, then the 'innocent' party becomes in turn guilty of a breach of contract.

As a general principle, the *bona fide* but mistaken exercise of a contractual right of rescission will not always and without more be deemed a repudiatory breach (*Woodar Investment Development Ltd* v *Wimpey Construction UK Ltd* [1980] 1 All ER 571). However, it is likely to be so held in construction cases, since its effects on the parties will usually be irreversible (see *Lubenham Fidelities and Investment Co Ltd* v *South Pembrokeshire DC* (1986) 33 BLR 39). The net result is that an originally innocent party who 'accepts a repudiation' or exercises a contractual determination provision will, if he turns out to have been mistaken, have committed a repudiatory breach. If so, he will be liable for all the resulting losses of the other party.

Turning to the matter of repudiation implied from breach of contract, this too poses severe practical problems. Few building contract provisions are given 'condition' status. This means that whether or not a breach is repudiatory will almost always be a question of fact and degree. As can be seen from some of the specific examples given below, the task of assessing whether or not a particular breach of contract is sufficient to justify termination is one of extreme difficulty and uncertainty. Any decision to terminate is consequently fraught with danger. The advice in general must be to rely on clear legal remedies (such as an action for damages, or the implementation of a contractual provision for determination) and to avoid self-help remedies altogether, except perhaps where there are real doubts as to the other party's solvency.

(b) Breach by the contractor

It is not possible to lay down any hard and fast rules as to what will constitute a repudiatory breach on the part of the contractor. Complete abandonment of the work will obviously do so (*Marshall* v *Mackintosh* (1898) 78 LT 750). However, an unjustified temporary suspension of work is far less certain (*JM Hill & Sons Ltd* v *Camden LBC* (1980) 18 BLR 31). Indeed, it has even been held that the temporary nature of suspension shows that the contractor's intention is not to repudiate the contract (*F Treliving & Co Ltd* v *Simplex Time Recorder Co (UK) Ltd* (1981, unreported)).

Delay by a contractor will not justify termination by the employer unless it is such as to demonstrate the contractor's intention not to be bound by the contract, or unless time is 'of the essence' (*Felton* v *Wharrie* (1906) HBC 4th ed, Vol 2, 398). This will seldom be the case in a building contract (especially where the contract clearly envisages the possibility of delay by making provision for liquidated damages). However, even where the contract itself does not make time of the essence, the employer can render it so by giving reasonable notice to the contractor after delay has occurred.

As a general rule, defective work will not amount to a repudiatory breach of contract (*Hoenig* v *Isaacs* [1952] 2 All ER 176), unless it is sufficiently serious to mean that the contractor has failed to achieve substantial performance of his obligations (as in *Bolton* v *Mahadeva* [1972] 2 All ER 1322). However, where a steadily increasing list of defects convinced the employer that the contractors did not have the ability, competence or the will to complete the work in accordance with the contract, it was held that the employer was justified in removing them from the site (*Sutcliffe* v *Chippendale & Edmondson* (1971) 18 BLR 149).

Apart from the above categories of breach, it has been held (on the particular facts of the respective cases) that failure to obtain a required performance bond was a repudiatory breach by the contractor (*Swartz & Son (Pty) Ltd* v *Wolmaranstadt Town Council* 1960 (2) SA 1), but that unauthorised sub-contracting was not (*Thomas Feather & Co (Bradford) Ltd* v *Keighley Corporation* (1953) 53 LGR 30).

(c) Breach by the employer

Of all the breaches of contract which an employer may commit, the one which is most frequently treated as a repudiation by contractors is undoubtedly that of failure to pay in accordance with the contract terms. In normal circumstances, however, failure to pay one or even several instalments as they fall due does not justify the other party in terminating a contract (*Mersey Steel & Iron Co* v *Naylor, Benzon & Co* (1884) 9 App Cas 434), far less so where the non-payment complained of relates to another contract between the same parties (*Small & Sons Ltd* v *Middlesex Real Estates Ltd* [1921] WN 245). It seems in truth that non-payment, underpayment or late payment will only be regarded as a repudiatory breach where its effect is to shatter the other party's confidence in ever receiving what is due (see *DR Bradley (Cable Jointing) Ltd* v *Jefco Mechanical Services Ltd* (1988) 6-CLD-07-19).

Closely linked with the question of underpayment is that of under-certification by the contract administrator. If this results from the employer's positive interference with or obstruction of the contract administrator in the exercise of his discretion, it will probably rank as a *repudiatory* breach. In other cases, even if the employer is held liable for the contract administrator's default (as to which see *Perini Corporation* v *Commonwealth of Australia* (1969) 12 BLR 82), this breach is unlikely to justify the contractor in terminating the contract. Indeed, it has even been held that a contractor's sole remedy for under-certification is to have the offending certificates corrected at arbitration, on the ground that the employer's insistence on paying only what is shown is not a breach of contract at all (*Lubenham Fidelities and Investment Co Ltd* v *South Pembrokeshire DC* (1986) 33 BLR 39).

Payment and certificates aside, breach by an employer of his general duties to co-operate with and not hinder the contractor may on occasion be sufficiently serious to justify the latter in leaving the site. Decisions to this effect have been reached (on the facts of particular cases) where an employer wrongfully ejected the contractor from the site (*Roberts* v *Bury Commissioners* (1870) LR 4 CP 755), ordered him to stop work (*Cort* v *Ambergate, Nottingham, Boston & Eastern Junction Railway Co* (1851) 17 QB 127), and failed to provide necessary drawings (*Kingdom* v *Cox* (1848) 5 CB 522). However, a mere partial interference with the contractor's possession of the site has been held insufficient to amount to repudiation (*Earth & General Contracts Ltd* v *Manchester Corporation* (1958) 108 LJ 665).

6 Determination under contractual provisions

(a) General

As mentioned earlier, many building contracts contain express provisions under which, if specified events occur, either the contract itself or the 'contractor's employment' may be terminated. The events specified will of course vary from one contract to another, and may range from natural disasters to insolvency, although they tend to be concerned mainly with serious breaches of contract. In this respect, determination clauses cover much of the same ground as the remedy of termination for repudiatory breach. However, they differ from that remedy in laying down in a much clearer fashion just what will be needed to permit termination. And clarity is of enormous importance in this context, since the purported exercise of a right of determination on insufficient grounds will normally be treated as a repudiatory breach (*Lodder* v *Slowey* [1904] AC 442; *Architectural Installation Services Ltd* v *James Gibbons Windows Ltd* (1989) 46 BLR 91).

Where an event occurs which falls within a contractual determination clause and which would also justify termination of the contract at common law, the innocent party has a choice of remedy unless the contract itself provides otherwise. In consequence, a purported exercise of the contractual right which fails on procedural grounds (eg as to the timing of a notice) may nonetheless be treated as the acceptance of a repudiatory breach (*Architectural Installation Services Ltd* v *James Gibbons Windows Ltd* (1989) 46 BLR 91). On the other hand, if a breach of contract is non-repudiatory at common law, the innocent party is limited to whatever remedy the contract provides—if this is 'determination or liquidated damages', he cannot bring the contract to an end and claim unliquidated damages (*Thomas Feather & Co (Bradford) Ltd* v *Keighley Corporation* (1953) 53 LGR 30).

As well as listing the events which will justify determination, contract terms of the kind now under discussion frequently lay down procedures which must be followed. These typically involve the service of a written notice or notices (eg a warning followed by the exercise of the power), and may well provide time limits and even methods of delivery. It is important that such provisions be complied with, for a determination clause will be construed strictly against the party seeking to rely on it (*Roberts* v *Bury Commissioners* (1870) LR 5 CP 310). Thus, where a warning notice was followed, after 11 months of silence, by a telex purporting to determine a sub-contract, it was held that this was invalid, since a reasonable person would have seen no connection between the two notices (*Architectural Installation Services Ltd* v *James Gibbons Windows Ltd* (1989) 46 BLR 91). However, the English courts have upheld notices which were proved actually to have arrived, notwithstanding that they were not sent by the prescribed method (*Goodwin* v *Fawcett* (1965) 175 EG 27; *JM Hill & Sons Ltd* v *Camden LBC* (1980) 18 BLR 31).

Finally, determination clauses often lay down in considerable detail the financial and other consequences which are to follow their implementation. Not surprisingly, these vary according to which party's default has led to the termination in question.

(b) Determination by the employer

The type of determination provision most commonly found in building contracts is one which entitles the employer either to determine the contract or to bring to an end the contractor's employment under it. Such provisions, sometimes called 'forfeiture clauses', are normally expressed to be triggered by the contractor's breach of certain provisions of the contract, and also by the contractor's insolvency.

JCT 80 clause 27 entitles the employer to 'determine the employment of the contractor' on various grounds, notably unjustified suspension of work, failure to proceed regularly and diligently, failure to remove defective work when ordered, unauthorised assignment or sub-contracting, corruption and insolvency. All but the last two require the contractor to be sent a warning notice as well as a notice of termination, and are subject to the proviso that termination must not be effected unreasonably or vexatiously (as to which see *John Jarvis* v *Rockdale Housing Association* (1987) 36 BLR 48).

ICE 6 clause 63, although headed 'Determination of the contractor's employment', in fact entitles the employer in certain circumstances to give notice and then to 'enter the site and the works and expel the contractor therefrom'. The circumstances listed (with the exception of sub-contracting) tend to follow those found in JCT 80; however, there is a general ground of the contractor's being, despite warnings from the engineer, 'persistently or fundamentally in breach of his obligations'.

GC/Works/1 clause 56 differs from other forms of contract in a number of important respects. In the first place, the employer is given power, by notice and without prior warning, to determine the contract (not, be it noted, the contractor's employment) for any reason whatsoever. Secondly, while the possibility of determining the contract without becoming liable to compensate the contractor is restricted to specified cases of contractor default or contractor insolvency, these cover a wider area than their equivalents under either JCT 80 or ICE 6. In particular, failure by the contractor to comply with *any* instruction of the PM, or with any of the conditions mentioned in the invitation to tender, can have this drastic effect.

The consequences of determination are broadly similar under all three forms of contract. The employer may employ others to complete the works, making use of the original contractor's temporary buildings, plant, tools, equipment and materials. The employer also has the option of taking an assignment of any sub-contracts. Most importantly, the contractor loses all rights to payment until the employer has completed the works, and even then will receive only the difference (if any) between what he would have earned under the contract and what it has cost the employer to take over.

(c) Determination by the contractor

With the exception of ICE 6 clause 40, which protects a contractor who is ordered by the engineer to suspend work for more than three months, only JCT 80 of the three contracts considered above entitles a contractor to determine his employment on the ground of employer default. Clause 28 of that contract confers such a right (which does not require advance warning) on the contractor where the employer fails to pay certificated sums within a certain period, where he interferes with or obstructs the issue of a certificate, or where the whole of the work is suspended for a period laid down in the Appendix (commonly one month) for various reasons which are the fault of the employer or the contract administrator.

Where a contractor exercises his right of determination (which again must not be done unreasonably or vexatiously), he will be entitled in effect to payment in full for work already done, compensation for anticipated profit on the remaining work and reimbursement of any other loss/expense suffered as a result of the termination.

(d) *Determination for 'neutral' causes*

Some contracts make provision for determination where the works are seriously affected by something beyond the control of either party. For example, JCT 80 (in clauses 22C, 28A and 32) provides that the contractor's employment may be determined by *either* party in the event of war breaking out, or if the whole of the work is suspended for one month by *force majeure* or civil commotion, or for three months by loss or damage resulting from a 'specified peril' (except where this is itself due to the default of the contractor or any sub-contractor). The consequences of any such determination are identical to those under clause 28 (described above), with the exception that the contractor is not entitled to reimbursement for any direct loss and/or expense caused by the determination.

Interestingly, while ICE 6 clause 65 also acknowledges the possibility of determining the contract on the outbreak of war, it only entitles the employer to take this step.

(e) *Determination provisions in sub-contracts*

As to this, little need be said, since the principles which govern determination clauses in main contracts apply with equal force where those provisions are stepped down into sub-contracts. However, one practical point which is worth making is that a sub-contract should always be made determinable in the event that either the main contract or the main contractor's employment is brought to an end. If this is not done, then a contractor who is, through no fault of his own, ejected from the site, may find that he incurs liability to his sub-contractors.

By and large, the determination clauses of both NSC/C and DOM/1 follow those of JCT 80, as regards both the grounds for and the consequences of determination. However, two quirks which may be noted are that NSC/C does not permit a nominated sub-contractor to determine for non-payment (presumably because he can instead seek direct payment from the employer), and that DOM/1 does not permit a domestic sub-contractor to claim for any loss/expense arising out of the determination, even where this has come about through the default of the main contractor or the employer.

Chapter 20

Settlement of Construction Disputes

It is an unfortunate but undeniable feature of building contracts that they engender a large number of disputes, both while the contract work is being carried out and after it has been completed. These disputes require settlement, and the techniques which are most commonly adopted for this fall into three main groups.

In the first place, and probably most familiar to legal practitioners, the twin possibilities of litigation and arbitration represent the adversarial approach to dispute resolution. This chapter is not the place for a detailed discussion of civil procedure, but it begins by briefly considering the more important differences between these methods, as well as their similarities.

The second main technique which is used for resolving construction disputes, and indeed for preventing disputes from arising in the first place, is that of contractual provisions for binding third party determination of certain contentious issues. In its best known form, this consists of certification by the contract administrator; however, some contracts also make use of external 'adjudicators' for this purpose.

Thirdly, and apparently enjoying a surge of popularity due to the perceived deficiencies of litigation and arbitration, there is a range of techniques whose common aim is to enable the parties to a dispute to reach a settlement of it through their own negotiations. These differ widely in terms of their formality (or lack of it), but are usually grouped under the general heading of 'Alternative Dispute Resolution'.

1 Litigation and arbitration compared

It should be emphasised from the outset that, while a comparison of these two procedures for resolving disputes may be of some interest, this does not mean that the parties to any given dispute will necessarily be in a position to choose between them. Depending upon the nature of the dispute, the terms of the contract under which it arises and the remedy which is being sought, it may well be that only one forum is available. These matters are further discussed in sections 2 and 3 below.

Where there *is* a choice between litigation and arbitration for a particular dispute, it may still be somewhat misleading to suggest that the two procedures can be easily compared. This is because, while litigation has a fairly constant and consistent meaning, arbitration can to a large extent be whatever the parties want it to be. In consequence, many of the perceived advantages or disadvantages of the two processes can alter radically, depending upon what sort of 'arbitration' is under discussion. That said, the following points are likely to arise in any discussion as to the 'best' forum.

First and foremost, supporters of arbitration frequently claim that it offers significant advantages over litigation in terms of both time and money. Unfortunately, this is where the question 'What is meant by arbitration?' really becomes crucial. It seems in truth that, while short informal arbitration procedures may indeed be quick, cheap and convenient, large-scale construction arbitrations on the litigation model are likely to last as long as proceedings in court and to cost even more. This is because, while a judge and a courtroom are provided free of charge by the legal system, arbitrators and arbitration rooms must be paid for by the parties.

There is perhaps something to be said for the view that certain types of dispute lend themselves to one or other method of settlement. Arbitration may be preferable for cases where what is in issue is not legal principle, but rather complex technical questions. Conversely, knotty legal problems may be better tried by a judge, especially if it is possible to bring it before an Official Referee on a 'construction summons'. In any event, disputes involving more than two parties are usually more suited to litigation since, without a considerable degree of goodwill on all sides, organising a multi-party arbitration is an almost impossible task.

It may be that any choice between arbitration and litigation must finally be made on the basis of rather less tangible and impressionistic criteria. For example, there is an undoubted feeling that, while litigation will almost always be a thoroughly confrontational experience (which is a great disadvantage where parties expect to work together again), arbitration need not necessarily be so. Again, if privacy is important, there is probably a greater chance of achieving this in arbitration (although it must be acknowledged that 'privacy' is a fairly relative concept, given the rather close-knit nature of the construction law world). These factors lean in favour of arbitration; on the other side there is a belief among some lawyers at least that arbitrators are 'softer' than judges, and thus less likely to rule entirely in favour of one party. If this is justified, it suggests that a party whose case is a very strong one is better off in court; a party defending a rather weak position may come away with at least something from arbitration.

2 Litigation

As mentioned above, the majority of building contract cases are tried before the Official Referees. This comes about either because the plaintiff's writ is marked 'Official Referees' business', or because a High Court action is transferred there. If the case is of any great size, it is almost certain to be tried before the full-time Official Referees in London; however, there are also circuit judges nominated to deal with Official Referees' business in some provincial centres.

The rules of procedure in building contract cases are in principle like those in other High Court litigation, although cases before the Official Referees are unusual in that the judge deals with all the interlocutory matters as well as with the trial itself. The details of procedure are not further discussed here, but there are two important aspects of litigation which require consideration.

(a) Limits of jurisdiction

In *Northern Regional Health Authority* v *Derek Crouch Construction Co Ltd* [1984] QB 644 it was held by the Court of Appeal that, where a building contract expressly gives power to an arbitrator to 'open up, review and revise any certificate, opinion, decision' of the contract administrator, this means that a court has no equivalent power. Hence, where a party to a construction dispute wishes to challenge a certificate or other decision of the contract administrator *on its merits*, arbitration will be the only available forum. However, it appears that a court has power to intervene where a certificate is *formally* invalid (for example because the contract administrator has colluded with the employer or has otherwise exceeded his jurisdiction), or where the entire certification procedure has broken down.

The precise extent of the ruling in *Crouch* is not clear. Official Referees have subsequently disclaimed any power in the courts to review certificates in cases where the contract did not explicitly give this power to the arbitrator (*Oram Builders Ltd* v *Pemberton* (1985) 29 BLR 23) and even where there was no arbitration clause at all (*Reed* v *Van der Vorm* (1985) 35 BLR 136; *JF Finnegan Ltd* v *Sheffield CC* (1988) 43 BLR 124). It seems, however, that this goes too far and that it is the conferring of jurisdiction on the arbitrator which is crucial in denying it to the court (*Benstrete Construction Ltd* v *Hill* (1987) 38 BLR 115).

A partial solution to the problems created by *Crouch* is offered by s 43A of the Supreme Court Act 1981 (inserted by s 100 of the Courts and Legal Services Act 1990). This provides that, if all the parties to an action agree, the judge can exercise those powers which the contract specifically confers on an arbitrator. It may be doubted whether the necessary agreement will be forthcoming once a case is in court (since, presumably, if one party wishes to challenge a certificate, the other party would prefer it not to be challenged). However, the inclusion of such an agreement in the contract itself would appear to be a sensible course of action, in case a subsequent dispute finds its way into court rather than to arbitration.

(b) Summary judgment and interim payment

A notable feature of modern construction litigation is the use made of applications for summary judgment under RSC Ord 14 and for interim payments under Ord 29. What these procedures have in common is that they offer a plaintiff the chance to receive payment on at least part of his claim at a much earlier date than can be achieved if either litigation or arbitration is pursued to a conclusion. Where they differ is that, whereas judgment for the plaintiff under Ord 14 represents a final decision on the claim, an award under Ord 29 assumes that a full trial on the merits will take place at a later stage.

To succeed under Ord 14, a plaintiff must convince the court that there is no arguable defence to the claim, or no defence except as to the quantum of damages. The burden of proof is a heavy one but, if it is satisfied, the plaintiff will have final judgment on the whole claim or, where quantum remains unproved, on the issue of liability.

The very nature of Ord 14 proceedings presupposes that there is not to be a full trial and, in consequence, any serious doubt as to the facts of the case will be enough to defeat the plaintiff's application. The same is true of disputes which raise complex issues of law, although a court will be prepared to deal with points of law which can be settled on the basis of brief argument from counsel (*Chatbrown* v *Alfred McAlpine (Southern) Ltd* (1986) 35 BLR 44; *Crown House Engineering Ltd* v *Amec Projects Ltd* (1989) 48 BLR 32).

The extent to which an application for summary judgment may be met by a defence of set off has been dealt with in Chapter 13, in the specific context of claims for payment. It is worth noting here that, where a party pleads a set off in this way, it frequently raises questions which appear to fall within the purview of the contractual arbitration clause. The question which then arises is whether the defendant can obtain a stay of the court proceedings (including the Ord 14 application) under s 4 of the Arbitration Act 1950, in order to have the entire case diverted to arbitration.

The answer to this question is that, if the court is satisfied that there is no arguable defence to the plaintiff's claim, there is no 'dispute' to be taken to arbitration and summary judgment will therefore be awarded (*Ellis Mechanical Services Ltd* v *Wates Construction Ltd* (1976) 2 BLR 57). Similarly, if only part of the claim is indisputable, summary judgment will be awarded on that part and the balance of the action stayed under s 4. Where, on the other hand, the alleged set off raises a genuine doubt, the defendant will be given leave to defend (*Hanak* v *Green* [1958] 2 QB 9), which may be made conditional on a payment into court if the judge is somewhat sceptical about the defence (*CM Pillings & Co Ltd* v *Kent Investments Ltd* (1985) 30 BLR 80).

A plaintiff will succeed in an application for interim payment under Ord 29 where the court is convinced that, if the action proceeded to trial, the plaintiff would obtain judgment against the defendant for a substantial sum of money. This procedure, which is in principle available even where any full 'trial' must take place at arbitration (*Imodco Ltd* v *Wimpey Major Products Ltd and Taylor Woodrow International Ltd* (1987) 40 BLR 1), results in an award to the plaintiff of whatever amount seems to the court to be just, but not exceeding a reasonable proportion of what will ultimately be recovered.

The burden of proof on a plaintiff who makes an application under Ord 29 closely resembles that under Ord 14. Thus, while a defendant who is granted only conditional leave to defend under Ord 14 may at the same time be ordered to make an interim payment (*British and Commonwealth Holdings plc* v *Quadrex Holdings Inc* [1989] 3 All ER 492), no such award can be made against a defendant who is given unconditional leave to defend (*Shanning Ltd* v *George Wimpey Ltd* [1988] 3 All ER 475). However, an important difference between the two remedies is that a mere counter-claim (ie not amounting to a set off) will be sufficient to exempt a defendant from having to make an interim payment (*Smallman Construction Ltd* v *Redpath Dorman Long Ltd* (1988) 47 BLR 15).

3 Arbitration

(a) Jurisdiction

Arbitration is based on the agreement of the parties, and the jurisdiction of an arbitrator is accordingly limited to what the parties choose to refer to him. In practice, this will mean all matters falling within the scope of the arbitration agreement under which the arbitrator's appointment is made. While this will necessarily turn on the construction of the particular arbitration clause, it may be said in general that the clauses found in building contracts are usually widely drafted. For example, JCT 80 Art 5 includes 'the construction of this contract, or any matter or thing of whatsoever nature arising hereunder or in connection herewith'. The formulation in ICE 6 clause 66 is 'a dispute of any kind whatsoever ... in connection with or arising out of the contract', while GC/Works/1 clause 60 refers to 'disputes, differences or questions ... arising out of or relating to the contract'.

Such wording clearly empowers the arbitrator to deal with any claim for breach of the contract. It also covers arguments over whether the contract has been determined on grounds of repudiation or frustration (*Heyman* v *Darwins Ltd* [1942] AC 356), and claims for misrepresentation, negligent misstatement and rectification on the ground of mistake (*Ashville Investments Ltd* v *Elmer Contractors Ltd* [1988] 2 All ER 577). However, claims of the latter kind will fall outside a clause which refers to disputes 'arising under' the contract (*Fillite (Runcorn) Ltd* v *Aqua-Lift* (1989) 45 BLR 27). Furthermore, no clause can give an arbitrator power to decide whether the contract is void from the beginning, since that is the very issue which will determine whether or not he has any jurisdiction at all.

(b) Staying proceedings

As a general principle, where a building contract contains an arbitration clause, any dispute which comes within the scope of that clause should be settled at arbitration. This is not to say that one of the parties may not institute legal proceedings; however, where this happens the other party may apply to have those proceedings stayed, by issuing a summons under s 4 of the Arbitration Act 1950 (s 1 of the Arbitration Act 1979 in the case of a 'non-domestic' arbitration agreement). Once such a summons is issued, and provided that certain conditions are met, the court in a non-domestic case *must* stay proceedings to allow arbitration to take place. In a domestic case the court has a discretion, but the onus on the party who seeks to avoid arbitration is nonetheless a heavy one.

The first of the conditions required for success under an s 4 summons is simply that the dispute in question must fall within the terms of the relevant arbitration agreement. As already noted, most building contract arbitration clauses are widely drafted, although they do not extend to disputes over whether the contract was validly made in the first place. Furthermore, a court which regards a claim as suitable, in whole or part, for summary judgment under RSC Ord 14 will not be thwarted by an s 4 summons; in such circumstances there is no real 'dispute' at all (*Ellis Mechanical Services Ltd* v *Wates Construction Ltd* (1976) 2 BLR 57).

The other two conditions imposed by s 4 are that the summons must be issued by the defendant 'before delivering any pleadings or taking any other step in the proceedings' (a trap into which many defendants have fallen); and that the defendant must be 'ready and willing to do all things necessary to the proper conduct of the arbitration'. This latter condition can be satisfied, and a stay therefore granted, even though it is not yet possible for arbitration to be commenced, for example because the necessary preliminary steps have not been taken (*Enco Civil Engineering Ltd* v *Zeus International Development Ltd* (1991) 56 BLR 43; *Channel Tunnel Group Ltd* v *Balfour Beatty Construction Ltd* [1992] 2 All ER 609).

Assuming that the conditions are satisfied, it is open to the plaintiff, at least in a domestic arbitration, to convince the court that proceedings should not be stayed to arbitration. In theory the court has a completely unfettered discretion in this matter, but the strong judicial bias in favour of holding the parties to their arbitration agreement has meant that the exceptional cases, in which a stay of proceedings is refused, tend to fall into recognisable groups. For example, court proceedings may well be allowed to continue where the arbitrator's impartiality is in doubt (Arbitration Act 1950, s 24); where there are allegations of fraud or professional negligence (*Turner* v *Fenton* [1982] 1 All ER 8); where there are more than two parties and a combined arbitration is not possible (*Taunton-Collins* v *Crombie* [1964] 2 All ER 332); and where the court suspects that the defendant is simply using s 4 as a delaying tactic (*Gilbert-Ash (Northern) Ltd* v *Modern Engineering (Bristol) Ltd* [1974] GC 689). However, the fact that a party will be able to obtain legal aid for litigation is no longer regarded as a reason for refusing a stay of proceedings (*Jones* v *Thyssen (Great Britain) Ltd and Taylor Woodrow Construction Ltd* (1991) 57 BLR 116). And the effect of *Northern Regional Health Authority* v *Derek Crouch Construction Co Ltd* [1984] QB 644 is that, where a dispute involves challenging a decision of the contract administrator, a stay will be almost inevitable.

(c) Arbitration procedure

In theory at least, an arbitrator may adopt any procedure he wishes, so long as it is consonant with the rules of natural justice. However, the Arbitration Acts appear to have been drafted on the assumption that arbitration will normally follow closely the procedure of litigation in the High Court, and this will almost invariably be so in the case of a building contract arbitration. Thus, unless the parties have clearly agreed otherwise, the proceedings will be adversarial in nature, usually involving an oral hearing at which the parties will be legally represented.

Certain of the bodies responsible for drafting standard form contracts have published rules of procedure which are intended to govern arbitrations arising out of those contracts. The JCT Arbitration Rules, for example, provide that the parties (or in default the arbitrator) can choose from different procedures depending on the type of dispute which is involved. The 'Full procedure with hearing' under rule 6 is the one which most closely approximates to litigation, and which will almost certainly be adopted in cases of any size and complexity. However, particular types of dispute may well not be suited to this procedure, in which case the rules offer two alternatives.

The first of these, the 'Procedure without hearing' under rule 5, is designed for such matters as valuations of work done, investigations into defects and interpretation of the contract. This is a 'documents only' arbitration, in which the parties submit written statements with supporting documentary evidence. The arbitrator is expected to decide on the basis of this evidence alone, although there is provision for a site inspection where necessary.

The second alternative, the 'short procedure with hearing' under rule 7, somewhat resembles the 'independent adjudication' provisions which are found in some contracts. Designed for disputes arising during the course of the works, in which a speedy decision is essential, it consists of a site visit and oral submissions by the parties. However, further evidence is expected to be kept to a minimum.

It is worth noting that the ICE Arbitration Procedure, which lays down a much more detailed code of rules than its JCT counterpart, also provides for as much flexibility as possible. The arbitrator is expressly given wide powers to control the course of the dispute, and can select from a useful range of remedies.

4 Third party determination

(a) Certification

Building and civil engineering contracts have for a long time given powers to the contract administrator to make various decisions which affect the rights and obligations of the contracting parties. These powers may for convenience be grouped together under the heading of 'certification', but it is important to appreciate that they also include decisions, for example on contractors' claims, which are not always evidenced by the issue of a formal certificate.

The range of certificates to be issued under any particular contract will vary, but it is common to find both *interim certificates*, which regulate the contractor's right to be paid during the course of the project, and a *final certificate*, which represents the contract administrator's final decision on a number of issues (see Chapter 13). In addition, certificates may be required to evidence the occurrence of various important events, such as the achievement of practical completion, the contractor's failure to complete on time, or the satisfactory making good of defects at the end of a Defects Liability Period.

A question of major practical importance is the extent to which the parties are legally bound by the issue (or non-issue) of certificates or by other decisions of the contract administrator. The true answer to this question, as to so many others, can only be found by examining the contract in question, for it is there that one will discover, for example, whether a final certificate is to be conclusive on any issues, or whether a certificate of practical completion can be reopened on subsequent discovery of defects in the work (see *Westminster CC* v *Jarvis & Sons Ltd* [1970] 1 All ER 942). Nonetheless, in general it is safe to say that only in relation to final certificates will true 'conclusiveness' be found. Interim certificates will rarely if ever have legally binding force, although the absence of a certificate of non-completion way well preclude the employer from deducting liquidated damages (*A Bell & Son (Paddington) Ltd* v *CBF Residential Care & Housing Association* (1989) 46 BLR 102).

As for final certificates, the contract terms are again paramount. Under both JCT 80 and IFC 84, for example, the final certificate is expressed to be conclusive on four particular matters, unless arbitration proceedings to challenge it have already been commenced or are commenced within 28 days of its issue. In view of the shortness of this period, it is important for a party to make absolutely clear his desire for arbitration. While any positive indication of this desire may suffice, the method usually adopted is to request the other party either to agree to the appointment of a named arbitrator or to join in the process of selecting one (*Emson Contractors Ltd* v *Protea Estates Ltd* (1987) 39 BLR 126).

If the above steps are not taken, the final certificate under JCT 80 becomes unchallengeable as to all adjustments of the contract sum and claims for both extensions of time and for loss and/or expense. Also included is the quality of workmanship and materials, but only in so far as the contract leaves this for the contract administrator to determine. However, the recent case of *Colbart* v *Kumar* [1992] CILL 752 suggests that the contract may impliedly as well as expressly leave 'quality' to the contract administrator, a ruling which greatly increases the practical importance of the final certificate.

In the absence of the type of clear wording provided by JCT 80, it can sometimes be a difficult question of construction as to whether a contract purports to make a certificate determinative of the parties' rights. What is more, there is the procedural issue of how, if at all, a certificate may be attacked. In this connection we have already noted the reluctance of the courts to investigate the merits of a certificate (see the earlier discussion of *Northern Regional Health Authority* v *Derek Crouch Construction Co Ltd* [1984] QB 644) which means that, at least where the contract has a wide-ranging arbitration clause, any challenge to a certificate or other decision can only be mounted at arbitration.

Assuming that a certificate is 'conclusive' in the sense described above, it cannot be challenged on its merits. Furthermore, decisions in other cases concerning third party determinations, such as share valuations or rent reviews, suggest that the courts will not intervene even where the decision is demonstrably wrong in law (*Jones* v *Sherwood Computer Services plc* [1992] 2 All ER 170). If this is so, then a certificate will lose its binding effect only where it is invalid on formal grounds, for example where the certifier has exceeded his jurisdiction or has colluded with one of the parties (see Chapter 13).

Parties faced with difficulties in overcoming a certificate have in the past sought redress by an alternative route, namely, by bringing an action for negligence against the certifier. At one time it was held that such actions must inevitably fail, since the contract administrator was entitled to immunity as a quasi-arbitrator, but this principle was overturned by the House of Lords in *Sutcliffe* v *Thackrah* [1974] AC 727. It was there held that an architect who negligently over-certified work could be made liable to compensate the employer when the latter, having paid out on the certificates, was unable to recover the money because the contractor had become insolvent.

It might be thought (and it was indeed suggested by Lord Salmon in *Sutcliffe* v *Thackrah*) that the contract administrator's duty to the client in respect of certification would be mirrored by one to the contractor, so that negligent *under-certification* could lead to liability in tort. However, a claim by a civil engineering contractor against the engineer, for alleged negligence in dealing with his claims for extra payment, was rejected by the Court of Appeal in *Pacific Associates Inc* v *Baxter* [1989] 2 All ER 159, and a Hong Kong court reached a similar decision in respect of an architect in *Leon Engineering & Construction Co Ltd* v *Ka Duk Investment Co Ltd* (1989) 47 BLR 139.

The Court of Appeal in the *Baxter* case stressed that there was no need to impose liability in tort, since a contractor aggrieved by decisions of the contractor administrator could simply challenge them at arbitration. It may therefore be that, where a contract contains no arbitration clause, or where it in some other way renders the contract administrator's decisions conclusive, an action in the tort of negligence will lie.

(b) Adjudication

A number of standard form building contracts and sub-contracts make provision for certain disputes which may arise during the currency of a project to be settled by an 'adjudicator'. This is an independent third party who is either named in the contract documents from the start or selected by agreement once the dispute has arisen. Such provisions are found for example in NSC/C and DOM/1, to deal with disputes over a main contractor's claim to refuse payment to a sub-contractor on the ground of a set off. There are also optional adjudication clauses, covering a wider range of issues, in the JCT design and build contract CD 81.

The purpose of an adjudication procedure of this kind is to avoid all the potential disadvantages of becoming involved in full-scale arbitration proceedings while the contract works are still in progress. It is thus common to provide that the adjudicator's decision is to be given within a very short time; that it is to be based on written statements from the parties but without a hearing; and that it is to be binding unless and until challenged at arbitration (which must wait until after practical completion of the works or determination of the contract).

The parties are in principle bound by the decision of an adjudicator, provided of course that it relates to a matter within his jurisdiction. As to this, it may be noted that the adjudicator under JCT sub-contracts has no power to declare that the sub-contractor's claim for payment is well founded. It was accordingly held by the Court of Appeal in *A Cameron Ltd* v *Mowlem & Co plc* (1990) 52 BLR 24 that, while the adjudicator may decide against the main contractor's claim to set off a cross-claim against the sub-contractor, there is no jurisdiction to strike out the main contractor's defence of abatement. The Court of Appeal further decided that, since adjudication does not itself constitute arbitration, the adjudicator's decision could not be enforced as if it were a court judgment under s 26 of the Arbitration Act 1950.

5 Alternative dispute resolution procedures (ADR)

A variety of techniques are available to help the parties come to some form of settlement without resorting to arbitration or litigation. These procedures are informal, and the terminology which is used to describe them is rather loose and vague. Their chief features are that they are cheap, non-binding, and investigatorial rather than accusatorial. Although they are informal, there are increasing efforts afoot to formalise them, by including various contractual procedures to encourage such approaches to agreement.

The terms most commonly found to describe these procedures are conciliation, mediation, quasi-conciliation, private enquiry, adjudication and mini-trial. These terms are often used interchangeably, and sometimes inconsistently, but basically they indicate private, non-adversarial methods of resolving disagreements. Since reconciliation is voluntary, either party may pull out at any time and refer the matter to the courts instead, if satisfactory progress is not being made. What is more, the parties are not bound to accept the decisions of the person seeking to resolve the dispute.

(a) Conciliation and mediation

There are two main approaches to concluding a reconciliation, which may be called ‘conciliation’ and ‘mediation’. The first requires the parties themselves, with the assistance of the conciliator, to reach an agreement and to decide upon the precise terms of that agreement. Impartiality in the conciliator is essential, since the purpose of this process is to precipitate an agreement by persuasion and suggestion. Conciliators do not take sides, take decisions or make judgments, but they talk to each party confidentially. The initial stages are often referred to as shuttle diplomacy, as the conciliator consults first with one party and then with the other. The conciliator may bring the parties together after a while for an open discussion, which he or she chairs and leads. The conciliator will be seeking to establish common ground, ascertaining the facts which are in dispute. In order to undertake this function effectively, the conciliator needs considerable knowledge of construction disputes.

The second process retains the flexibility of pure conciliation, whilst encouraging a slightly more interventionist role for the mediator, in that it requires him or her to come to a decision. As a result, it tends to be less open-ended. It is expected that neither party will pull out and that both will accept such a decision. It is also expected that this process will give the parties a useful indication of the outcome of an arbitration. This is probably why recourse to arbitration seldom follows mediation.

It should be noted that, although the terms 'conciliation' and 'mediation' are used by writers to distinguish between these two procedures, many of the contracts which incorporate what are in fact mediation procedures use the term 'conciliation'.

(b) Quasi-conciliation

As a variation on the procedure described above, quasi-conciliation starts differently. It comes about when one of the parties unilaterally appoints an expert professional to advise on a dispute, perhaps in order to obtain a second opinion. The purpose of the appointment is not simply to maximise the return on a claim, as would be the case where a claims consultant is engaged, but rather to help the party to overcome some technical or contractual difficulty. The investigator may be appointed to discover the facts and to make a recommendation to the party about how to proceed. It is often the case that this quasi-conciliator will need to talk to the other party and find out exactly what is at issue. If the other party also appoints such a professional, then the two of them may get together and compare their findings and their conclusions. In theory at least, they ought to do this impartially.

Once the quasi-conciliator has reached a decision, a report is made to the client which can then be used as a negotiating instrument. In addition, if the dispute continues and goes to court, the report may be used in evidence.

(c) Private enquiry

This procedure involves the appointment of an independent professional to investigate some aspect of the project. It is commonly used for highly technical disputes, but is also valuable where the issues to be resolved are sensitive. Because the uses to which they are put are so wide-ranging, there is no fixed procedure for such an enquiry. On the basis of the report produced, the parties are in a much better position to negotiate and reach a settlement.

It is very important that the appointee is given precise terms of reference in order that he or she can identify and carry out the intended task. Where this is done, it is usually found that private enquiries discover technical facts much more quickly than would a judicial enquiry. This is partly at least because arbitrators and judges are prohibited from using their own experience, and must reach a decision purely on the basis of what is put before them. This is by contrast with a private enquiry, where the person conducting the enquiry can make use of his own knowledge and professional expertise in arriving at a conclusion.

(d) Mini-trial

This procedure involves the disputing parties in presenting their cases to a board which consists of themselves! To be more precise, it means that representatives of the employer's and contractor's organisations will conduct something like a trial in front of a panel of senior executives from those organisations. It is important that this group should have the necessary authority to reach and implement decisions, and also that its members should not have been personally involved in the dispute up to this point.

Strictly speaking, this does not really fit the definition of ADR given above, because it is adversarial in nature. The two parties are expected to take opposite stances and to argue their cases in front of the panel. Having heard the evidence, the panel can then negotiate their respective positions until they reach agreement.

6 Incorporating alternative dispute resolution procedures

Although most of the techniques discussed above are introduced *ad hoc* when a construction dispute actually arises, there are a number of current standard form building contracts in which they are incorporated from the outset. As mentioned above, dispute resolution by 'adjudication' is found in several JCT sub-contracts (and the Government sub-contract GW/S), and also in the ACA form of contract which is designed for use under the BPF procurement system. Conciliation has recently been introduced formally into the ICE contract.

One of the first contracts to make specific provision for ADR was the main New Zealand standard form construction contract (*Conditions of Contract for Building and Civil Engineering Construction* (NZS 3910:1987)). This states in clause 12.3.3 that, where a notice requiring arbitration is issued by either party, that notice may include a request for conciliation. If the other party agrees to this request, the employer and the contractor must then try to agree on a conciliator, to whom the matter in dispute can be submitted. It is intended that the conciliator should discuss the matter with the parties, in the hope that the issue can be resolved by agreement. Such discussions are to be held 'without prejudice', and are not to be referred to in any later proceedings. If an agreement cannot be reached between the parties, the conciliator may issue a written decision, thus adopting the more pro-active of the two approaches to conciliation.

Although, for this process to take place at all, both parties have to agree to submit to it, the conciliator's decision is not binding on both parties, as either can reject it within ten working days. These provisions do not prevent arbitration from being pursued, but are intended to be an intermediate stage before the parties resort to arbitration. Additionally, it is clear that the conciliator is regarded as a neutral expert whose judgment is likely to predict the most likely outcome of an arbitration.

The ICE 6 contract contains similar provisions, which are entirely new to British main contracts. At clause 66 the procedures for the settlement of disputes are outlined. This clause starts by defining the types of disputes which are covered by these provisions. The definition is wide-ranging, and includes most potential sources of dispute. The second part of the clause requires that a dispute be commenced by either party serving the engineer with a Notice of Dispute. This notice may only be served if the person issuing it has first taken all steps or procedures described elsewhere in the contract to overcome the dispute, and has allowed sufficient time for reasonable steps to have been taken. This clause, then, is clearly intended to be a last resort. The engineer shall decide the issue whenever a notice of dispute is served, and this decision is stated to be final and binding upon the contractor and the employer, unless the recommendation of a conciliator has been accepted by both parties, or an arbitrator has revised an engineer's decision, and this award has been published. This removes any doubt about the status of an engineer's decision. It takes a very definite and serious step on the part of the employer or contractor to go against a decision of the engineer. If either party does not agree with the engineer's decision, or if the engineer has failed to reach a decision within the time limit (one month), then there are two courses of action available; conciliation or arbitration.

Arbitration must be commenced by a Notice to Refer. If no such notice has been given, then either party can refer the dispute to conciliation. This must be undertaken in accordance with the ICE conciliation procedure which was published in 1988, and is enclosed with the contract.

The conciliation procedure is very clear, and is not intended to be adversarial. The conciliator is bound to begin the process as soon as possible, and to reach a decision as quickly as possible. The rules invite written submissions from the parties, stating their version of the case, and the conciliator may allow each party to respond to specific points in writing. The conciliator may wish to visit the site, or may generally collect any information thought fit. Whilst the conciliator may meet the parties separately, there is also the option to convene a meeting at which evidence may be sought, and submissions invited from the disputers. The rules make it clear that the rules of evidence are not applicable. The decision of the conciliator is to be delivered in writing. If either party refuses to accept this decision, they can still commence arbitration within one month.

Since the decision of the conciliator can be referred to arbitration within one month of it being reached, this clause effectively opens up different time limits for pursuing arbitration. Under clause 66(6) the time limits for issuing a notice to refer may have elapsed, but disagreement with the decision of a conciliator will enable a party to begin arbitration proceedings anyway.

The FIDIC International Standard Form of Civil Engineering Contract, 4th edition, contains a provision for the amicable settlement of disputes at clause 67.2. This clause is only operable where notice of intention to proceed to arbitration has already been issued. When this happens, arbitration cannot start unless the parties have attempted to settle the dispute amicably. The parties then have 56 days within which to come to a settlement (unless they otherwise agree), after which time arbitration will commence.

In English law, these words do not impose an obligation on the parties to attempt to reach a settlement, and could possibly simply prolong the period before which arbitration commences. However, there is of course nothing to stop the parties from attempting to reach agreement without going to arbitration. This clause in fact only serves as a timely reminder to the parties that they really ought to try.

A further development of adjudication is currently being offered as a service for use on any construction projects. There are firms now who specialise in offering Contract Management Adjudication services, based on the model used by the BPF in their system of construction procurement. The idea is that the adjudicator becomes a permanent part of the project team, and is there to avoid disputes occurring in the first place. Such a scheme is said to be complementary to the presence of a strong project manager.

Index